Administering SQL Server 7

The Cram Sheet

This Cram Sheet contains the distilled, key information for the Administering SQL Server 7.0 exam. Review this information last thing before entering the test room, paying special attention to those areas where you feel you need the most review. If you transfer any of the tasks from this sheet onto a blank piece of paper before beginning the exam, you can refer to it while taking the test.

SERVER INSTALLATION

1. Installation Requirements:

- **CPU** Intel Pentium 166 (or higher) or DEC Alpha AXP.

- **Memory** 32MB (64MB for Enterprise Edition).

- **CD-ROM** Required. (However, it also can be installed from the hard drive or network share).

- **Free hard-disk space for software** 180MB for full installation, 170MB for typical installation, and 90MB for management tools.

- **Operating System** MS Windows NT 4 SP4, Windows 95/98, or Windows NT Enterprise SP4 for Enterprise SQL Server.

- **Internet Explorer** Version 4.01 SP1 or later required.

SECURITY

2. SQL Server supports two types of login authentication: SQL Server authentication and NT authentication.

- SQL Server authentication stores logins and their associated passwords in the SQL Server.

- NT authentication uses the NT Security to validate the user.

3. SQL Server supports two types of roles for granting permissions to groups of users: server roles and database roles.

- Server roles are fixed roles that grant server-wide rights.

- Database roles are used to give database-wide rights.

4. Database roles are classified into two types: fixed and user-defined.

- Fixed database roles are predefined and created for each database.

- User-defined database roles are created by users of a database.

- **Subscriber** Servers that store copies of replicated data and receive updates.
- **Article** Data that will be replicated.
- **Publication** A collection of articles.
- **Push Subscription** Replication initiated by the Publisher.
- **Pull Subscription** Replication initiated by the Subscriber.

5. SQL Server supports three types of replication:

- **Snapshot** Takes data from Publishers and copies it to Subscribers, replacing existing data.
- **Transactional** Takes changes from the Publisher and repeats the changes at the Subscriber.
- **Merge** Allows changes to be made at the Publisher or the Subscriber.

REMOTE DATA SOURCES

6. RPC only lets you call stored procedures; linked server lets you directly access the tables.

7. You must also configure security to allow for the connections.

TROUBLESHOOTING

8. SQL Server will write errors to the SQL Server error log or the NT Application log or both if the Server was started as an NT Service.

39. SQL Server will write errors to the SQL Server error log only if the Server was started at the NT command prompt.

40. When clients fail to connect to a server, check network connectivity to the server with ping or makepipe.

41. Never forget the simple solutions to problems. (For example, sometimes, people fail to access servers because they type the wrong password.)

42. If deadlocking becomes a problem, look in the SQL code and monitor the server for the following:

- Excessively long transactions
- The use of holdlock
- Different SQL scripts or stored procedures that are accessing the same data in different orders

19. A filegroup backup copies groups of files used to make up a database.

20. Backup strategy is based on the length of time you have to perform a backup and how long you want a database recovery to take.

MONITORING

21. The NT Performance Monitor can be used to chart up to the second performance of servers on the network.

22. The Performance Monitor can track performance counters defined by SQL Server.

23. The Performance Monitor also has alert capabilities.

24. The Profiler collects information on traces (specified events) on the SQL Server.

25. Events can include:
- Connections and disconnections
- Transact-SQL batches
- Statements within stored procedures
- Deadlocks
- Errors

26. Trace information can be stored in a file or in a database.

27. Trace information can include:
- The event being traced
- The name of the user performing traced task

- The stored procedure or SQL Statement being executed
- The duration of the event
- The severity of any Error messages

28. The output from sp_who indicates whether a user's process is being blocked by another. The blocking process' spid is displayed in the BLK column.

29. The output from sp_lock output will indicate the type of locks being held by a process and on what objects the locks are being held.

30. SET SHOWPLAN_ALL and SET SHOWPLAN_TEXT will display information about how SQL Statements will be executed rather than executing them.

31. SET SHOWPLAN_ALL ON returns data in the form of a table.

32. SET SHOWPLAN_TEXT ON returns data in the form of printed messages.

REPLICATION

33. SQL Server 7 uses a Publisher/Subscriber metaphor as a model for replication.

34. The Publisher/Subscriber components are as follows:
- **Publisher** Makes data available to other servers or database.
- **Distributor** The server that contains the distribution database.

5. Application roles do not have users; instead, access to the role is controlled by your application.

6. Understand the use of the following server roles:

sysadmin Can perform any activity in SQL Server.

securityadmin Manages server logins.

serveradmin Configures server wide settings.

setupadmin Adds and removes linked servers.

processadmin Manages processes.

diskadmin Manages disk files.

dbcreator Creates and alters databases.

7. If you grant an NT User or Group to a database role, the NT User or Group becomes a user of that database.

8. Understand the use of the following fixed database roles:

db_owner Performs activity of all other database roles and other maintenance activities

db_accessadmin Adds and removes database users.

db_securityadmin Manages database roles and statement and object permissions.

db_ddladmin Adds, modifies, and drops objects.

db_backupoperator Backs up the database.

db_datareader Can see all data from every table in the database.

db_datawriter Can add, change, and delete data from every table in the database.

- **db_denydatareader** Bars access to read data.
- **db_denydatawriter** Bars access to write data.

DATABASES

9. If you separate the data, indexes, and transaction log to separate disks, it can improve your performance.

10. Unless you limit a file, a file can grow until it uses all the space on a drive.

TRANSFERRING DATA

11. The **INSERT** statement is used to load one row at a time.

12. **BULK INSERT** is a SQL statement that loads from a file into an existing table.

13. bcp performs similar to **BULK INSERT,** but can also export a table.

14. Neither bcp or **BULK INSERT** can load data into a temporary table.

15. The **SELECT INTO** statement creates a table.

BACKUP

16. A full back up creates a complete copy of a database.

17. A transaction log backup copies and truncates the database log, removing all transactions before the oldest open transaction. Transaction log backups support restoration of a database to the point of failure.

18. A differential backup copies the changes that have been made to a database since its last full backup.

Differential backups can be used in place of transaction log backups but doesn't support recovery of a database to the point of failure.

MCSE
Administering
SQL Server 7

Jeffrey Garbus
David Pascuzzi
Alvin Chang

The Coriolis Group, LLC
14455 N. Hayden Road, Suite 220
Scottsdale, Arizona 85260

480/483-0192
FAX 480/483-0193
http://www.coriolis.com

Library of Congress Cataloging-in-Publication Data
Garbus, Jeffrey R.
    MCSE administering SQL Server 7 exam cram / by Jeffrey Garbus, David Pascuzzi, and Alvin Chang.
        p.   cm.
    Includes index.
    ISBN 1-57610-227-0
    1. Electronic data processing personnel--Certification.   2. Microsoft software--Examinations--Study guides.   I. SQL server.
QA76.3.G37   1999
005.75'85--DC21
                                                    98-50747
                                                    CIP

Printed in the United States of America
10 9 8 7 6 5 4 3 2 1

Publisher
Keith Weiskamp

Acquisitions Editor
Shari Jo Hehr

Marketing Specialist
Cynthia Caldwell

Project Editor
Don Eamon

Technical Reviewer
Michael Yocca

**Production
Coordinator**
Kim Eoff

Cover Design
Jody Winkler
Jesse Dunn

Layout Design
April Nielsen

14455 North Hayden Road, Suite 220 • Scottsdale, Arizona 85260

Coriolis: The Training And Certification Destination ™

Thank you for purchasing one of our innovative certification study guides, just one of the many members of the Coriolis family of certification products.

Certification Insider Press™ has long believed that achieving your IT certification is more of a road trip than anything else. This is why most of our readers consider us their *Training And Certification Destination*. By providing a one-stop shop for the most innovative and unique training materials, our readers know we are the first place to look when it comes to achieving their certification. As one reader put it, "I plan on using your books for all of the exams I take."

To help you reach your goals, we've listened to others like you, and we've designed our entire product line around you and the way you like to study, learn, and master challenging subjects. Our approach is *The Smartest Way To Get Certified™*.

In addition to our highly popular *Exam Cram* and *Exam Prep* guides, we have a number of new products. We recently launched Exam Cram Live!, two-day seminars based on *Exam Cram* material. We've also developed a new series of books and study aides—*Practice Test Exam Crams* and *Exam Cram Flash Cards*—designed to make your studying fun as well as productive.

Our commitment to being the *Training And Certification Destination* does not stop there. We just introduced *Exam Cram Insider*, a biweekly newsletter containing the latest in certification news, study tips, and announcements from Certification Insider Press. (To subscribe, send an email to **eci@coriolis.com** and type "subscribe insider" in the body of the email.) We also recently announced the launch of the Certified Crammer Society and the Coriolis Help Center—two new additions to the Certification Insider Press family.

We'd like to hear from you. Help us continue to provide the very best certification study materials possible. Write us or email us at **cipq@coriolis.com** and let us know how our books have helped you study, or tell us about new features that you'd like us to add. If you send us a story about how we've helped you, and we use it in one of our books, we'll send you an official Coriolis shirt for your efforts.

Good luck with your certification exam and your career. Thank you for allowing us to help you achieve your goals.

Keith Weiskamp
Publisher, Certification Insider Press

For Penny.
—Jeff Garbus

I dedicate this book to the memory of my mother, Shirley Pascuzzi.
—David Pascuzzi

For my parents.
—Alvin Chang

&

About The Authors

With a B.S. from Rensselaer Polytechnic Institute, **Jeff Garbus** has experience with PCs to mainframes, and back again. Jeff has many years of client/server and Sybase experience, with a special emphasis on assisting clients in migrating from existing systems to pilot and large-scale projects. Jeff has spoken at user conferences and user groups for many years, written articles and columns for national and international magazines, and has written over 10 books, among them *Sybase System 11 DBA Survival Guide, Sybase System 11 Unleashed, Optimizing SQL Server 7.0,* and the soon-to-be-published *MCSE Database Design On SQL Server 7 Exam Cram,* also published by the Coriolis Group.

Jeff is currently president of Tampa-based Soaring Eagle Consulting, an RDBMS consulting and training firm specializing in solving business problems. He can be reached at **jeffg@soaringeagleltd.com**.

David Pascuzzi is a technical trainer, author, and consultant in computer-related technologies specializing in database technologies for more than 10 years. He has written training courses for the government and private industries, and has written various articles on database technologies.

In his consulting work, David has performed tasks ranging from production database support to database performance tuning to database design. He currently is an MCP for SQL Server. Since attaining his MCP, he has concentrated on developing SQL Server courseware and SQL Server consulting. He can be reached at **pascuzzi@concentric.net**.

Alvin Chang is a technical trainer, author, and consultant working for Soaring Eagle Consulting, a Tampa-based consulting and training firm. An MCP for SQL Server, he has taught SQL Server and consulted throughout the United States. Currently specializing in Microsoft and Sybase System Administration, Alvin started as a technical trainer for products like Microsoft Office, Lotus Smartsuite, and Lotus Notes before moving into RDBMSs. He can be reached at **alvin@soaringeagleltd.com**.

Acknowledgments

I'd like to thank all of the people whose time and support helped make this possible, from my agent who found Coriolis for us, to the editorial and production team at Coriolis who made this a better product.

Most of all, I'd like to thank my family, for giving me the time and space to get the work done.

Thank you all.

—*Jeff Garbus*

I would like to thank Jeff Garbus for including me in this book. Thanks to my parents, Frank and Shirley Pascuzzi, who instilled into me my thirst for knowledge and for teaching me how to analyze problems and get results. Specials thanks to my wonderful wife Paula for letting me do this book, in addition to my full-time job. And, thanks to my daughter Bailey and son Conner for letting daddy work on this book when they wanted to play.

—*David Pascuzzi*

I would like to thank Jeff Garbus for providing me the opportunity to contribute to this book. Thanks to Gary Tyrrell, who listened to me when I needed a break. Thanks to my brother Basil, whose late night phone calls ran up my phone bill, but kept me sane. And a special thanks to my parents Yuling and Yuching Chang, who got me started on computers in the first place.

—*Alvin Chang*

Contents At A Glance

Table Of Contents

Introduction

Welcome to the *MCSE Administrating SQL Server 7 Exam Cram*! This book aims to help you get ready to take—and pass—the Microsoft certification test numbered "Exam 70-028," titled "Administering Microsoft SQL Server 7.0." This Introduction explains Microsoft's certification programs in general and talks about how the Exam Cram series can help you prepare for Microsoft's certification exams.

Exam Cram books help you understand and appreciate the subjects and materials you need to pass Microsoft certification exams. Exam Cram books are aimed strictly at test preparation and review. They do not teach you everything you need to know about a topic (such as the ins and outs of designing or programming the SQL Server). Instead, we (the authors) present and dissect the questions and problems we've found that you're likely to encounter on a test. We've worked from Microsoft's own training materials, preparation guides, and tests, and from a battery of third-party test preparation tools. Our aim is to bring together as much information as possible about Microsoft certification exams.

Nevertheless, to completely prepare yourself for any Microsoft test, we recommend that you begin by taking the Self-Assessment included in this book immediately following this Introduction. This tool will help you evaluate your knowledge base against the requirements for an MCSE under both ideal and real circumstances.

Based on what you learn from that exercise, you might decide to begin your studies with some classroom training, or that you pick up and read one of the many study guides available from Microsoft or third-party vendors, including The Coriolis Group's Exam Prep series.

We also strongly recommend that you install, configure, and play with the software or environment that you'll be tested on, because nothing beats hands-on experience and familiarity when it comes to understanding the questions you're likely to encounter on a certification test. Book learning is essential, but hands-on experience is the best teacher of all!

The Microsoft Certified Professional (MCP) Program

The MCP Program currently includes seven separate tracks, each of which boasts its own special acronym (as a would-be certificant, you need to have a high tolerance for alphabet soup of all kinds):

➤ **MCP (Microsoft Certified Professional)** This is the least prestigious of all the certification tracks from Microsoft. Attaining MCP status requires an individual to pass one exam. Passing any of the major Microsoft exams (except the Networking Essentials Exam) qualifies an individual for MCP credentials. Individuals can demonstrate proficiency with additional Microsoft products by passing additional certification exams.

➤ **MCP + I (Microsoft Certified Professional plus Internet)** This mid-level certification is attained by completing three core exams: Windows NT Server, TCP/IP, and Internet Information Server.

➤ **MCP + SB (Microsoft Certified Professional + Site Building)** This new certification program is designed for individuals who are planning, building, managing, and maintaining Web sites. Individuals with the MCP + SB credential will have demonstrated the ability to develop Web sites that include multimedia and searchable content and Web sites that connect to and communicate with a back-end database. It requires one MCP exam, plus two of these three exams: Designing and Implementing Commerce Solutions with Microsoft Site Server 3.0 Commerce Edition, Designing and Implementing Web Sites with Microsoft FrontPage 98, and Designing and Implementing Web Solutions with Microsoft Visual InterDev 6.0.

➤ **MCSE (Microsoft Certified Systems Engineer)** Anyone who has a current MCSE is warranted to possess a high level of expertise with Windows NT (either version 3.51 or 4) and other Microsoft operating systems and products. This credential is designed to prepare individuals to plan, implement, maintain, and support information systems and networks built around Microsoft Windows NT and its BackOffice family of products.

To obtain an MCSE, an individual must pass four core operating system exams, plus two elective exams. The operating system exams require individuals to demonstrate competence with desktop and server operating systems and with networking components.

You must pass at least two Windows NT-related exams to obtain an MCSE: one on Implementing and Supporting Windows NT Server (version 3.51 or 4) and the other on Implementing and Supporting Windows NT Server in the Enterprise (version 3.51 or 4). These tests are intended to indicate an individual's knowledge of Windows NT in smaller, simpler networks and in larger, more complex, and heterogeneous networks, respectively.

You must pass two additional tests as well. These tests are networking and desktop operating system related. At present, the networking requirement can only be satisfied by passing the Networking Essentials test. The desktop operating system test can be satisfied by passing a Windows 95, Windows NT Workstation (the version must match whichever core curriculum is pursued), or Windows 98 test.

The two remaining exams are elective exams. An elective exam may fall in any number of subject or product areas, primarily BackOffice components. These include tests on IE4, SQL Server, IIS, SNA Server, Exchange Server, Systems Management Server, and the like. However, it is also possible to test out on electives by taking advanced networking topics like Internetworking with Microsoft TCP/IP (but here again, the version of Windows NT involved must match the version for the core requirements taken). If you are on your way to becoming an MCSE and have already taken some exams, visit **www.microsoft.com/mcp/certstep/mcse.htm** for information about how to proceed with your MCSE certification.

Whatever mix of tests is completed toward MCSE certification, individuals must pass six tests to meet the MCSE requirements. It's not uncommon for the entire process to take a year or so, and many individuals find that they must take a test more than once to pass. Our primary goal with the Exam Cram series is to make it possible, given proper study and preparation, to pass all of the MCSE tests on the first try. Table 1 shows the required and elective exams for the MCSE certification.

➤ **MCSE + I (Microsoft Certified Systems Engineer + Internet)** This is a newer Microsoft certification and focuses not just on Microsoft operating systems, but also on Microsoft's Internet servers and TCP/IP.

To obtain this certification, an individual must pass seven core exams, plus two elective exams. The core exams include not only the server operating systems (NT Server and Server in the Enterprise) and a desktop OS (Windows 95, Windows 98, or Windows NT Workstation), but also include Networking Essentials, TCP/IP, Internet Information Server (IIS), and the Internet Explorer Administration Kit (IEAK).

Table 1 MCSE Requirements*

Core

All 3 of these are required	
Exam 70-067	Implementing and Supporting Microsoft Windows NT Server 4.0
Exam 70-068	Implementing and Supporting Microsoft Windows NT Server 4.0 in the Enterprise
Exam 70-058	Networking Essentials
Choose 1 from this group	
Exam 70-064	Implementing and Supporting Microsoft Windows 95
Exam 70-073	Implementing and Supporting Microsoft Windows NT Workstation 4.0
Exam 70-098	Implementing and Supporting Microsoft Windows 98

Elective

Choose 2 from this group	
Exam 70-088	Implementing and Supporting Microsoft Proxy Server 2.0
Exam 70-079	Implementing and Supporting Microsoft Internet Explorer 4.0 by Using the Internet Explorer Administration Kit
Exam 70-087	Implementing and Supporting Microsoft Internet Information Server 4.0
Exam 70-081	Implementing and Supporting Microsoft Exchange Server 5.5
Exam 70-059	Internetworking with Microsoft TCP/IP on Microsoft Windows NT 4.0
Exam 70-028	Administering Microsoft SQL Server 7.0
Exam 70-029	Designing and Implementing Databases on Microsoft SQL Server 7.0
Exam 70-056	Implementing and Supporting Web Sites Using Microsoft Site Server 3.0
Exam 70-086	Implementing and Supporting Microsoft Systems Management Server 2.0
Exam 70-085	Implementing and Supporting Microsoft SNA Server 4.0

* This is not a complete listing—you can still be tested on some earlier versions of these products. However, we have included mainly the most recent versions so that you may test on these versions and thus be certified longer. We have not included any tests that are scheduled to be retired.

The two remaining exams are elective exams. These elective exams can be in any of four product areas: SQL Server, SNA Server, Exchange Server, or Proxy Server. Table 2 shows the required and elective exams for the MCSE+I certification.

➤ **MCSD (Microsoft Certified Solution Developer)** The new MCSD credential reflects the new skills required to create multitier, distributed, and COM-based solutions, in addition to desktop and Internet applications, using new technologies. To obtain an MCSD, an individual must demonstrate the ability to analyze and interpret user requirements; select and integrate products, platforms, tools, and technologies; design and implement code and customize applications; and perform necessary software tests and quality assurance operations.

Table 2   MCSE+Internet Requirements*

Core

All 6 of these are required	
Exam 70-067	Implementing and Supporting Microsoft Windows NT Server 4.0
Exam 70-068	Implementing and Supporting Microsoft Windows NT Server 4.0 in the Enterprise
Exam 70-058	Networking Essentials
Exam 70-059	Internetworking with Microsoft TCP/IP on Microsoft Windows NT 4.0
Exam 70-087	Implementing and Supporting Microsoft Internet Information Server 4.0
Exam 70-079	Implementing and Supporting Microsoft Internet Explorer 4.0 by Using the Internet Explorer Administration Kit
Choose 1 from this group	
Exam 70-064	Implementing and Supporting Microsoft Windows 95
Exam 70-073	Implementing and Supporting Microsoft Windows NT Workstation 4.0
Exam 70-098	Implementing and Supporting Microsoft Windows 98

Elective

Choose 2 from this group	
Exam 70-088	Implementing and Supporting Microsoft Proxy Server 2.0
Exam 70-081	Implementing and Supporting Microsoft Exchange Server 5.5
Exam 70-028	System Administration for Microsoft SQL Server 7.0
Exam 70-029	Implementing a Database Design on Microsoft SQL Server 7.0
Exam 70-056	Implementing and Supporting Web Sites Using Microsoft Site Server 3.0
Exam 70-085	Implementing and Supporting Microsoft SNA Server 4.0

* This is not a complete listing—you can still be tested on some earlier versions of these products. However, we have included mainly the most recent versions so that you may test on these versions and thus be certified longer. We have not included any tests that are scheduled to be retired.

To become an MCSD, you must pass a total of four exams: three core exams (available fall 1998) and one elective exam. The required exam is Analyzing Requirements and Defining Solution Architectures (Exam 70-100). Each candidate must also choose one of these two desktop application exams—Designing and Implementing Desktop Applications with Microsoft Visual C++ 6.0 (Exam 70-016) or Visual Basic 6.0 (Exam 70-176)—PLUS one of these two distributed application exams—Designing and Implementing Distributed Applications with Visual C++ 6.0 (Exam 70-015) or Visual Basic 6.0 (Exam 70-175).

Elective exams cover specific Microsoft applications and languages, including Visual Basic, C++, the Microsoft Foundation Classes, Access, SQL Server, Excel, and more. If you are on your way to becoming an MCSD and have already taken some exams, visit **Microsoft.com/ train_cert** for information about how to proceed with your MCSD certification under this new track.

➤ **MCDBA (Microsoft Certified Database Administrator)** The MCDBA credential reflects the skills required to implement and administer Microsoft SQL Server databases. To obtain an MCDBA, an individual must demonstrate the ability to derive physical database designs, develop logical data models, create physical databases, create data services by using Transact-SQL, manage and maintain databases, configure and manage security, monitor and optimize databases, and install and configure Microsoft SQL Server.

To become an MCDBA, you must pass a total of five exams: four core exams and one elective exam. The required core exams are "Administering Microsoft SQL Server 7.0," "Designing and Implementing Databases with Microsoft SQL Server 7.0," "Implementing and Supporting Microsoft Windows NT Server 4.0," and "Implementing and Supporting Microsoft Windows NT Server 4.0 in the Enterprise."

The elective exams that you can choose from cover specific uses of SQL Server and include "Designing and Implementing Distributed Applications with Visual Basic 6.0," "Designing and Implementing Distributed Applications with Visual C++ 6.0," "Designing and Implementing Data Warehouses with Microsoft SQL Server 7.0 and Microsoft Decision Support Services 1.0," and two exams that relate to NT: "Internetworking with Microsoft TCP/IP on Microsoft Windows NT 4.0" and "Implementing and Supporting Microsoft Internet Information Server 4.0".

Note that the exam covered by this book can be used as the elective for the MCDBA certification. Table 3 shows the requirements for the MCDBA certification.

➤ **MCT (Microsoft Certified Trainer)** Microsoft Certified Trainers are individuals who are deemed capable of delivering elements of the official Microsoft training curriculum, based on technical knowledge and instructional ability. Thus, it is necessary for an individual seeking MCT credentials (which are granted on a course-by-course basis) to pass the related certification exam for a course and successfully complete the official Microsoft training in the subject area, as well as demonstrate an ability to teach.

This latter criterion may be satisfied by proving that one has already attained training certification from Novell, Banyan, Lotus, the Santa Cruz Operation, or Cisco, or by taking a Microsoft-sanctioned workshop on instruction. Microsoft makes it clear that MCTs are important cogs in the Microsoft training channels. Instructors must be MCTs before Microsoft will allow them to teach in any of its official training

Table 3   MCDBA Requirements

Core

All 4 of these are required	
Exam 70-028	Administering Microsoft SQL Server 7.0
Exam 70-029	Designing and Implementing Databases with Microsoft SQL Server 7.0
Exam 70-067	Implementing and Supporting Microsoft Windows NT Server 4.0
Exam 70-068	Implementing and Supporting Microsoft Windows NT Server 4.0 in the Enterprise

Elective

Choose 1 from this group	
Exam 70-015	Designing and Implementing Distributed Applications with Microsoft Visual C++ 6.0
Exam 70-019	Designing and Implementing Data Warehouses with Microsoft SQL Server 7.0 and Microsoft Decision Support Services 1.0
Exam 70-059	Internetworking with Microsoft TCP/IP on Microsoft Windows NT 4.0
Exam 70-087	Implementing and Supporting Microsoft Internet Information Server 4.0
Exam 70-175	Designing and Implementing Distributed Applications with Microsoft Visual Basic 6.0

channels, including Microsoft's affiliated Certified Technical Education Centers (CTECs) and the Microsoft Online Institute (MOLI).

Certification is an ongoing activity. Once a Microsoft product becomes obsolete, MCSEs (and other MCPs) typically have 12 to 18 months in which they may recertify on current product versions. (If individuals do not recertify within the specified time period, their certification becomes invalid.) Because technology keeps changing and new products continually supplant old ones, this should come as no surprise.

The best place to keep tabs on the MCP Program and its various certifications is on the Microsoft Web site. The current root URL for the MCP program is titled "Microsoft Certified Professional Web site" at **www.microsoft.com/mcp**. But Microsoft's Web site changes frequently, so if this URL doesn't work, try using the Search tool on Microsoft's site with either "MCP" or the quoted phrase "Microsoft Certified Professional Program" as the search string. This will help you find the latest and most accurate information about the company's certification programs.

You can also obtain a special CD-ROM from Microsoft that contains a copy of the Microsoft Education And Certification Roadmap. The Roadmap covers much of the same information as the Web site, and it is updated quarterly. To obtain your copy of the CD-ROM, call Microsoft at 1 (800) 636-7544, Monday through Friday, 6:30 A.M. through 7:30 P.M. Pacific Time.

Taking A Certification Exam

Alas, testing is not free. You'll be charged $100 for each test you take, whether you pass or fail. In the U.S. and Canada, tests are administered by Sylvan Prometric. Sylvan Prometric can be reached at 1 (800) 755-3926 or 1 (800) 755-EXAM, any time from 7:00 A.M. to 6:00 P.M., Central Time, Monday through Friday. If this number doesn't work, please try (612) 896-7000 or (612) 820-5707.

To schedule an exam, call at least one day in advance. To cancel or reschedule an exam, you must call at least 12 hours before the scheduled test time (or you may be charged regardless). When calling Sylvan Prometric, please have the following information ready for the telesales staffer who handles your call:

➤ Your name, organization, and mailing address.

➤ Your Microsoft Test ID. (For most U.S. citizens, this will be your social security number. Citizens of other nations can use their taxpayer IDs or make other arrangements with the order taker.)

➤ The name and number of the exam you wish to take. (For this book, the exam number is 70-028, and the exam name is "Administering Microsoft SQL Server 7.0.")

➤ A method of payment must be arranged. (The most convenient approach is to supply a valid credit card number with sufficient available credit. Otherwise, payments by check, money order, or purchase order must be received before a test can be scheduled. If the latter methods are required, ask you order taker for more details.)

When you show up to take a test, try to arrive at least 15 minutes before the scheduled time slot. You must bring and supply two forms of identification, one of which must be a photo ID.

All exams are completely closed-book. In fact, you will not be permitted to take anything with you into the testing area, but you will be furnished with a blank sheet of paper and a pen. We suggest that you immediately write down on that sheet of paper all the information you've memorized for the test.

In Exam Cram books, this information appears on a tear-out sheet inside the front cover of each book. You will have some time to compose yourself, to record this information, and even to take a sample orientation exam before you must begin the real thing. We suggest you take the orientation test before taking your first exam, but because they're all more or less identical in layout, behavior, and controls, you probably won't need to do this more than once.

When you complete a Microsoft certification exam, the software will tell you whether you've passed or failed. All tests are scored on a basis of 1,000 points, and results are broken into several topic areas. Even if you fail, we suggest you ask for—and keep—the detailed report that the test administrator should print for you. You can use this report to help you prepare for another go-round, if needed.

If you need to retake an exam, you'll have to call Sylvan Prometric, schedule a new test date, and pay another $100 to take it again. Microsoft has recently implemented a new policy regarding failed tests. The first time you fail a test, you are able to retake the test the next day. However, if you fail a second time, you must wait 14 days before retaking that test. The 14-day waiting period is in effect for all tests after the first failure.

Tracking MCP Status

As soon as you pass any Microsoft exam other than Networking Essentials, you'll attain Microsoft Certified Professional (MCP) status. Microsoft also generates transcripts that indicate which exams you have passed and your corresponding test scores. You can order a transcript by email at any time by sending an email addressed to **mcp@msprograms.com**. You can also obtain a copy of your transcript by downloading the latest version of the MCT Guide from the Web site and consulting the section titled "Key Contacts" for a list of telephone numbers and related contacts.

Once you pass the necessary set of exams (six for MCSE or nine for MCSE+I), you'll be certified. Official certification normally takes anywhere from four to six weeks, so don't expect to get your credentials overnight. When the package arrives, it will include a Welcome Kit that contains a number of elements, including:

➤ An MCSE or MCSE+I certificate, suitable for framing, along with a Professional Program Membership card and lapel pin.

➤ A license to use the MCP logo, thereby allowing you to use the logo in advertisements, promotions, and documents, and on letterhead, business cards, and so on. Along with the license comes an MCP logo sheet, which includes camera-ready artwork. (Note: before using any of the artwork, individuals must sign and return a licensing agreement that indicates they'll abide by its terms and conditions.)

➤ A one-year subscription to TechNet, a collection of CDs that includes software, documentation, service packs, databases, and more technical information than you can possibly ever read. In our opinion, this is the best and most tangible benefit of attaining MCSE or MCSE + I status.

➤ A subscription to *Microsoft Certified Professional Magazine*, which provides ongoing data about testing and certification activities, requirements, and changes to the program.

➤ A free Priority Comprehensive 10-pack with Microsoft Product Support, and a 25 percent discount on additional Priority Comprehensive 10-packs. This lets you place up to 10 free calls to Microsoft's technical support operation at a higher-than-normal priority level.

➤ A one-year subscription to the Microsoft Beta Evaluation program. This subscription will get you all beta products from Microsoft for the next year. (This does not include developer products. You must join the MSDN program or become an MCSD to qualify for developer beta products.)

Many people believe that the benefits of MCP certification go well beyond the perks that Microsoft provides to newly anointed members of this elite group. We're starting to see more job listings that request or require applicants to have an MCSE, MCSE + I, MCSD, etc., and many individuals who complete the program can qualify for increases in pay or responsibility. As an official recognition of hard work and broad knowledge, one of the MCP credentials is a badge of honor in many IT organizations.

How To Prepare For An Exam

Preparing for any SQL Server 7-related test (including Administration) requires that you obtain and study materials designed to provide comprehensive information about SQL Server 7 and the specific exam for which you are preparing. The following list of materials will help you study and prepare:

➤ The Microsoft SQL Server 7 manuals (or Books Online, the CD-ROM online documentation) and help files, which ship on the CD-ROM with the product and also appear on the TechNet CD-ROMs).

➤ *The Microsoft SQL Server 7.0 System Administration Training Kit*, published by Microsoft Press, Redmond, WA, 1996. ISBN: 1-57231-827-9. Even though it costs $99.95 (list price), it's worth every penny—not just for the documentation, but also for the utilities and other software included (which add considerably to the base functionality of SQL Server 7).

➤ The exam prep materials, practice tests, and self-assessment exams on the Microsoft Training And Certification Download page (www.microsoft.com/Train_Cert/download/downld.htm). Find the materials, download them, and use them!

In addition, you'll probably find any or all of the following materials useful in your quest for SQL Server expertise:

➤ **Study Guides** Publishers such as Certification Insider and Sybex offer MCSE study guides of one kind or another. We've reviewed them and found the Certification Insider Press and Sybex titles to be informative and helpful for learning the materials necessary to pass the tests. The Certification Insider Press series includes:

 ➤ **The Exam Cram series** These books give you information about the material you need to know to pass the tests.

 ➤ **The Exam Prep series** These books provide a greater level of detail than the Exam Crams.

Together, the two series make a perfect pair.

➤ **Classroom Training** ATECs, AATPs, MOLI, and unlicensed third-party training companies (like Wave Technologies, American Research Group, Learning Tree, Data-Tech, and others) all offer or will soon be offering classroom training on SQL Server 7 system administration. These companies aim to help prepare system administrators to run SQL Server 7 and pass the MCSE tests. While such training runs upward of $350 per day in class, most of the individuals lucky enough to partake (including your humble authors, who've even taught such courses) find them to be quite worthwhile.

➤ **Other Publications** You'll find direct references to other publications and resources in this text, but there's no shortage of materials available about SQL Server 7. To help you sift through some of the publications out there, we end each chapter with a "Need To Know More?" section that provides pointers to more complete and exhaustive resources covering the chapter's information. This should give you an idea of where we think you should look for further discussion.

➤ **The TechNet CD-ROM** TechNet is a monthly CD subscription available from Microsoft. TechNet includes all the Windows NT BackOffice Resource Kits and their product documentation. In addition, TechNet provides the contents of the Microsoft Knowledge Base and many kinds of software, white papers, training materials, and other good stuff. TechNet also contains all service packs, interim release patches, and supplemental driver software released since the last major version for most Microsoft programs and all Microsoft operating systems. A one-year subscription costs $299—worth every penny, even if only for the download time it saves.

By far, this set of required and recommended materials represents a nonpareil collection of sources and resources for all SQL Server 7 topics and software. We anticipate that you'll find that this book belongs in this company. In the section that follows, we explain how this book works, and we give you some good reasons why this book counts as a member of the required and recommended materials list.

About This Book

Each topical Exam Cram chapter follows a regular structure, along with graphical cues about important or useful information. Here's the structure of a typical chapter:

➤ **Opening Hotlists** Each chapter begins with a list of the terms, tools, and techniques that you must learn and understand before you can be fully conversant with that chapter's subject matter. We follow the hotlists with one or two introductory paragraphs to set the stage for the rest of the chapter.

➤ **Topical Coverage** After the opening hotlists, each chapter covers a series of at least four topics related to the chapter's subject title. Throughout this section, we highlight topics or concepts likely to appear on a test using a special Study Alert layout, like this:

 This is what a Study Alert looks like. Normally, a Study Alert stresses concepts, terms, software, or activities that are likely to relate to one or more certification test questions. For that reason, we think any information found offset in Study Alert format is worthy of unusual attentiveness on your part. Indeed, most of the information that appears on the Cram Sheet appears as Study Alerts within the text.

Occasionally, you may see tables called "Vital Statistics." The contents of Vital Statistics tables are worthy of an extra once-over. These tables usually contain informational tidbits that might show up in a test question, but they're not quite as important as Study Alerts.

Pay close attention to material flagged as a Study Alert; although all the information in this book pertains to what you need to know to pass the exam, we flag certain items that are really important. You'll find what appears in the meat of each chapter to be worth knowing, too, when preparing for the test. Because this book's material is very condensed, we recommend that you use this book along with other resources to achieve the maximum benefit.

In addition to the Study Alerts and Vital Statistics tables, we have provided tips that will help build a better foundation for SQL Server knowledge. Although the information may not be on the exam, it is certainly related and will help you become a better test taker.

This is how tips are formatted. Keep your eyes open for these, and you'll become an SQL Server guru in no time!

➤ **Practice Questions** Although we talk about test questions and topics throughout each chapter, this section presents a series of mock test questions and explanations of both correct and incorrect answers. We also try to point out especially tricky questions by using a special icon, like this:

Ordinarily, this icon flags the presence of a particularly devious inquiry, if not an outright trick question. Trick questions are calculated to be answered incorrectly if not read more than once, and carefully, at that. Although they're not ubiquitous, such questions make regular appearances on the Microsoft exams. That's why we say exam questions are as much about reading comprehension as they are about knowing your material inside out and backwards.

➤ **Details And Resources** Every chapter ends with a section titled "Need To Know More?", which provides direct pointers to Microsoft and third-party resources offering more details on the chapter's subject. In addition, this section tries to rank or at least rate the quality and thoroughness of the topic's coverage by each resource. If you find a resource you like in this collection, use it, but don't feel compelled to use all the resources. On the other hand, we only recommend resources we use on a regular basis, so none of our recommendations will be a waste of your time or money (but purchasing them all at once probably represents an expense that many network administrators and would-be MCSEs might find hard to justify).

The bulk of the book follows this chapter structure slavishly, but there are a few other elements that we'd like to point out. Chapter 14 includes a sample test that provides a good review of the material presented throughout the book to ensure you're ready for the exam. Chapter 15 provides an answer key to the sample test that appears in Chapter 14. Additionally, you'll find the Glossary, which explains terms, and an index that you can use to track down terms as they appear in the text.

Finally, the tear-out Cram Sheet attached next to the inside front cover of this *Exam Cram* book represents a condensed and compiled collection of facts, figures, and tips that we think you should memorize before taking the test. Because you can dump this information out of your head onto a piece of paper before answering any exam questions, you can master this information by brute force—you only need to remember it long enough to write it down when you walk into the test room. You might even want to look at it in the car or in the lobby of the testing center just before you walk in to take the test.

How To Use This Book

If you're prepping for a first-time test, we've structured the topics in this book to build on one another. Therefore, some topics in later chapters make more sense after you've read earlier chapters. That's why we suggest you read this book from front to back for your initial test preparation. If you need to brush up on a topic or you have to bone up for a second try, use the index or table of contents to go straight to the topics and questions that you need to study. Beyond the tests, we think you'll find this book useful as a tightly focused reference to some of the most important aspects of SQL Server 7.

Given all the book's elements and its specialized focus, we've tried to create a tool that will help you prepare for—and pass—Microsoft Certification Exam 70-028, "Administering SQL Server 7.0." Please share your feedback on the book with us, especially if you have ideas about how we can improve it for future test-takers. We'll consider everything you say carefully, and we'll respond to all suggestions.

Thanks, and enjoy the book!

Self-Assessment

Based on recent statistics from Microsoft, as many as 250,000 individuals are at some stage of the certification process but haven't yet received an MCP or other Microsoft certification. We also know that three or four times that number may be considering whether or not to obtain a Microsoft certification of some kind. That's a huge audience!

The reason we included a self-assessment in this *Exam Cram* book is to help you evaluate your readiness to tackle MCSE (and MCSE+I) certification. It should also help you understand what you need to master the topic of this book—namely, Exam 70-028, "Administrating Microsoft SQL Server 7.0." But before you tackle this self-assessment, let's talk about concerns you may face when pursuing an MCSE, and what an ideal MCSE candidate might look like.

MCSEs In The Real World

In the next section, we describe an ideal MCSE candidate, knowing full well that only a few real candidates will meet this ideal. In fact, our description of that ideal candidate might seem downright scary. But take heart: Although the requirements to obtain an MCSE may seem pretty formidable, they are by no means impossible to meet. However, you should be keenly aware that it does take time, requires some expense, and consumes substantial effort to get through the process.

More than 90,000 MCSEs are already certified, so it's obviously an attainable goal. You can get all the real-world motivation you need from knowing that many others have gone before, so you will be able to follow in their footsteps. If you're willing to tackle the process seriously and do what it takes to obtain the necessary experience and knowledge, you can take—and pass—all the certification tests involved in obtaining an MCSE. In fact, we've designed these *Exam Crams*, and the companion *Exam Preps*, to make it as easy on you as possible to prepare for these exams. But prepare you must!

The same, of course, is true for other Microsoft certifications, including:

➤ MCSE+I, which is like the MCSE certification but requires seven core exams, and two electives drawn from a specific pool of Internet-related topics, for a total of nine exams.

➤ MCSD, which is aimed at software developers and requires one specific exam, two more exams on client and distributed topics, plus a fourth elective exam drawn from a different, but limited, pool of options.

➤ Other Microsoft certifications, whose requirements range from one test (MCP or MCT) to many tests (MCP+I, MCP+SB, MCDBA).

The Ideal MCSE Candidate

Just to give you some idea of what an ideal MCSE candidate is like, here are some relevant statistics about the background and experience such an individual might have. Don't worry if you don't meet these qualifications, or don't come that close—this is a far from ideal world, and where you fall short is simply where you'll have more work to do.

➤ Academic or professional training in network theory, concepts, and operations. This includes everything from networking media and transmission techniques through network operating systems, services, and applications.

➤ Three-plus years of professional networking experience, including experience with Ethernet, token ring, modems, and other networking media. This must include installation, configuration, upgrade, and troubleshooting experience.

➤ Two-plus years in a networked environment that includes hands-on experience with Windows NT Server, Windows NT Workstation, and Windows 95 or Windows 98. A solid understanding of each system's architecture, installation, configuration, maintenance, and troubleshooting is also essential.

➤ A thorough understanding of key networking protocols, addressing, and name resolution, including TCP/IP, IPX/SPX, and NetBEUI.

➤ A thorough understanding of NetBIOS naming, browsing services, and file and print services.

➤ Familiarity with key Windows NT-based TCP/IP-based services, including HTTP (Web servers), DHCP, WINS, DNS, (these topics are especially important for this exam, for what we hope are obvious reasons) plus familiarity with one or more of the following: Internet Information Server (IIS), Index Server, and Proxy Server.

➤ Working knowledge of NetWare 3.x and 4.x, including IPX/SPX frame formats, NetWare file, print, and directory services, and both Novell and Microsoft client software. Working knowledge of Microsoft's Client Services for NetWare (CSNW), Gateway Services for NetWare

(GSNW), the NetWare Migration Tool (NWCONV), and the NetWare Client for Windows (NT, 95, and 98) is essential.

Fundamentally, this boils down to a bachelor's degree in computer science, plus three years of work experience in a technical position involving network design, installation, configuration, and maintenance. We believe that well under half of all certification candidates meet these requirements, and that, in fact, most meet less than half of these requirements—at least, when they begin the certification process. But because all 90,000 people who already have been certified have survived this ordeal, you can survive it too—especially if you heed what our self-assessment can tell you about what you already know and what you need to learn.

Put Yourself To The Test

The following series of questions and observations is designed to help you figure out how much work you must do to pursue Microsoft certification and what kinds of resources you may consult on your quest. Be absolutely honest in your answers, or you'll end up wasting money on exams you're not yet ready to take. There are no right or wrong answers, only steps along the path to certification. Only you can decide where you really belong in the broad spectrum of aspiring candidates.

Two things should be clear from the outset, however:

➤ Even a modest background in computer science will be helpful.

➤ Hands-on experience with Microsoft products and technologies is an essential ingredient to certification success.

Educational Background

1. Have you ever taken any computer-related classes? [Yes or No]

   If Yes, proceed to question 2; if No, proceed to question 4.

2. Have you taken any classes on computer operating systems? [Yes or No]

   If Yes, you will probably be able to handle Microsoft's architecture and system component discussions. If you're rusty, brush up on basic operating system concepts, especially virtual memory, multitasking regimes, user mode versus kernel mode operation, and general computer security topics.

   If No, consider some basic reading in this area. We strongly recommend a good general operating systems book, such as *Operating System Concepts*, by Abraham Silberschatz and Peter Baer Galvin (Addison-Wesley, 1997,

ISBN 0-201-59113-8). If this title doesn't appeal to you, check out reviews for other, similar titles at your favorite online bookstore.

3. Have you taken any networking concepts or technologies classes? [Yes or No]

If Yes, you will probably be able to handle Microsoft's networking terminology, concepts, and technologies (brace yourself for frequent departures from normal usage). If you're rusty, brush up on basic networking concepts and terminology, especially networking media, transmission types, the OSI Reference model, and networking technologies such as Ethernet, token ring, FDDI, and WAN links.

If No, you might want to read one or two books in this topic area. The two best books that we know of are *Computer Networks, 3rd Edition*, by Andrew S. Tanenbaum (Prentice-Hall, 1996, ISBN 0-13-349945-6) and *Computer Networks and Internets*, by Douglas E. Comer (Prentice-Hall, 1997, ISBN 0-13-239070-1).

Skip to the next section, "Hands-On Experience."

4. Have you done any reading on operating systems or networks? [Yes or No]

If Yes, review the requirements stated in the first paragraphs after questions 2 and 3. If you meet those requirements, move on to the next section. If No, consult the recommended reading for both topics. A strong background will help you prepare for the Microsoft exams better than just about anything else.

Hands-On Experience

The most important key to success on all of the Microsoft tests is hands-on experience, especially with Windows NT Server and Workstation, plus the many add-on services and BackOffice components around which so many of the Microsoft certification exams revolve. If we leave you with only one realization after taking this self-assessment, it should be that there's no substitute for time spent installing, configuring, and using the various Microsoft products upon which you'll be tested repeatedly and in depth.

5. Have you installed, configured, and worked with:

   ➤ Windows NT Server? [Yes or No]

   If Yes, make sure you understand basic concepts as covered in Exam 70-067 and advanced concepts as covered in Exam 70-068. You should also study the TCP/IP interfaces, utilities, and services for this test, for Exam 70-059, plus Internet Information Server capabilities for Exam 70-087.

You can download objectives, practice exams, and other information about Microsoft exams from the company's Training and Certification page on the Web at **www.micr osof t.com/tr ain_c ert/**. Use the "Find an Exam" link to get specific exam info.

If you haven't worked with Windows NT Server, TCP/IP, and IIS (or whatever product you choose for your final elective), you must obtain one or two machines and a copy of Windows NT Server. Then, learn the operating system, and do the same for TCP/IP and whatever other software components on which you'll also be tested.

In fact, we recommend that you obtain two computers, each with a network interface, and set up a two-node network on which to practice. With decent Windows NT-capable computers selling for about $500 to $600 apiece these days, this shouldn't be too much of a financial hardship. You can order a BackOffice Trial Kit from Microsoft, which includes evaluation copies of both Workstation and Server, for under $50 from **www.backoffice.microsoft.com/downtrial/**.

➤ Windows NT Workstation? [Yes or No]

If Yes, make sure you understand the concepts covered in Exam 70-073.

If No, you will want to obtain a copy of Windows NT Workstation and learn how to install, configure, and maintain it. You can use *MCSE NT Workstation 4 Exam Cram* to guide your activities and studies, or work straight from Microsoft's test objectives if you prefer.

 For all of these Microsoft exams, the Resource Kits for the topics involved are a good study resource. You can purchase softcover Resource Kits from Microsoft Press (search for them at **http:// mspr ess.micr osof t.com/**), but they're also included on the TechNet CD subscription (**www.micr osof t.com/t echnet**). We believe that Resource Kits are among the best preparation tools available, along with the *Exam Crams* and *Exam Preps*, that you can use to get ready for Microsoft exams.

You have the option of taking the Window 95 (70-064) exam or the Windows 98 (70-098) exam, instead of Exam 70-073, to fulfill your desktop operating system requirement for the MCSE. Although we don't recommend these others (because studying for Workstation helps you prepare for the Server exams), we do recommend that you obtain Resource Kits and other tools to help you prepare for those exams if you decide to take one or both of them for your own reasons.

6. For any specific Microsoft product that is not itself an operating system (for example, FrontPage 98, SQL Server, and so on), have you installed, configured, used, and upgraded this software? [Yes or No]

If the answer is Yes, skip to the next section. If it's No, you must get some experience. Read on for suggestions on how to do this.

Experience is a must with any Microsoft product exam, be it something as simple as FrontPage 98 or as challenging as Exchange 5.5 or SQL Server 7. You can grab a download of BackOffice at **www.backoffice. microsoft.com/downtrial/**; for trial copies of other software, search Microsoft's Web site using the name of the product as your search term.

 If you have the funds, or your employer will pay your way, consider taking a class at a Certified Training and Education Center (CTEC) or at an Authorized Academic Training Partner (AATP). In addition to classroom exposure to the topic of your choice, you get a copy of the software that is the focus of your course, along with a trial version of whatever operating system it needs (usually, NT Server), with the training materials for that class.

Before you even think about taking any Microsoft exam, make sure you've spent enough time with the related software to understand how it may be installed and configured, how to maintain such an installation, and how to troubleshoot that software when things go wrong. This will help you in the exam, and in real life!

Testing Your Exam-Readiness

Whether you attend a formal class on a specific topic to get ready for an exam or use written materials to study on your own, some preparation for the Microsoft certification exams is essential. At $100 a try, pass or fail, you want to do everything you can to pass on your first try. That's where studying comes in. If you still don't hit a score of at least 70 percent after these tests, you'll want to investigate the other practice test resources we mention in this section.

For any given subject, consider taking a class if you've tackled self-study materials, taken the test, and failed anyway. The opportunity to interact with an instructor and fellow students can make all the difference in the world, if you can afford that privilege. For information about Microsoft classes, visit the Training and Certification page at **www.microsoft.com/train_cert/** (use the "Find a Course" link).

If you can't afford to take a class, visit the Training and Certification page anyway, because it also includes pointers to free practice exams. And even if you can't afford to spend much at all, you should still invest in some low-cost practice exams from commercial vendors, because they can help you assess your readiness to pass a test better than any other tool. All of the following Web sites offer practice exams online for less than $100 apiece (some for significantly less than that):

➤ Beachfront Quizzer at **www.bfq.com/**

➤ Hardcore MCSE at **www.hardcoremcse.com/**

➤ LANWrights at **www.lanw.com/books/examcram/order.htm**

➤ MeasureUp at **www.measureup.com/**

7. Have you taken a practice exam on your chosen test subject? [Yes or No]

If Yes, and you scored 70 percent or better, you're probably ready to tackle the real thing. If your score isn't above that crucial threshold, keep at it until you break that barrier.

If No, obtain all the free and low-budget practice tests you can find (see the list above) and get to work. Keep at it until you can break the passing threshold comfortably.

When it comes to assessing your test readiness, there is no better way than to take a good-quality practice exam and pass with a score of 70 percent or better. When we're preparing ourselves, we shoot for 80-plus percent, just to leave room for the "weirdness factor" that sometimes shows up on Microsoft exams.

Assessing Readiness For Exam 70-028

In addition to the general exam-readiness information in the previous section, there are several things you can do to prepare for the Administrating Microsoft SQL Server 7.0 exam. As you're getting ready for Exam 70-028, visit the MCSE mailing list. Sign up at **www.sunbelt-software.com** (look for the "Subscribe to..." button). This is a great place to ask questions and get good answers, or simply to watch the questions that others ask (along with the answers, of course).

You should also cruise the Web looking for "braindumps" (recollections of test topics and experiences recorded by others) to help you anticipate topics you're likely to encounter on the test. The MCSE mailing list is a good place to ask where the useful braindumps are, or you can check Shawn Gamble's list at **www.commandcentral.com** (he's also got some peachy—and free—practice tests on this subject) or Herb Martin's Braindump Heaven at **http:// 209.207.167.177/.**

When using any braindump, it's OK to pay attention to information about questions. But you can't always be sure that a braindump's author will also be able to provide correct answers. Thus, use the questions to guide your studies, but don't rely on the answers in a braindump to lead you to the truth. Double-check everything you find in any braindump.

Microsoft exam mavens also recommend checking the Microsoft Knowledge Base (available on its own CD as part of the TechNet collection, or on the Microsoft Web site at **http://support.microsoft.com/support/**) for "meaningful technical support issues" that relate to your exam's topics. Although we're not sure exactly what the quoted phrase means, we have also noticed some overlap between technical support questions on particular products and troubleshooting questions on the exams for those products.

One last note: It might seem counterintuitive to talk about hands-on experience in the context of the Administrating Microsoft SQL Server 7.0 exam. But as you review the material for that exam, you'll realize that hands-on experience with SQL Server 7 will be invaluable. Surprisingly, you'll also benefit from hands-on experience with Windows NT Server, particularly when it comes to configuring files and file groups, using Windows NT Integrated Security, and monitoring SQL Server.

Onward, Through The Fog!

Once you've assessed your readiness, undertaken the right background studies, obtained the hands-on experience that will help you understand the products and technologies at work, and reviewed the many sources of information to help you prepare for a test, you'll be ready to take a round of practice tests. When your scores come back positive enough to get you through the exam, you're ready to go after the real thing. If you follow our assessment regime, you'll not only know what you need to study, but when you're ready to make a test date at Sylvan or VUE. Good luck!

Microsoft Certification Exams

Terms you'll need to understand:

√ Radio button

√ Checkbox

√ Exhibit

√ Multiple-choice question formats

√ Careful reading

√ Process of elimination

Techniques you'll need to master:

√ Assessing your exam-readiness

√ Preparing to take a certification exam

√ Practicing (to make perfect)

√ Making the best use of the testing software

√ Budgeting your time

√ Saving the hardest questions until last

√ Guessing (as a last resort)

Exam taking is not something that most people anticipate eagerly, no matter how well prepared they may be. In most cases, familiarity helps ameliorate test anxiety. In plain English, this means you probably won't be as nervous when you take your fourth or fifth Microsoft certification exam as you'll be when you take your first one.

Whether it's your first exam or your tenth, understanding the details of exam taking (how much time to spend on questions, the environment you'll be in, and so on) and the exam software will help you concentrate on the material rather than on the setting. Likewise, mastering a few basic exam-taking skills should help you recognize—and perhaps even outfox—some of the tricks and gotchas you're bound to find in some of the exam questions.

This chapter, besides explaining the exam environment and software, describes some proven exam-taking strategies that you should be able to use to your advantage.

Assessing Exam-Readiness

Before you take any more Microsoft exams, we strongly recommend that you read through and take the Self-Assessment included with this book (it appears just before this chapter). This will help you compare your knowledge base to the requirements for obtaining an MCSE, and it will also help you identify parts of your background or experience that may be in need of improvement, enhancement, or further learning. If you get the right set of basics under your belt, obtaining Microsoft certification will be that much easier.

After you've gone through the Self-Assessment, you can remedy those topical areas where your background or experience may not measure up to an ideal certification candidate. But you can also tackle subject matter for individual tests at the same time, so you can continue making progress while you're catching up in some areas.

After you've worked through an *Exam Cram*, have read the supplementary materials, and have taken the practice test, you'll have a pretty clear idea of when you should be ready to take the real exam. We strongly recommend that you keep practicing until your scores top the 70 percent mark; 75 percent is a good goal to give yourself some margin for error in a real exam situation (where stress will play more of a role than when you practice). When you hit that point, you should be ready to go. But if you get through the practice exam in this book without attaining that score, you should keep taking practice tests and studying the materials until you get there. You'll find more information about other practice test vendors in the Self-Assessment, along with even more pointers on how to study and prepare. But now, on to the exam!

The Exam Situation

When you arrive at the testing center where you scheduled your exam, you'll need to sign in with an exam coordinator. He or she will ask you to show two forms of identification, one of which must be a photo ID. After you've signed in and your time slot arrives, you'll be asked to deposit any books, bags, or other items you brought with you. Then, you'll be escorted into a closed room. Typically, the room will be furnished with anywhere from one to half a dozen computers, and each workstation will be separated from the others by dividers designed to keep you from seeing what's happening on someone else's computer.

You'll be furnished with a pen or pencil and a blank sheet of paper, or, in some cases, an erasable plastic sheet and an erasable felt-tip pen. You're allowed to write down any information you want on both sides of this sheet. Before the exam, you should memorize as much of the material that appears on The Cram Sheet (inside the front cover of this book) as you can so you can write that information on the blank sheet as soon as you are seated in front of the computer. You can refer to your rendition of The Cram Sheet anytime you like during the test, but you'll have to surrender the sheet when you leave the room.

Most test rooms feature a wall with a large picture window. This permits the exam coordinator standing behind it to monitor the room, to prevent exam takers from talking to one another, and to observe anything out of the ordinary that might go on. The exam coordinator will have preloaded the appropriate Microsoft certification exam—for this book, that's Exam 70-028—and you'll be permitted to start as soon as you're seated in front of the computer.

All Microsoft certification exams allow a certain maximum amount of time in which to complete your work (this time is indicated on the exam by an onscreen counter/clock, so you can check the time remaining whenever you like). Exam 70-028 consists of 52 randomly selected questions. You may take up to 90 minutes to complete the exam.

All Microsoft certification exams are computer generated and use a multiple-choice format. Although this may sound quite simple, the questions are constructed not only to check your mastery of basic facts and figures about Administering SQL Server 7, but they also require you to evaluate one or more sets of circumstances or requirements. Often, you'll be asked to give more than one answer to a question. Likewise, you might be asked to select the best or most effective solution to a problem from a range of choices, all of which technically are correct. Taking the exam is quite an adventure, and it involves real thinking. This book shows you what to expect and how to deal with the potential problems, puzzles, and predicaments.

Exam Layout And Design

Some exam questions require you to select a single answer, whereas others ask you to select multiple correct answers. The following multiple-choice question requires you to select a single correct answer. Following the question is a brief summary of each potential answer and why it is either right or wrong.

Question 1

When is a trigger fired?

- ○ a. When the trigger fire statement is executed
- ○ b. Before data modification
- ○ c. Before constraint validation
- ○ d. After the transaction completes
- ○ e. After constraint validation but before the transaction commits

The correct answer to this question is e. A trigger is an integral part of the transaction that fires it, and it needs access to the before and after image of the data to do its work.

This sample question format corresponds closely to the Microsoft certification exam format—the only difference on the exam is that questions are not followed by answer keys. To select an answer, position the cursor over the radio button next to the answer. Then, click the mouse button to select the answer.

Let's examine a question that requires choosing multiple answers. This type of question provides checkboxes rather than radio buttons for marking all appropriate selections.

Question 2

How long does a trigger persist in a database? [Check all correct answers]

- ❑ a. Until the session is terminated
- ❑ b. Until it is dropped
- ❑ c. Until a new trigger is created without the append option
- ❑ d. Until another trigger replaces it
- ❑ e. None of the above

The correct answers to this question are b, c, and d. Triggers are permanent projects in a database, so answer a is not true.

For this type of question, more than one answer is required. As far as the authors can tell (and Microsoft won't comment), such questions are scored as wrong unless all the required selections are chosen. In other words, a partially correct answer does not result in partial credit when the test is scored. For Question 2, you have to check the boxes next to answers a and d to obtain credit for a correct answer. Notice that picking the right answers also means knowing why the other answers are wrong!

Although these two basic types of questions can appear in many forms, they constitute the foundation on which all the Microsoft certification exam questions rest. More complex questions include so-called exhibits, which are usually screenshots of SQL Server Enterprise Manager. For some of these questions, you'll be asked to make a selection by clicking on a checkbox or radio button on the screenshot itself. For others, you'll be expected to use the information displayed therein to guide your answer to the question. Familiarity with the underlying utility is your key to choosing the correct answer(s).

Other questions involving exhibits use charts or network diagrams to help document a workplace scenario that you'll be asked to troubleshoot or configure. Careful attention to such exhibits is the key to success. Be prepared to toggle frequently between the exhibit and the question as you work.

The Fixed-Length Exam Strategy

A well-known principle when taking fixed-length exams is to first read over the entire exam from start to finish while answering only those questions you feel absolutely sure of. On subsequent passes, you can dive into more complex questions more deeply, knowing how many such questions you have left.

Fortunately, Microsoft exam software for fixed-length tests makes the multiple-visit approach easy to implement. At the top-left corner of each question is a checkbox that permits you to mark that question for a later visit. (Note: Marking questions makes review easier, but you can return to any question if you are willing to click the Forward or Back button repeatedly.) As you read each question, if you answer only those you're sure of and mark for review those that you're not sure of, you can keep working through a decreasing list of questions as you answer the trickier ones in order.

There's at least one potential benefit to reading the exam over completely before answering the trickier questions: Sometimes, information in later questions will shed more light on earlier questions. Other times, information you read on later questions might jog your memory about SQL Server 7 administration facts, figures, or behavior that also will help with earlier questions. Either way, you'll come out ahead if you defer those questions about which you're not absolutely sure.

Here are some question-handling strategies that apply to fixed-length tests. Use them if you have the chance:

➤ When returning to a question after your initial read-through, read every word again—otherwise, your mind can fall quickly into a rut. Sometimes, revisiting a question after turning your attention elsewhere lets you see something you missed, but the strong tendency is to see what you've seen before. Try to avoid that tendency at all costs.

➤ If you return to a question more than twice, try to articulate to yourself what you don't understand about the question, why the answers don't appear to make sense, or what appears to be missing. If you chew on the subject for awhile, your subconscious might provide the details that are lacking, or you might notice a "trick" that will point to the right answer.

As you work your way through the exam, another counter that Microsoft provides will come in handy—the number of questions completed and questions outstanding. For fixed-length tests, it's wise to budget your time by making sure that you've completed one-quarter of the questions one-quarter of the way through the exam period (or the first 17 questions in the first 26 minutes) and three-quarters of them three-quarters of the way through (51 questions in the first 78 minutes).

If you're not finished when 100 minutes have elapsed, use the last 5 minutes to guess your way through the remaining questions. Remember, guessing is potentially more valuable than not answering, because blank answers are always wrong, but a guess may turn out to be right. If you don't have a clue about any of the remaining questions, pick answers at random, or choose all a's, b's, and so on. The aim is to submit an exam for scoring that has an answer for every question.

At the very end of your exam period, you're better off guessing than leaving questions unanswered.

The Adaptive Exam Strategy

If there's one principle that applies to taking an adaptive test, it could be summed up as "Get it right the first time." You cannot elect to skip a question and move on to the next one when taking an adaptive test because the testing software uses your answer to the current question to select whatever question it plans to present next. Nor can you return to a question once you've moved on, because the software gives you only one chance to answer the question.

Also, when you answer a question correctly, you are presented with a more difficult question next, to help the software gauge your level of skill and ability. When you answer a question incorrectly, you are presented with a less difficult question, and the software lowers its current estimate of your skill and ability. This continues until the program settles into a reasonably accurate estimate of what you know and can do, and it takes you on average through somewhere between 25 and 35 questions as you complete the test.

The good news is that if you know your stuff, you'll probably finish most adaptive tests in 30 minutes or so. The bad news is that you must really, really know your stuff to do your best on an adaptive test. That's because some questions are so convoluted, complex, or hard to follow that you're bound to miss one or two, at a minimum, even if you do know your stuff. So the more you know, the better you'll do on an adaptive test, even accounting for the occasionally weird or unfathomable questions that appear on these exams.

 Because you can't tell in advance if a test is fixed-length or adaptive, you will be best served by preparing for the exam as if it were adaptive. That way, you should be prepared to pass no matter what kind of test you take. But if you do take a fixed-length test, remember our tips from the preceding section. They should help you improve on what you could do on an adaptive test.

If you encounter a question on an adaptive test that you can't answer, you must guess an answer immediately. Because of the way the software works, you may have to suffer for your guess on the next question if you guess right, because you'll get a more difficult question next!

Exam-Taking Basics

The most important advice about taking any exam is this: Read each question carefully. Some questions are deliberately ambiguous, some use double negatives, and others use terminology in incredibly precise ways. The authors have taken numerous exams—both practice and live—and in nearly every one have missed at least one question because they didn't read it closely or carefully enough.

Here are some suggestions on how to deal with the tendency to jump to an answer too quickly:

➤ Make sure you read every word in the question. If you find yourself jumping ahead impatiently, go back and start over.

➤ As you read, try to restate the question in your own terms. If you can do this, you should be able to pick the correct answer(s) much more easily.

➤ When returning to a question after your initial read-through, read every word again—otherwise, your mind can fall quickly into a rut. Sometimes, revisiting a question after turning your attention elsewhere lets you see something you missed, but the strong tendency is to see what you've seen before. Try to avoid that tendency at all costs.

➤ If you return to a question more than twice, try to articulate to yourself what you don't understand about the question, why the answers don't appear to make sense, or what appears to be missing. If you chew on the subject for awhile, your subconscious might provide the details that are lacking or you might notice a "trick" that will point to the right answer.

Above all, try to deal with each question by thinking through what you know about SQL Server 7 administration—the characteristics, behaviors, facts, and figures involved. By reviewing what you know (and what you've written down on your information sheet), you'll often recall or understand things sufficiently to determine the answer to the question.

Question-Handling Strategies

Based on exams we have taken, some interesting trends have become apparent. For those questions that take only a single answer, usually two or three of the answers will be obviously incorrect, and two of the answers will be plausible—of course, only one can be correct. Unless the answer leaps out at you (if it does, reread the question to look for a trick; sometimes those are the ones you're most likely to get wrong), begin the process of answering by eliminating those answers that are most obviously wrong.

Things to look for in obviously wrong answers include spurious menu choices or utility names, nonexistent software options, and terminology you've never seen. If you've done your homework for an exam, no valid information should be completely new to you. In that case, unfamiliar or bizarre terminology probably indicates a totally bogus answer.

Numerous questions assume that the default behavior of a particular utility is in effect. If you know the defaults and understand what they mean, this knowledge will help you cut through many Gordian knots.

Mastering The Inner Game

In the final analysis, knowledge breeds confidence, and confidence breeds success. If you study the materials in this book carefully and review all the exam prep questions at the end of each chapter, you should become aware of those areas where additional learning and study are required.

Next, follow up by reading some or all of the materials recommended in the "Need To Know More?" section at the end of each chapter. The idea is to become familiar enough with the concepts and situations you find in the sample questions that you can reason your way through similar situations on a real exam. If you know the material, you have every right to be confident that you can pass the exam.

After you've worked your way through the book, take the practice exam in Chapter 14. This will provide a reality check and help you identify areas you need to study further. Make sure you follow up and review materials related to the questions you miss on the practice exam before scheduling a real exam. Only when you've covered all the ground and feel comfortable with the whole scope of the practice exam should you take a real one.

> If you take the practice exam and don't score at least 75 percent correct, you'll want to practice further. Though one is not available for SQL Server administration yet, Microsoft usually provides free Personal Exam Prep (PEP) exams and the self-assessment exams from the Microsoft Certified Professional Web site's download page (its location appears in the next section). If you're more ambitious or better funded, you might want to purchase a practice exam from a third-party vendor.

Armed with the information in this book and with the determination to augment your knowledge, you should be able to pass the certification exam. However, you need to work at it, or you'll spend the exam fee more than once before you finally pass. If you prepare seriously, you should do well. Good luck!

Additional Resources

A good source of information about Microsoft certification exams comes from Microsoft itself. Because its products and technologies—and the exams that go with them—change frequently, the best place to go for exam-related information is online.

If you haven't already visited the Microsoft Certified Professional site, do so right now. The MCP home page resides at **www.microsoft.com/mcp** (see Figure 1.1).

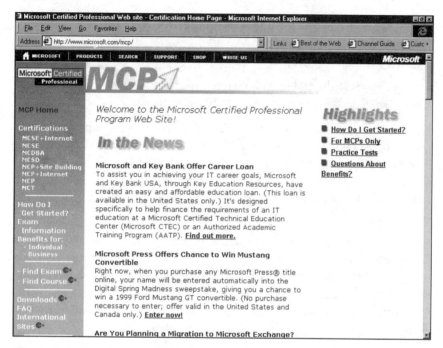

Figure 1.1 The Microsoft Certified Professional home page.

Note: This page might not be there by the time you read this, or it might have been replaced by something new and different, because things change regularly on the Microsoft site. Should this happen, please read the sidebar titled "Coping With Change On The Web."

The menu options in the left column of the home page point to the most important sources of information in the MCP pages. Here's what to check out:

➤ **Certification Choices** Use these links to read about the various certification programs that Microsoft offers.

➤ **Find Exam** Use this menu entry to pull up a search tool that lets you list all Microsoft exams and locate all exams relevant to any Microsoft certification (MCPS, MCSE, MCT, and so on) or those exams that cover a particular product. This tool is quite useful not only to examine the options but also to obtain specific exam preparation information, because each exam has its own associated preparation guide. This is Exam 70-028.

➤ **Downloads** Use this menu entry to find a list of the files and practice exams that Microsoft makes available to the public. These include several items worth downloading, especially the Certification Update, the Personal Exam Prep (PEP) exams, various assessment exams, and a general exam study guide. Try to make time to peruse these materials before taking your first exam.

These are just the high points of what's available in the Microsoft Certified Professional pages. As you browse through them—and we strongly recommend that you do—you'll probably find other informational tidbits mentioned that are every bit as interesting and compelling.

Coping With Change On The Web

Sooner or later, all the information we've shared with you about the Microsoft Certified Professional pages and the other Web-based resources mentioned throughout the rest of this book will go stale or be replaced by newer information. In some cases, the URLs you find here might lead you to their replacements; in other cases, the URLs will go nowhere, leaving you with the dreaded "404 File not found" error message. When that happens, don't give up.

There's always a way to find what you want on the Web if you're willing to invest some time and energy. Most large or complex Web sites—and Microsoft's qualifies on both counts—offer a search engine. Looking back at Figure 1.1, you can see that a Search button appears along the top edge of the page. As long as you can get to Microsoft's site (it should stay at **www.microsoft.com** for a long while yet), you can use this tool to help you find what you need.

The more focused you can make a search request, the more likely the results will include information you can use. For example, you can search for the string "training and certification" to produce a lot of data about the subject in general, but if you're looking for the preparation guide for Exam 70-028, "Administering Microsoft SQL Server 7.0," you'll be more likely to get there quickly if you use a search string similar to the following:

```
"Exam 70-028" AND "preparation guide"
```

Likewise, if you want to find the Training and Certification downloads, try a search string such as this:

```
"training and certification" AND "download page"
```

Finally, feel free to use general search tools—such as **www.search.com**, **www.altavista.com**, and **www.excite.com**—to search for related information. Although Microsoft offers the best information about its certification exams online, there are plenty of third-party sources of information, training, and assistance in this area that need not follow Microsoft's party line. The bottom line is this: If you can't find something where the book says it lives, start looking around. If worse comes to worst, you can always email us. We just might have a clue.

SQL Server Overview

Terms you'll need to understand:

✓ Client

✓ Server

✓ Transact SQL

Techniques you'll need to master:

✓ Identifing the uses of the master database

✓ Identifing the uses of the model database

✓ Identifing the uses of the msdb database

✓ Identifing the uses of the tempdb database

Introduction To Application Architectures

Two basic application architectures are available: mainframe (or monolithic) architecture and distributed architecture. Every application developed uses one of these architectures.

Mainframe or monolithic systems generally consist of a single central computer and "dumb" terminals. The mainframe contains all the processing power. The terminals simply display screen images and transfer keystrokes. In monolithic systems, all application components (user interface, program logic, integrity logic, and data access) are contained in the mainframe system.

In distributed architecture, processing is distributed among applications that are linked through a communications network. The most common distributed architecture is a two-tier architecture known as *client/server*. Other common application environments are three-tiered and Web environments. A three-tiered application will separate the display logic, business logic, and data access logic into separate applications, or tiers. A Web environment is not significantly different from other environments. The main difference is that, with a Web environment, you can have many clients connecting from diverse hardware platforms.

Client/Server Architecture

In client/server architecture, a central server platform performs all the data-access tasks. Client/server architecture is a branch of computing in which one process requests information from another process. In this architecture, processing power is distributed among clients and servers. The application platform typically performs all tasks related to user interface, program logic, and integrity logic. The server can perform the program logic and the integrity logic. These software processes can be on the same computer or in different countries. All components can have varying processing capabilities and are connected via a network.

A *client* is a process that issues requests and presents data. A *server* is a process that responds to and processes requests. Typical servers include fax servers, mail servers, gateway servers, database servers, and communications servers.

A server controls data or resources in a central location. The server is optimized to process data and to deliver result sets or responses, if applicable. A server typically returns raw data independent of how the data will be presented. The server is usually scaleable, with comparable capabilities available on a variety of hardware and operating platforms.

A client requests data or some other service from the server, and presents the data to the user, frequently with a graphical user interface (GUI). It is the client's responsibility to present the data to the end user. Because presentation and application services reside on the client and, therefore, consume client CPU and RAM resources, the server's resources are freed for processing data and requests.

Client applications can run on a number of platforms. Some common client platforms include the following:

➤ PC-DOS/MS-DOS

➤ 16-bit Windows

➤ Windows 95/98

➤ Windows NT/2000

➤ Macintosh OS

➤ Novell NetWare

➤ UNIX

➤ OS/2

SQL Server Architecture Overview

The SQL Server architecture consists of clients and database servers communicating via network protocols, even if the client and server exist on the same computer. The data presentation and user interface are always controlled by the client software. The SQL Server always manages the data access. Either the client or the SQL Server can control application program logic and data integrity logic. The benefits of SQL Server's approach are shown in the following list:

➤ Application maintenance is simplified by allowing you to change the database structure independent of the display logic.

➤ Business rules can be consistently enforced.

➤ Duplication of programming efforts can be minimized.

➤ Each platform can be optimized for the task it performs.

➤ Distributed processing improves multiuser access and performance.

Microsoft SQL Server uses native operating-system services to perform much of the underlying processing. It uses the following functions from the OS:

➤ Disk I/O

➤ Memory management

➤ Networking services

➤ Symmetric multiprocessing (SMP) support

➤ Threads

Microsoft's Symmetric Server Architecture relies on native 32-bit thread services to provide memory protection, SMP support, and greater server reliability. User connections are dynamically scheduled to available threads, which are then scheduled by the OS to available processors. Figure 2.1 shows the interaction between SQL Server connections and an operating thread.

SQL Server Functions And Features

SQL Server provides different pools of threads for different purposes, including parallel table scanning, backup striping, disk-device management, and user

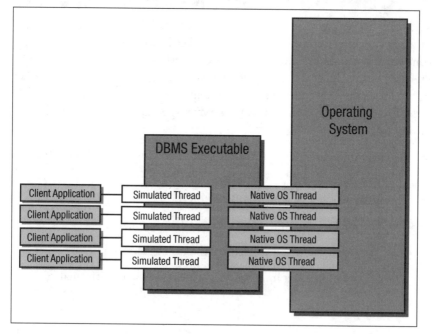

Figure 2.1 SQL Server threading.

connections. SQL Server can have multiple tasks running, even if only one CPU exists in the computer. SQL Server will dynamically round-robin the user connections to available threads, even if the number of user connections exceeds the threads available.

SQL Server 7 will dynamically configure many options while it is running, for example, the number of user connections. Either you can allow SQL Server to configure itself, or you can override SQL Server and set your own configuration. SQL Server performs its own internal memory management for caching data and stored procedures based on the configuration variables. Usually, you want to let SQL Server manage most of its configurable parameters.

SQL Server was built around the network environment. It supports many types of clients, running on many different hardware platforms, like those shown earlier in the "Client/Server Architecture" section.

SQL Server manages multiple databases in an instance of SQL Server. Each database has different configuration options, objects, users, and transaction logs.

SQL Server dynamically optimizes queries by using a built-in cost-based optimizer that will automatically determine the best way to access the data needed for your query. You don't have to write your SQL statements in any special order to get optimal performance.

Transact SQL

SQL Server provides a number of enhancements (stored procedures, triggers, rules, defaults, and procedural statements) to the ANSI Structured Query Language (SQL) standard called Transact SQL, or TSQL.

TSQL provides full support of ANSI SQL and also includes the following:

➤ Server-resident programs such as stored procedures and triggers

➤ Control of flow statements

➤ Additional data types

➤ Various types of built-in integrity such as rules, defaults, and triggers

➤ Additional built-in functions

The Four System Databases In SQL Server 7

SQL Server stores data in databases. Each database contains its own users, tables, procedures, and database files. Developers and end users work with the logical objects in the database. The system administrator deals with the physical database files. SQL Server has four system databases: master, model, msdb, and tempdb.

The *master* database holds all the system-wide information, including login accounts, server configuration information, and information about other databases. All system-stored procedures, such as **sp_who**, are stored in the master database.

model is a template database used when creating other databases. It contains all the database objects that will be created in any new databases. (When you want to add database objects, you add them first to the model database.) The model database also has the database settings that will be used by any new databases, and it has a copy of all database system tables.

The SQL Server Agent uses the *msdb* database to store all job and alert information.

tempdb is a special temporary working database. Each time the SQL Server restarts, tempdb is dropped and then reinitialized from the model database. tempdb grows automatically as needed to meet any temporary storage needs.

Practice Questions

Question 1

> What is the *model* database used for?
>
> ○ a. A test database to test changes to your other databases
>
> ○ b. A template for creating all new databases
>
> ○ c. A container for server-wide information
>
> ○ d. A temporary working storage area
>
> ○ e. None of the above

The correct answer is b. Model is a template for all new databases. Answer a is incorrect because MS SQL Server doesn't provide a test database for testing your changes. Answer c is incorrect because the master database contains server-wide information, while the model database contains only database-specific information. Answer d is incorrect because tempdb is the temporary storage area. Answer e is incorrect because the correct answer is provided.

Question 2

> Which one of the following is a valid client platform?
>
> ○ a. Windows NT 3.5.1
>
> ○ b. Sun Solaris
>
> ○ c. Windows 95
>
> ○ d. Windows NT Server 4
>
> ○ e. All of the above

The correct answer is e. All the answers are valid client platforms.

Question 3

> To allow more than one user to access a database, what special
> SQL Server configuration must be performed?
>
> ○ a. Start multiple instances of SQL Server.
>
> ○ b. Start multiple databases on the same devices in one
>   instance of SQL Server.
>
> ○ c. Do nothing.
>
> ○ d. It cannot be done.
>
> ○ e. Start multiple instances of SQL Server on different
>   computers.

The correct answer is c. SQL Server will automatically allow more than one
user to access a database. All other answers are incorrect because the correct
response is given.

Question 4

> In client/server architecture, what is the normal purpose of a
> server? [Check all the correct answers]
>
> ❑ a. Format data for displaying to the end user
>
> ❑ b. Handle data storage
>
> ❑ c. Enforce data integrity
>
> ❑ d. Control the graphical user interface
>
> ❑ e. Supply the end user with automatic corrections to
>   misspelled words as they are typed

The correct answers are b and c. Answers a, d, and e are incorrect because the
client should format the data, control the GUI, and correct data entry .

Need To Know More?

 McGehee, Brad and Shepker, Matthew, *Using Microsoft SQL Server 7.0*, (Indianapolis, IN, QUE, 1998, ISBN 0-7897-1628-3). Chapters 1 and 2 provide a good overview of SQL Server architecture.

 MS SQL Server Books Online.

 Search the TechNet CD-ROM (or its online version through **www.microsoft.com**)

 www.microsoft.com/sql has up to date information on using SQL Server.

Server Installation, Configuration, And Upgrades

3

Terms you'll need to understand:

√ SQL Server

√ Decision Support Service

√ English Query

√ SQL Server Enterprise

√ SQL Server Profiler

√ SQL Server Query

√ MS DTC Client

√ Replication Conflict Resolver

√ Services

√ Network libraries

√ Clustering

√ Failover

√ Network protocol

√ Net-Libraries

√ Client connectivity

√ Character set

√ Sort order

√ Side-by-side upgrade

√ Computer-to-computer upgrade

√ Import server

√ Export server

√ Warm backup

Techniques you'll need to master:

√ Planning the installation

√ Installing SQL Server

√ Upgrading an existing server and migrating your databases

√ Performing an unattended installation

√ Configuring SQL Server

√ Configuring SQL Mail

√ Setting up clustering for failover

√ Setting up standby servers for failover

√ Installing and configuring a client

√ Uninstalling SQL Server

Overview Of Installing SQL Server

SQL Server is easy and fast to install. It comes with the tools needed to install SQL Server, to upgrade a previous version of SQL Server, to migrate from other systems to SQL Server, and to integrate SQL Server with other products. The installation process has four main stages: planning, preparing, doing, and testing. The work done in each stage varies, depending on whether you are installing a new instance of SQL Server, upgrading from a previous version of SQL Server, or migrating to SQL Server from another product.

Planning For Installation

The first step in installing SQL Server is to plan your SQL Server installation. You need to evaluate your hardware, ensure that the hardware meets SQL Server minimum installation requirements, choose the components to install, decide when to install the software, select the network protocols to use, and decide on character sets and sort orders.

Variations Of SQL Server

If you run the autorun.exe provided with SQL Server, you have three installation options. You can install SQL Server, Decision Support Services, and English Query.

English Query is an application development tool that allows users to use Standard English when writing basic data-access queries. (You have to develop your own applications to use this tool.) English Query runs on SQL Server 6.5 SP3 or higher.

The Decision Support Services (DSS) option converts a standard database into a structure that the business user can analyze. DSS is a multitiered database engine. You use DSS in developing data-warehouse applications.

SQL Server is the option that will be covered in detail here. You can install three flavors of SQL Server: Desktop, Standard, and Enterprise. Table 3.1 describes the differences among the three types.

System Requirements

To run efficiently, SQL Server requires certain minimum hardware and OS combinations. Table 3.2 lists the minimum hardware and software requirements for running SQL Server 7.

You will need additional free disk space for your databases. This requirement is covered in "Types Of SQL Server Installations," a following section in this chapter.

Table 3.1 Vital SQL Server variations.

Option	Desktop	Standard	Enterprise
Operating System	Windows 95/98 All NT 4	NT Server	NT Server Enterprise Edition
Supports Memory (2GB)	No	No	Yes
Failover Support	No	No	Yes
Merger Replication	Full	Full	Full
Transaction Replication	Subscriber	Full	Full
Maximum CPUs	2	4	32
Max Database Size	4GB	No Max	No Max
Full-Text Search	No	Yes	Yes

Table 3.2 Vital SQL Server hardware and software requirements.

Component	Requirement
CPU	Intel Pentium Pro or Pentium II 133 (or compatible) or DEC Alpha AXP.
Memory	32MB (64MB for Enterprise).
CD-ROM	Any.
Free Hard-Disk Space	180MB for full installation, 170MB for typical installation, and 90MB for management tools.
Operating System	MS Windows NT 4 SP4, Windows 95, Windows 98, Windows 95 OSR2, or Windows 2000 (when released).
Network Software	Software provided with OS. Additional networking software is required if you use Banyan VINES or AppleTalk.
Network Adapters	Any supported by the operating system.

Components Of SQL Server

You need to decide which components of SQL Server you want to install. SQL Server comes with six components: SQL Server program files, management tools, online documentation, development tools, sample files, and client connectivity tools.

SQL Server Program Files

SQL Server program files are the files needed to run SQL Server. You can install different combinations of program files, which you can see in the following list:

➤ SQL Server installs the SQL Server RDBMS and other tools, including bcp, isql, osql, ODBC, and DB-Library.

➤ Upgrade Tools installs the 6.x To 7 Upgrade Wizard.

 The Upgrade Wizard can be installed only under Windows NT.

➤ Replication Support installs the pieces needed for replication.

➤ Full-Text Search installs the full-text search engine, which provides more complex character column searches.

Management Tools

Management tools help you to manage SQL Server. These tools can be installed in the Management Tools category in SQL Server Setup. The following list details each tool:

➤ **SQL Server Enterprise Manager** Performs standard database administration tasks.

➤ **SQL Server Profiler** Monitors and records SQL Server database activity.

➤ **SQL Server Query Analyzer** Provides a graphical interface for entering Transact-SQL statements and procedures.

➤ **MS DTC Client Support** Extends database transactions across multiple servers.

➤ **Replication Conflict Resolver** Displays and helps you reconcile replication conflicts.

Online Documentation

Online documentation is the electronic documentation for SQL Server. The following documentation is installed:

➤ **Books Online** Consists of the entire SQL Server documentation set.

➤ **Quick Tour** Helps familiarize new users with SQL Server.

➤ **What's New** Lists the new features in SQL Server 7.

Development Tools

Development tools are the libraries and DLLs used for developing applications that use SQL Server. The following list explains these tools:

➤ **Headers and Libraries** Installs the included files and library files needed to create SQL Server applications.

➤ **Virtual Device Interface** Installs the DLLs req|≈red to back up to and restore from a virtual device.

Samples

The samples component installs sample files for the various ways to develop code with SQL Server. You can install any of the following sample files:

➤ **DBLIB** DB-Library examples

➤ **DTS** Data Transformation Services examples

➤ **ESQLC** Embedded SQL for C examples

➤ **MS DTC** Microsoft Distributed Transaction Coordinator examples

➤ **ODBC** Open Database Connectivity examples

➤ **ODS** Open Data Services examples

➤ **OLEAut** Object Linking and Embedding Automation examples

➤ **Repl** Replication examples

➤ **SQL-DMO** SQL Distributed Management Objects examples

Client Connectivity

Client connectivity tools let you connect from a client application to SQL Server. This component installs all the pieces needed to connect from a client application. This includes the client configuration utilities, ODBC, and the network libraries.

Choosing Network Protocols

SQL Server communicates with the client through network protocols, the communication layer used to talk between applications over a network. For every network protocol you want to use, the corresponding SQL Server network library must be installed. These libraries must be installed, even if the client is running on the server. The server can support more than one network library. The server must be configured to communicate using the network libraries that you want to use. After SQL Server is installed, you can change the network protocols that it uses.

The following network protocols are available:

➤ **Named Pipes** By default, uses the pipe \\.\pipe\sql\query for Named Pipes communications. SQL Server on Windows 95 or Windows 98 cannot use the Named Pipes protocol. Clients on Windows 95 or Windows 98 can used named pipes to communicate with a SQL Server running on Windows NT. This is one of the default server protocols for Windows NT.

➤ **TCP/IP Sockets** Serves as the default network protocol. The default TCP/IP port number is 1433. This is one of the default server protocols for Windows 95/98/NT.

➤ **Multiprotocol** Uses the Windows NT remote procedure call (RPC) facility. No client configuration is needed to use Multiprotocol. It runs on top of TCP/IP Sockets, NWLink IPX/SPX, and Named Pipes. This is one of the default server protocols for Windows 95/98/NT.

➤ **NWLink IPX/SPX** Allows SQL Server to communicate by using the NWLink IPX/SPX protocol.

➤ **AppleTalk ADSP** Enables Apple Macintosh clients to connect to SQL Server by using native AppleTalk. The only other option for Macintosh clients is TCP/IP.

➤ **Banyan VINES** Allows SQL Server to use the Banyan VINES Sequenced Packet Protocol (SPP). It is not currently available on the Alpha AXP platform.

➤ **Shared Memory** Applies when the SQL Server and the client application are on the same computer. This protocol requires no configuration.

Choosing A Character Set

A *character set*, also known as a code page, determines which characters SQL Server can use in character data. The printable characters, the first 128, are the same for all character sets. The last 128 characters vary in each character set. You should have a standard character set, or server-to-server queries may fail.

 After you choose a character set, you have to rebuild the database and reload the data, if you want to change the character set. A database backup and restore will not change the character set of the data.

Choosing A Sort Order

A *sort order* determines the order in which SQL Server returns rows when you use the **ORDER BY** clause. SQL Server allows you to choose one sort order to configure for the entire server. You should have a standard sort order, or server-to-server queries may fail.

After you choose a sort order, you have to rebuild the database and reload the data if you want to change the sort order. A database backup and restore under the new sort order will not change the order of the data. If you are changing both the sort order and the character set, you can make both changes, and then rebuild the database and reload the data.

Choosing File Locations

When installing SQL Server, you have to decide where to place the different files. You can specify the locations of program files and data files, but the system files will always be placed in the system directory.

> *Note: If you want to run both SQL Server version 6.x and Version 7 on the same computer, do not install SQL Server 7 in the same directory as 6.x. The new version will overwrite the old.*

The *Unicode collation sequence* is the sort order to use with Unicode data. The Unicode collation sequence consists of two parts—locale and style. The locale is used to specify the country or location. The style describes how to handle the differences between characters.

Types Of SQL Server Installations

SQL Server provides three types of installations: typical, compact, and custom. Use your choices for these options to determine which type of installation to perform.

A typical installation installs SQL Server by using the default installation options. A typical installation includes the SQL Server management tools and SQL Server online documentation. A typical installation doesn't include full-text search, development tools, or samples. Most users will use this installation type. Table 3.3 lists the components installed with a typical installation.

A compact installation installs only the minimum configuration necessary to run SQL Server with the default installation options. A compact installation does not include SQL Server management tools or online documentation. This installation is recommended for computers that have little free disk space.

A custom installation enables you to change any of the default options. This installation is recommended for expert users or if you are installing a cliet computer. You can specify any of the following options:

➤ Upgrade tools

➤ Replication support

Table 3.3 A typical installation.	
Option	**Value**
Upgrade Tools	Installed
Replication Support	Installed
Full-Text Search	Not installed
Client Management Tools	Installed
Online Documentation	Installed
Development Tools	Not installed
Samples	Not installed
Character Set	ISO 1252
Sort Order	Dictionary Order, case-insensitive
Unicode Collation	General, case-insensitive
NT Network Protocols	Named Pipes, TCP/IP, and Multiprotocol
95/98 Network Protocols	TCP/IP and Multiprotocol

➤ Full-text search support

➤ Client management tools

➤ Online documentation

➤ Development tools

➤ Samples

➤ Character set

➤ Sort order

➤ Unicode collation

➤ Network protocols

 If you want to use full-text services, use a custom installation and add the Full-Text Search Support to the server components.

Preparing For Installation

Before installing SQL Server, preplan. To do so, follow these steps:

1. If you want SQL Server to communicate with other clients and/or servers, set up domain accounts.

2. If you are performing an upgrade, back up the previous version of SQL Server.

3. Shut down all services dependent on SQL Server.

4. Shut down Microsoft Windows NT Event Viewer and regedt32.exe and regedit.exe.

5. Review the hardware and software requirements for installing SQL Server.

6. Log on to the system under a user account that has administrative privileges.

7. Write down all your decisions from the planning stage.

Installing SQL Server

Installing SQL Server is a fairly simple and straightforward process. To do so, take these steps:

1. Insert the SQL Server CD-ROM into your drive, and then click on Install SQL Server 7. If the CD-ROM does not Autorun, double-click on Setup.bat in the root directory of the CD or use the Autorun feature to select what you want to install (Database server, DSS, or English Query).

2. After choosing the Database component, select the variation of SQL Server that meets your organization's needs.

3. After reading the software license agreement, click on Yes if you accept the agreement. If you click on No, the installation will stop.

4. Enter your name, company, and serial number.

5. Select the type of installation: Custom, Typical, or Compact.

6. If you chose a custom installation, select the components and sub-components to install.

7. If you chose a custom installation, select a character set, a sort order, and a Unicode collation.

8. If you chose a custom installation, select the network libraries to install, and then click on OK.

9. Enter a user name and a password for the SQL Server service, or click on the Use The Local System Account option.

10. If you want the SQL Server Agent and MSDTC to use a different account than SQL Server, enter the accounts to use. Otherwise, the

SQL Server Agent and MSDTC services will default to the same account entered for the SQL Server.

11. The setup program installs SQL Server.

Installation Results

After an installation, SQL Server will be on your hard drive, and system databases will be created. Table 3.4 lists the databases created during the installation process.

Unless you change the file locations, the database and log files install in the \MSSQL7\DATA directory. All other files install in the directories, as listed in Table 3.5.

Upgrading SQL Server

You can upgrade SQL Server version 6.x to SQL Server 7 by using the SQL Server Upgrade Wizard. This wizard can upgrade all or some of your databases at a time. It can also migrate replication settings, SQL Executive settings, and most of the SQL Server 6.x configuration options to SQL version 7.

The SQL Server Upgrade Wizard does not remove the 6.x version of the software from the computer. It can remove the 6.x database devices. You should leave SQL Server 6.x on the computer until you are sure the upgrade was successful.

Upgrade Requirements

When you upgrade from SQL Server 6.x to 7, additional minimum requirements exist in addition to the standard installation requirements. Table 3.6 lists these requirements.

Table 3.4 Databases created by installation.			
Database	**Description**	**Database File**	**Log File**
master	Stores system-wide configuration information	master.mdf	mastlog.ldf
model	Provides a template for all new databases	model.mdf	modellog.ldf
msdb	Schedules jobs and alerts	msdbdata.mdf	msdblog.ldf
tempdb	Provides a temporary work area	tempdb.mdf	templog.ldf
pubs	Contains a sample database	pubs.mdf	pubs_log.ldf
northwind	Contains a sample database	northwnd.mdf	northwnd.ldf

Table 3.5 Directories used by SQL Server installation.	
Directory	**Contents**
\Mssql7\Backup	Default location for backup files
\Mssql7\Binn	Client and server executable files, online help files, and DLL files for extended stored procedures
\Mssql7\Books	Online Book files
\Mssql7\Data	Default location for system and sample database files
\Mssql7\Ftdata	Full-text catalog files
\Mssql7\DevTools\Include	Include (*.h) files used to create programs
\Mssql7\DevTools\Lib	Library (*.lib) files used to create programs
\Mssql7\DevTools\Samples	Program examples
\Mssql7\Html	Microsoft Management Console (MMC) and SQL Server HTML files
\Mssql7\Install	Scripts run during setup and the result from running the setup scripts
\Mssql7\Jobs	Storage location for temporary job output files
\Mssql7\Log	Error log files
\Mssql7\Repldata	Working area for replication tasks
\Mssql7\Upgrade	Files used for upgrading from SQL Server version 6.x to SQL Server 7

Table 3.6 Upgrade requirements.	
Component	**Minimum Requirements**
Hard-Disk Space	1.5 times the size of the 6.x database that is being upgraded
Operating System	NT Server 4 SP4
SQL Server Version	6 with SP3, 6.5 with SP3 or higher
Network Protocol	Named Pipes, using the default pipe for the SQL Server 7

 To upgrade from SQL Server 6.x to 7, you must have enough available disk space, no matter what type of upgrade you are performing. The SQL Server Upgrade Wizard estimates how much disk space is needed to perform the upgrade. This is only an estimate.

Preparing For The Upgrade

Before you upgrade, you have some steps to take and decisions to make. You must follow these steps:

1. Install SQL Server 7.

2. Back up your SQL Server 6.x databases.

3. If you are upgrading servers to be used in replication, install the latest SQL Server Service Pack.

   ➤ For the 6.x SQL Server, tempdb needs to be at least 25MB.

   ➤ Memory for the 6.x SQL Server should be less than half the total memory.

   ➤ All database users must have a login.

   ➤ All logins must have a default database that already exists in the SQL Server 7 installation or that is being created as part of the upgrade.

4. Assign a user name and a password to the MSSQLServer service for both the SQL Server 6.x and SQL Server 7 installations.

5. If replication is running, stop replication, and make sure that the log is empty.

6. Shut down all applications, and have all users disconnect from the server.

Upgrading Your Databases

After preparing to upgrade a database from 6.x to 7, you then have to perform the actual upgrade. When you upgrade a database, all the 6.x database objects and all the data in the database are upgraded to a 7 structure and migrated to the 7 database.

You can perform the upgrade with one computer or two computers. A one-computer upgrade is known as a *side-by-side* upgrade. A two-computer upgrade is known as a *computer-to-computer* upgrade. Both a side-by-side upgrade and a computer-to-computer upgrade have an import server and an export server. The import server is the SQL Server 7 server. The export Server is the 6.x server. The export server defaults to the server on which you are running the Upgrade Wizard. When you perform a computer-to-computer upgrade, both computers must be in the same network domain.

Note: If you want to migrate replication settings, you must perform a side-by-side upgrade.

There are two methods of data migration: Named Pipes and Tape Backup.

The Named Pipes Method

The Named Pipes method sets up a direct connection to both databases. Data is moved directly from the 6.x to the 7 database. This method is faster than the Tape Backup method. You must run the upgrade from the computer that contains the target SQL Server 7.

Note: The Named Pipes method cannot be used with SQL Server 6.

After you perform a Named Pipes upgrade, both the 6.x and the 7 databases will exist. To use the Named Pipes method of migrating your databases, follow these steps:

1. Start the SQL Server Upgrade Wizard.

2. Choose the Named Pipes option.

3. Enter the 6.x SQL Server computer's name, not the SQL Server alias.

4. Enter the sa password for the 6.x SQL Server and for the 7 SQL Server.

5. Select the databases to upgrade.

6. Either accept the default disk configuration, or override it by using the layout utility.

7. Select the system objects to transfer. The object areas are server configuration, replication settings, and SQL Executive settings.

8. Set ANSI nulls to the desired value.

9. Set quoted identifiers to the desired value. If you have keywords or special characters in object names, you must turn on this option.

10. Perform the upgrade.

Then, the Upgrade Wizard performs the following steps:

1. Starts SQL Server 6.*x*.

2. Checks the SQL Server 6.*x* databases.

3. Exports the system objects selected for migration.

4. Exports logins.

5. Exports all objects for all databases chosen.

6. Shuts down SQL Server 6.*x*.

7. Starts SQL Server 7.

8. Creates databases and database files.

9. Modifies SQL Executive objects and settings so they can be loaded into SQL Server 7.

10. Creates logins.

11. Creates database objects.

12. Migrates data from the SQL Server 6.*x* databases and imports it into the SQL Server 7 databases.

13. Loads the modified SQL Executive objects and settings into SQL Server 7.

14. Verifies that the upgrade was successful.

The Tape Backup Method

The Tape Backup method backs up the 6.x databases you want to migrate, removes all database devices for every database, and then loads the SQL Server 7 databases.

After you perform a Tape Backup upgrade, only the SQL Server 7 databases will exist. All databases—even the ones that you did not migrate—will be removed from SQL Server 6.x.

To perform a Tape Backup upgrade, following these steps:

1. Start the SQL Server Upgrade Wizard.

2. Choose the Tape option.

3. Enter the 6.x SQL Server computer's name, not the SQL Server alias.

4. Enter the sa password for SQL Server 6.x and SQL Server 7.

5. Select the databases to upgrade.

6. Specify the location of the tape drive.

7. Optionally, have the Upgrade Wizard perform a regular database backup.

8. Either accept the default disk configuration, or override it by using the layout utility.

9. Select the system objects to transfer. The object areas are server configuration, replication settings, and SQL Executive settings.

10. Set ANSI nulls to the correct value.

11. Set quoted identifiers to the correct value.

12. Perform the upgrade.

The Upgrade Wizard then performs the following steps:

1. Starts SQL Server 6.*x*.

2. Checks the SQL Server 6.*x* databases.

3. Exports the system objects selected for migration.

4. Exports logins.

5. Exports all objects for all databases chosen.

6. Shuts down SQL Server 6.*x*.

7. Moves the SQL Server 6.x data to tape.

8. Optionally, backs up the 6.x databases.

9. Deletes all the 6.x database devices.

10. Starts SQL Server 7.

11. Creates databases and database files.

12. Modifies SQL Executive objects and settings so they can be loaded into SQL Server 7.

13. Creates logins.

14. Creates database objects.

15. Imports data from tape into the SQL Server 7 databases.

16. Loads the modified SQL Executive objects and settings into SQL Server 7.

17. Verifies that the upgrade was successful.

Configuring Data Files During Upgrades

When you perform an upgrade, SQL Server uses a default location for the database and log files. You have three options here: You can use the default database and log files, you can use database and log files that you have already created in SQL Server 7, or you can use a script file to create a new database and its database and log files.

If you use the default files, the SQL Server Upgrade Wizard will estimate the space needed to hold all the data from the 6.x databases. The log file will be created at twice the size of the log segment in the 6.x database.

The database file will be in the same directory as the first data device assigned to the database. The log file will be in the same directory as the first device assigned to the log segment.

The default configuration can be modified. You can change the name and location of the file, the initial size of the file, and the auto-growth information.

 If you want to specify existing files, you must create the database and the files before running the Upgrade Wizard.

Verifying The Upgrade

The Upgrade Wizard will perform validation to make sure that the upgrade ran successfully. The wizard generates a list of all the objects in the 7 database and compares this list with the objects that were in the 6.x database. The wizard also runs a checksum on each column of every table to verify that the upgrade was successful.

When errors are checked, any differences between the databases are not reported if those differences are present because of the change in SQL Server design. Errors generated from stored procedures that will not load because of SQL differences will be reported twice, once when the stored procedure was being created and again when the Upgrade Wizard verifies the upgrade.

Unattended Installations

There are two ways to perform an unattended installation. You can use System Management Server version 1.2, or later, to install SQL Server on multiple computers, or you can use an initialization file to answer all of the prompts.

Four programs are available for installing and uninstalling SQL Server. A sample initialization file is provided for the installation programs.

➤ The program sql70ins.cmd installs SQL Server. It uses the sql70ins.iss initialization file to perform a typical SQL Server installation, and it calls the program setupsql.exe to perform the actual installation.

➤ The program sql70cli.cmd installs SQL Server management tools. It uses the Sql70cli.iss initialization file to perform a typical SQL Server management tools installation.

➤ The program sql70rem.exe removes SQL Server.

Note: You can also create custom setup initialization files that set any installation options.

➤ The first two installation programs (sql7ins.cmd and sql70cli.cmd) call the correct version of setupsql.exe for your platform, which performs the actual installation. You can also call the setupsql.exe program directly.

Running An Unattended Installation

The setupsql.exe program is located in the platform directory\setup directory. It has the following three parameters:

➤ The first parameter, -f1, is the name of the initialization file to use when running an unattended installation.

➤ When you use the **start/wait** command to run the program with the -SMS setupsql.exe option, control is not returned to the command prompt until the installation is complete.

➤ The -s parameter runs setupsql.exe in a silent mode, with no user interface.

The following example shows how to use the setupsql.exe program:

```
start /wait D:\x86\setup\setupsql.exe
        -f1C:\SQLServerInstall\sql7_oinst.iss -SMS -s
```

Installing SQL Server With SMS

If you need to install SQL Server on multiple Windows NT computers from a central location, SMS provides this functionality. You use a package definition Format (.pdf) file to create a SMS package for SQL Server. This file contains the instructions for running the SQL Server installation programs.

To install SQL Server using SMS, follow these steps:

1. Copy all files and the directory structure from the SQL Server 7 installation disk to a directory on a shared network drive.

2. Create an unattended setup initialization (.iss) file.

3. Using SMS, import the .pdf file as a new package.

4. Using SMS, select the new .pdf file from the package source directory.

5. Enter the server and the share name of the share to which you copied SQL Server installation files.

6. Use a query to locate the computers on which you want to install SQL Server.

7. In the jobs screen, enter the query or computer group from Step 6.

8. Select the RUN workstation command and the name of the installation file.

Troubleshooting The Installation

The installation of SQL Server usually goes smoothly. When a problem occurs, it is usually fairly simple to fix. Normally, you can fix a problem by doing one of the following: freeing up disk space, stopping the application that was reported as causing the problem, or rebooting the computer.

If an installation fails, the setup program will remove all installed components. When you have an error in installing SQL Server, follow these steps to determine the source of the problem:

1. Read the error messages. Most installation error messages are meaningful and easily identify the problem.

2. Analyze the sqlstp.log file to see if any errors occurred before the last error message.

3. Try to continue past the error, as it might be only a warning.

4. If you cannot resolve the problem, save a copy of the sqlstp.log and sqlstp.iss files so you can give them to Microsoft.

Troubleshooting An Upgrade

Besides the standard information about the installation, an upgrade will log extra information for you. The MSQL7\Upgrade directory will contain a folder for each upgrade performed. This folder will contain folders for each database being upgraded. There will be files containing all information about the upgrade, including all errors that occurred.

Testing An Installation

The simplest way to test an installation is to connect with osql, Microsoft's interactive SQL program, check the SQL Server version, and, if you did an upgrade, verify that the databases are there.

Starting And Stopping SQL Server

SQL Server can run as a service or as an executable file. In Windows 95/98, SQL Server can run only as an executable file. In Windows NT, SQL Server is usually run as a service.

The main advantage of running SQL Server as a service is that you can manage SQL Server like any other service. When the account that starts SQL Server logs off, the service will not stop running. When SQL Server is running as a service, you can manage it in five ways:

➤ You can use the Windows NT Service Manager to start and stop the service.

➤ The service can be configured to start automatically.

➤ You can use a specialized application to manage the service, like net start, net stop, net pause, and net continue.

➤ The SQL Server Control Manager can start and stop the service.

➤ The SQL Server Enterprise Manager can start and stop the service.

All the options have the same results. Besides starting and stopping the service, you can also pause a service. A paused SQL Server will accept no new connections.

You can start SQL Server from the command prompt by running the sqlsrvr.exe file. If you start SQL Server this way, you cannot use Enterprise Manager, SQL Server Service Manager, the operating system service manager, or any of the net commands to pause, stop, or resume the service. These programs will show the service stopped. When running SQL Server from the command prompt, all system messages appear in the window used to start SQL Server. Also, if you log off or close the window from which the SQL Server was started, SQL Server will shut down.

Whatever way you run SQL Server, you can set the startup parameters. Table 3.7 lists all the startup parameters.

You can also shut down SQL Server with the TSQL **SHUTDOWN** command. This command can be used, no matter which method you use to start the SQL Service. The **SHUTDOWN** command has an optional parameter—**WITH NOWAIT**—which causes the server to shut down immediately, without allowing users to finish their work.

Table 3.7 SQL Server startup parameters.	
Parameter	**Description**
-dmaster_file_ path	Specifies the fully qualified file name for the master database data file. If you do not provide this option, the existing Registry parameter is used.
-eerror_log_ path	Identifies he fully qualified path for the error log file. If you do not provide this option, the Registry is read.
-lmaster_log_path	Specifies the fully qualified file for the master database data file. If you do not provide this option, the existing Registry parameter is used.
-c	Shortens startup time by causing SQL Server not to run as a Windows NT service.
-f	Starts SQL Server with minimal configuration. Used when the server configuration stops SQL Server from starting.
-m	Starts SQL Server in single-user mode.
-n	Turns off logging to the Windows NT application event log.
-pprecision_level	Specifies the maximum level of precision, 1 to 38, to be supported by **decimal** and **numeric** data types.
-sregistry_key	Identifies a Registry key to be used when starting SQL Server.
/Ttrace#	Starts SQL Server with the trace flag (**trace#**) turned on.
-x	Disables the keeping of CPU time and cache-hit ratio statistics. Allows maximum performance.

Configuring SQL Server

SQL Server provides many configuration options. The way in which you set these options affects the behavior of SQL Server. These options are set with the **sp_configure** command, as shown in the following syntax:

```
sp_configure 'option', 'value'
reconfigure {with override}
```

The configuration options do not take effect until you run the reconfigure command. The **with override** option is used to override validation checking of the parameters. You can set any of the options listed in Table 3.8.

The Allow Updates option lets you directly modify system tables. Any stored procedure created while this option is set can modify system tables after the option is turned off.

Table 3.8 Configuration options.

Option	Minimum	Maximum	Default	Restart
affinity mask	0	2,147,483,647	0	Y
allow updates	0	1	0	N
cost threshold for parallelism	0	32,767	5	N
cursor threshold	−1	2,147,483,647	-1	N
default language	0	9,999	0	N
default sortorder ID	0	255	52	Y
fill factor	0	100	0	Y
index create memory	704	1,600,000	1216	N
language in cache	3	100	3	Y
lightweight pooling	0	1	0	N
locks*	5,000	2,147,483,647	0	Y
max async IO	1	255	32	Y
max degree of parallelism	0	32	0	N
max query wait	0	2,147,483,647	600	N
max server memory*	0	2,147,483,647	2,147,483,647	Y
max text repl size	0	2,147,483,647	65,536	N
max worker threads	10	1,024	255	N
media retention	0	365	0	Y
min memory per query	0	2,147,483,647	1,024	N
min server memory*	0	2,147,483,647	0	N
nested triggers	0	1	1	N
network packet size	512	32,767	4,096	N
open objects*	0	2,147,483,647	500	Y
priority boost	0	1	0	Y
query governor cost limit	0	2,147,483,647	0	Y
recovery interval*	0	32,767	0	N
remote access	0	1	1	Y
remote login timeout	0	2,147,483,647	5	N

(continued)

Table 3.8 Configuration options (continued).

Option	Minimum	Maximum	Default	Restart
remote proc trans	0	1	0	Y
remote query timeout	0	2,147,483,647	0	N
resource timeout	5	2,147,483,647	10	N
scan for startup procs	0	1	0	Y
set working set size	0	1	0	Y
show advanced options	0	1	1	N
spin counter	0	2,147,483,647	10,000	Y
time slice	50	1,000	100	Y
Unicode comparison style	0	2,147,483,647	0	Y
Unicode locale ID	0	2,147,483,647	1,033	Y
user connections*	0	32,767	0	Y
user options	0	4,095	0	N
VLM size	0	2,147,483,647	0	N

* These are self-configuring options. SQL Server will set the option value, depending on the needs of the system.

Besides the **sp_configure** option, you will need to configure which version of SQL Server can run. The vswitch.exe program allows you to specify whether version 6, 6.5, or 7 of SQL Server is active. The syntax of the **vswitch** command is:

```
Syntax
vswitch   -SwitchTo [60|65|70} {-Slient [0|1]}
```

Following is an example using the **vswitch** command:

```
c:\mssql7\binn\vswitch -SwitchTo 65 -Silent 1
```

Configuring SQL Mail

SQL Mail allows SQL Server to communicate with an Exchange Server. SQL Mail is useful for sending errors, performance-monitor thresholds, and the results from scheduled tasks.

Before you can use SQL Mail, you have to configure the system. The computer on which SQL Server is running must be set up to use mail. A mail post office must be active. Also, SQL Server must be set up as a mail client.

To set up SQL Mail, follow these steps:

1. Start the mail client, using the same mail profile that SQL Mail will use.

2. Using SQL Server Enterprise Manager, select the server.

3. Open the SQL Server Agent properties dialog box.

4. Select a valid mail profile.

5. Open the SQL Mail Properties dialog box and select a valid profile name.

6. If you want a SQL Mail session to start when SQL Server starts, select the Auto-Start SQLMail When SQL Server Starts option.

Setting Up A Failover Server

Failover is the means of switching to a different SQL Server when a disaster occurs. Failover prepares you for what SQL Server will need to do if the SQL Server, or the computer SQL Server is on, stops running. Two types of failover can be used with SQL Server: clustering and warm backup. Both failover scenarios use a primary server and a secondary server. The primary server is the SQL Server that is actively processing requests. The secondary server is the SQL Server that will process requests when the primary server is not available.

Clustering allows you to set up two computers that shares disk drives containing SQL Server and SQL Server data files. If the SQL Server on the primary server stops or if the computer that is running SQL Server stops, SQL Server automatically starts on the secondary computer.

Warm backup, also called a standby server, occurs when you have a second server ready to bring online when SQL Server stops. In this scenario, the system administrator must keep the standby server in sync with the primary server. When the primary server stops working, the system administrator must manually bring the standby server online.

The main differences between using a clustered failover and using a warm backup are as follows:

➤ A standby server can run on any supported hardware and OS.

➤ A standby server does not have automatic failover.

➤ A standby server might not have up-to-date data when the failover occurs.

➤ You can perform periodic database maintenance on the standby server.

Clustering—Sharing Disk Drives

You can use clustering with Microsoft Cluster Service (MSCS) on Windows NT Server Enterprise Edition. To use clustering, you must have hardware that supports MSCS by using shared disk space between both servers in the cluster.

The first step in setting up a failover server is to install MSCS. Next, you need to install SQL Server on the primary MSCS node on a shared device. All database files also must be installed on shared devices.

Warm Backup—Setting Up A Standby Server

You can perform a warm backup with any hardware and OS that SQL Server will run on. You create a standby server by installing SQL Server on a second computer and periodically loading the primary server's contents onto the standby server.

To set up a standby server, follow these steps:

1. Back up the database.

2. Back up the transaction.

3. Periodically back up the transaction log.

4. If the primary server fails, execute the **BACKUP LOG** statement, using the **NO_TRUNCATE** clause to back up the currently active transaction log.

On the standby server:

1. Restore the database by using the **STANDBY** clause.

2. Restore the log by using the **STANDBY** clause for every log backup made.

3. If the primary server fails, execute the **RESTORE DATABASE WITH RECOVERY** statement to restore the database and bring up the standby server.

Installing A Client Computer

You use the server installation with a custom installation to install a client computer. The custom installation will allow you to install the development libraries, network libraries, ODBC, and other tools that you may want to run on a client machine.

After installing the client software, use the Client Network Utility to configure the client machine to connect to the server. The Client Network Utility allows you to give the SQL Server an alias—a name that the client computer will use when referencing the SQL Server instance. It also enables you define the network protocol and network address to use when communicating with the SQL Server.

> *Note: If you configured the SQL Server to use the default Named Pipes for network communication, you do not have to configure the client computer's network connection.*

If you are going to use ODBC to communicate with SQL Server, you will need to configure the SQL Server ODBC driver, using the ODBC administration tool.

Uninstalling SQL Server

There are three basic methods of uninstalling SQL Server: You can use the Control Panel Add/Remove Programs application, use sqlrem.exe with an installation file similar to an unattended installation, or use the Uninstall SQL Server menu option. When you uninstall SQL Server, the SQL Server home directory might not be completely removed. If the home directory isn't removed, you can remove it manually.

As with an upgrade, you need to shut down all applications and services that currently use SQL Server. Remember, if you have the SQL Server Manager on your Taskbar, you must exit the program so that you can uninstall it. Data and log files for user databases might not be removed with an uninstall operation.

Practice Questions

Question 1

> Microsoft SQL Server 7 will run on which of the following operating systems? [Check all the correct answers]
>
> ❑ a. Windows 95
>
> ❑ b. Windows 3.11
>
> ❑ c. Windows NT 4
>
> ❑ d. Windows NT 3.5.1
>
> ❑ e. Windows 98

The correct answers are a, c, and e. Answers d and b are incorrect because SQL Server 7 will not run on Windows NT 3.5.1 or Windows 3.11.

Question 2

> Which of the following can be done during an upgrade? [Check all the correct answers]
>
> ❑ a. You can set the ANSI null behavior for the databases being upgraded.
>
> ❑ b. You can pick which databases to upgrade.
>
> ❑ c. You can selectively migrate logins.
>
> ❑ d. You can migrate replication settings.
>
> ❑ e. You can select which tables to migrate.

The correct answers are a, b, and d. Answer c is incorrect because you cannot pick which logins to migrate. All logins that are users in the databases being migrated will be migrated. Answer e is incorrect because you cannot select which tables to migrate. The migration granularity is at a database.

Question 3

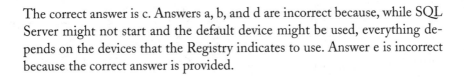

When running SQL Server, if the -d option is not set, what will happen?

- ○ a. SQL Server will not start.
- ○ b. The default device will be used.
- ○ c. The Registry will be read for the devices to be used.
- ○ d. The database will start in read-only mode.
- ○ e. None of the above.

The correct answer is c. Answers a, b, and d are incorrect because, while SQL Server might not start and the default device might be used, everything depends on the devices that the Registry indicates to use. Answer e is incorrect because the correct answer is provided.

Question 4

Which of the following options can be used to remove an installation of SQL Server? [Check all the correct answers]

- ❑ a. Use the Uninstall option from the SQL Server 7 menu
- ❑ b. Use the Remove SQL Server option in Enterprise Manager
- ❑ c. Use the Add/Remove Programs application in the Control Panel
- ❑ d. Use the Add/Remove Services application in the Control Panel
- ❑ e. Use sql70rem.exe to perform an unattended uninstallation
- ❑ f. Use the SQL Server switch utility

The correct answers are a, c, and e. Answer b is incorrect because you cannot uninstall SQL Server from Enterprise Manager. answer d is incorrect because there is no Add/Remove Services control panel application. Answer f is incorrect because the switch utility is used to switch between running a 6.x SQL Server and a 7 SQL Server. It does not perform an uninstallation.

Question 5

> Under which of the following conditions should you install the
> Desktop edition of SQL Server?
>
> O a. When you want to run SQL Server on Windows 98
>
> O b. If the machine has more than 2GB of memory
>
> O c. If you want to use failover
>
> O d. If you want to assign four CPUs to the server
>
> O e. If the database size is less than 12GB

The correct answer is a. Answer b is incorrect because SQL Server Desktop
edition supports only 2GB of memory. Answer c is incorrect because it does
not use failover. You need to use the Standard or Enterprise edition to use four
CPUs. Answer d is incorrect because the database size limit for the Desktop
edition is 4GB.

Question 6

> What of the following statements are true about a standby server?
> [Check all the correct answers]
>
> ❑ a. Standby server databases will automatically be kept in
>   sync with the primary server.
>
> ❑ b. Standby server can be used to keep a warm backup of a
>   database.
>
> ❑ c. Standby server can run only with Windows NT Enterprise
>   edition.
>
> ❑ d. Standby server can run on any operating system that will
>   run SQL Server.
>
> ❑ e. Standby server shares database files with the primary
>   server.

The correct answers are b and d. Standby server databases are not automatically kept in sync with the primary server, making answer a incorrect. Answer
c is incorrect because a standby server can be on any platform that runs SQL
Server (although a cluster server can run only on Windows NT Enterprise
edition). Answer e is incorrect; a cluster server—not a standby server—shares
database files with the primary server.

Question 7

> To connect from a client computer (a different computer than the one running SQL Server) to SQL Server, you must take which of the following steps? [Check all correct answers]
>
>
>
> ❑ a. Install the ODBC drivers on the client computer
>
> ❑ b. Configure SQL Server to use Named Pipes protocol
>
> ❑ c. Install Net-Library on the client computer
>
> ❑ d. Configure the client computer to connect by using the protocol(s) installed on the SQL Server
>
> ❑ e. None of the above

The correct answer is c. The Net-Libraries must be installed on the client computer. Answer a is incorrect because you need to install only the ODBC drivers if you plan on using ODBC to connect to the SQL Server. Answer b is incorrect; you can use any supported protocol to connect from a client computer to SQL Server. Answer d is incorrect; you don't need to configure the client computer to connect to the SQL Server, if the SQL Server is using the default Named Pipes network connection. Answer e is incorrect because the correct answer is provided.

Need To Know More?

 SQL Server *7: The Complete Reference*; Coffman, Gayle; Osborne/ McGraw-Hill; Berkley, CA, 1999; ISBN 0-07-882494-X. Chapters 11 through 13 cover installing SQL Server, upgrading SQL Server, and installing SQL Mail.

 Using Microsoft SQL Server 7.0; McGehee, Brad and Shepker, Matthew; QUE,Indianapolis, Indiana, 1998; ISBN 0-7897-1628-3. Chapter 3 does a good job of describing everything that you needs to consider when planning to install SQL Server. Chapters 4 and 5 cover installing the SQL Server and clients.

 MS SQL Server books Online.

 Search the TechNet CD-ROM (or its online version through **www.microsoft.com**).

 www.microsoft.com/ntserver/info/hwcompatibility.htm lists hardware that is compatible with Windows NT.

 www.microsoft.com/sql has up to date information on using SQL Server.

4

Security

Security Overview

To access SQL Server objects and data, users must pass through two security layers: authentication and permission validation. In addition to the two security layers provided by SQL Server, the operating system also provides a level of security.

Operating-system security limits a user's access to operating-system resources. For example, the operating-system security controls who can access a file or physically logon to a computer. On a computer running SQL Server, the users accessing SQL Server do not need access to any operating-system resource.

SQL Server requires an operating system account to access system resources. Any resources accessed by SQL Server will be accessed using SQL Server's operating-system login. The exception is when using the **xp_cmdshell**, extended stored procedure operating-system resources are accessed with the account used by SQL Server Agent. The account used by SQL Server can be a specifically assigned account, or it can be the System Account.

> *Note: If you do not start SQL Server with the System Account, it's the responsibility of the operating-system administrator to provide SQL Server with a login and to grant the correct operating-system permissions to the account.*

Authentication

SQL Server login authentication is the process that allows a user to connect with SQL Server. SQL Server has two authentication functions: SQL Server Authentication and NT Authentication. You can configure SQL Server to use only NT Authentication or to use mixed mode, which uses both NT Authentication and SQL Server Authentication. (You cannot configure SQL Server to use only SQL Server Authentication.)

 It's possible to have SQL Server running in mixed mode and not have any NT accounts configured to access SQL Server with NT Authentication. But if a user tries to access SQL Server with NT Authentication, the NT Authentication processes will deny the user access to SQL Server.

Access to SQL Server is controlled by logins. A login can be thought of as a SQL Server account. Logins should not be confused with users. In SQL Server's security paradigm, a user is granted access to a database, while a login is granted access to the server.

SQL Server Authentication

SQL Server Authentication allows a user to specify a login name and a password when connecting to SQL Server. SQL Server authentication also allows a user to connect to SQL Server when the user does not have a Windows NT account. These login names and passwords are distinct from any network logins, and are distinct from SQL Server to SQL Server.

When SQL Server is first installed, only one account—the sa (system administrator) login—is created. The sa login has full access to all objects in every database. The sa login performs all system-administration (sa) functions in SQL Server. You use the sa login to control the SQL Server configuration, resources, environment, and operations. The sa login is a member of the sysadmin fixed server role (roles are covered later in this chapter).

When SQL Server is installed, the sa login will have a null password. We recommend that you change the sa login's password immediately.

Adding Logins

SQL Server logins are added to SQL Server with the **sp_addlogin** stored procedure. Only members of the sysadmin and securityadmin SQL Server roles can run the **sp_addlogin** stored procedure. The syntax of **sp_addlogin** is as follows:

```
sp_addlogin [@loginame =] 'login'
   [,[@passwd =] 'password']
   [,[@defdb =] 'database']
   [,[@deflanguage =] 'language']
   [,[@sid =] 'sid']
   [,[@encryptopt =] {NULL | skip_encryption | skip_encryption_old]
```

The parameters of **sp_addlogin** are as follows:

➤ **@loginame** The unique name for the new login.

➤ **@passwd** The password for the new login.

Passwords are not required for SQL Server logins, but they are highly recommended.

➤ **@defdb** The default database for the new login. When the login connects, SQL Server will try to switch the login's active database to the login's default database. If the **@defdb** parameter is not set, the default database for the login will be the master database.

 Setting a default database does not grant the login access to the database. The login still must be given access before it can actually use the database.

➤ **@deflanguage** The default language for the login. If the **@deflanguage** parameter is not set, the default language will be the language set with the **sp_configure** stored procedure.

➤ **@sid** The unique security identification number (sid) for the login. If the **@sid** parameter is not set, SQL Server will generate a sid automatically.

➤ **@encryptopt** The parameter that determines how the password is stored. If **@encryptopt** is null, the password is encrypted. If **@encryptopt** is **skip_encryption**, the password isn't encrypted. If **@encryptopt** is **skip_encryption_old**, the password was encrypted by an earlier version of SQL Server.

The following example creates a login and password for John and sets the login's default database to accounting:

```
EXEC sp_addlogin john, johnspwd, accounting
```

Dropping Logins

Any member of the sysadmin or securityadmin roles can remove other logins from the SQL Server with the **sp_droplogin** stored procedure. The syntax of **sp_droplogin** is as follows:

```
sp_droplogin login_name
```

 A login cannot be dropped if the login is mapped to a user or aliased to a user in a database (users are covered later in this chapter), the login owns a database, the login owns jobs in msdb, or the login is currently connected. Also, you cannot drop the sa login. You can drop only logins that were added with the **sp_addlogin** stored procedure.

Changing A Login's Password

For security purposes, you will want to occasionally change a password. This is done with the **sp_password** stored procedure. The syntax of **sp_password** is as follows:

```
sp_password [[@old =] 'old_password',]
   {[@new =] 'new_password'}
   [,[@loginame =] 'login']
```

Login accounts can change their own passwords, but if the login account has the sysadmin role, then he or she can change the password for other logins. If you change the password for another login, the **@old** parameter must be the login's current password.

The stored procedure **sp_password** will change the password for only those logins added with **sp_addlogin**.

NT Authentication

NT Authentication allows SQL Server login names and passwords to be defined based on Windows NT network login names and passwords. Users can then supply just one network login that will connect them to the network *and* to SQL Server. Windows NT Authentication is also called *integrated security*.

Adding NT Users And Groups

The **sp_grantlogin** stored procedure allows a Windows NT login or group to connect to SQL Server without providing a SQL Server login. The syntax of **sp_grantlogin** is as follows:

```
sp_grantlogin [@loginame = ] 'login'
```

The loginame is an NT login or group in the format 'domainname\user'.

Stopping An NT User And Group From Connecting

To explicitly stop a user from connecting to a SQL Server, you use **sp_denylogin**. The syntax of **sp_denylogin** is as follows:

```
sp_denylogin {[@loginname = ]'login'}
```

To allow a user access to SQL Server after you have used **sp_denylogin** to block access, you must grant the user access with the **sp_grantlogin** stored procedure.

Removing NT Users' And Groups' Access Permissions

After a login has been either granted or denied access, you can remove the grant or denied access with the **sp_revokelogin** stored procedure. The syntax of **sp_revokelogin** is as follows:

```
sp_revokelogin {[@loginame = ]'login'}
```

If you use **sp_revokelogin** to stop a user from connecting to SQL Server, that user can still connect if he or she belongs to a group that has access.

Viewing Logins

SQL Server provides a stored procedure for viewing login information. To see all the login names created, use the **sp_helplogins** stored procedure. The following statement retrieves all the login information:

```
sp_helplogins [[@LoginNamePattern =] 'login' ]
```

If you specify an **@LoginNamePattern** when calling the stored procedure **sp_helplogins**, **sp_helplogins** displays information about the login specified in the **@LoginNamePattern**. Otherwise, **sp_helplogins** displays information about every login.

Setting The Default Database

If you want to change a login's default database, you use the **sp_defaultdb** stored procedure. The syntax of **sp_defaultdb** is as follows:

```
sp_defaultdb [@loginname = ] 'login',
   [@defdb = ] 'default database name'
```

If you are in the sysadmin or securityadmin roles, you can change the default database for other logins. Otherwise, you can change only your own default database.

 If the login is a Windows NT user or group and has not been added to SQL Server, the procedure **sp_defaultdb** will add the user or group to SQL Server.

Setting The Default Language

To change a login's default language, use the **sp_defaultlanguage** stored procedure. The syntax of **sp_defaultlanguage** is as follows:

```
sp_defaultlanguage [@loginname = ] 'login',
   [@defdb = ] 'default database'
```

If you are in the sysadmin or securityadmin roles, you can change the default language for other logins. Otherwise, you can change only your own default language.

If the login is a Windows NT user or group and has not been added to SQL Server, the procedure **sp_defaultlanguage** will add the user or group to SQL Server.

If a user passes SQL Server Authentication, he or she will then be connected to SQL Server. By itself, however, this connection doesn't allow the user access to any resources. You must still provide access to SQL Server resources by using roles, allowing login access to databases, and granting permissions.

Accessing Databases

The database is an important unit of security in SQL Server. Access to a database can be granted or denied to specific logins, NT users, and NT groups. When you grant access to a database, you create a database user.

Creating Database Users

Typically, to access a database, your login must be defined as a user of the database. There are two stored procedures to add users: **sp_adduser** and **sp_grantdbaccess**. The **sp_adduser** stored procedure is part of SQL Server to provide backward compatibility. The **sp_adduser** stored procedure calls the **sp_grantdbaccess** stored procedure. The syntax of **sp_adduser** and **sp_grantdbaccess** is as follows:

```
sp_adduser [@loginname = ] 'login_name'
   [,[@name_in_db = ] 'user_name' ]
   [,[@grpname = ] 'role_name']
      -- or --
sp_grantdbaccess [@loginname = ] 'login_name'
   [,[@name_in_db = ] 'user_name' ]
```

The only difference between **sp_adduser** and **sp_grantdbaccess** is that **sp_adduser** allows you to assign an initial fixed database role or user-defined database role to the new user.

When adding a user, you must first use the database that you want the user to be allowed in. You cannot add a user if the login name has already been added as a user or as an alias to a user in the current database.

The following code snippet illustrates how to add to a database a user that is a SQL Server login and a user that is a Windows NT user:

```
/* must be using correct database ... */
use accounting
```

```
go
/* ... then add users */
exec sp_grantdbaccess John
exec sp_grantdbaccess 'MYDOMAIN\User1',user1
go
```

Removing Users

You remove a user from a database with **sp_dropuser** or **sp_revokedbaccess**. The syntax of **sp_dropuser** and **sp_revokedbaccess** is as follows:

```
sp_dropuser [@name_in_db = ] 'user_name'
```

```
sp_revokedbaccess [@name_in_db = ] 'user_name'
```

When a user is removed, all aliases and permissions are automatically removed. Users cannot be dropped if they currently own objects within the database.

Using Aliases

Another way to allow a login to access a database is to alias the login to an existing user. This is done with the **sp_addalias** stored procedure. The syntax of the **sp_addalias** is as follows:

```
sp_addalias [@loginame = ] 'login' ,
       [@name_in_db = ] 'alias_user'
```

The **sp_dropalias** stored procedure is used to remove an alias. The syntax of **sp_dropalias** is as follows:

```
sp_dropalias [@loginame = ] 'login'
```

> *Note: Aliases are provided for compatibility with earlier versions of SQL Server. Microsoft recommends that roles be used instead of aliases with SQL Server 7.*

Viewing Users

SQL Server provides a stored procedure that allows you to see a list of users in the current database. The stored procedure that displays user information is **sp_helpuser**. The syntax of **sp_helpuser** is as follows:

```
sp_helpuser [[@name_in_db = ] 'user_name']
```

Special Users

SQL Server has two special users in a database: the database owner (dbo) and guest. The database owner (dbo) has overall control and responsibility for each database. Logins that have the sysadmin fixed server role automatically become dbos in any database they use. When creating a database, the login that created the database becomes the dbo. To change a database owner, you use the **sp_changedbowner** stored procedure. The syntax of **sp_changedbowner** is as follows:

```
sp_changedbowner [@loginame = ] 'login'
   [,[@map = ] {'true'|'false'}]
```

You cannot change the database owner to any login that is a user in the database or to any login that is aliased to a user in the database. The owner of the system database cannot be changed. If the **@map** flag is false, then all logins that were aliased to dbo will be unaliased. If the **@map** flag is true or not provided, then all logins that were aliased to dbo will be aliased to dbo after the database owner is changed.

You can create a special user account called *guest* in any database. If you create a guest account, then all logins can use the database. If the login was not specifically added as a user of the database, the login will access the database as the guest account.

Roles

Roles allow you to group together logins and permissions with two kinds of roles—server and database.

> *Note: In prior versions of SQL Server, the SQL Server database groups provided a similar functionality to roles. Even though groups are currently supported in SQL Server 7, we recommend that you use roles, rather than groups, because roles provide a more robust capability.*

Roles allow you to set up a hierarchical security structure in which a role is a member of another role. You can also assign permissions to a role; that way, when a user takes a new position in your organization, you can just assign the user a new role.

Fixed Server Roles

SQL Server provides seven fixed server roles. These roles are used to assign standard SQL Server server-wide jobs to logins. The fixed server roles are listed in Table 4.1.

You can assign logins to fixed server roles, giving the login the permissions of the fixed server role. You cannot remove fixed server roles from the system, nor can you create new fixed server roles.

Assigning Fixed Server Roles

To assign a login to a fixed server role, use the **sp_addsrvrolemember** stored procedure. The syntax of **sp_addsrvrolemember** is as follows:

```
sp_addsrvrolemember [@loginame =] 'login'
   [,[@rolename =] 'role']
```

If the login is a Windows NT user or group that has not been granted access to SQL Server, the user or login will be granted access when you run the **sp_addsrvrolemember** stored procedure.

 You can change the sa login's role membership.

Unassigning Logins From Fixed Server Roles

If you no longer want a login to be a member of a fixed server role, you use the **sp_dropsrvrolemember** stored procedure. The **sp_dropsrvrolemember** stored procedure syntax is as follows:

```
sp_dropsrvrolemember [@loginame =] 'login'
   [,[@rolename =] 'role']
```

Viewing Information About Fixed Server Roles

SQL Server provides three stored procedures to retrieve information about fixed server roles: **sp_helpsrvrole, sp_helpsrvrolemember,** and **sp_srvrolepermission**.

The **sp_helpsrvrole** stored procedure returns a list of the fixed server roles and a description of each role. The syntax of **sp_helpsrvrole** is as follows:

```
sp_helpsrvrole [[@srvrolename =] 'role']
```

Vital Table 4.1	Fixed server roles.	
Role	**Login Type**	**Description**
sysadmin	System administrators	Can perform any activity in SQL Server
securityadmin	Security administrators	Manages server logins
serveradmin	Server administrators	Configures server-wide settings
setupadmin	Setup administrators	Adds and removes linked servers
processadmin	Process administrators	Manages processes
diskadmin	Disk administrators	Manages disk files
dbcreator	Database creators	Creates and alters databases

The **sp_helpsrvrolemember** stored procedure returns a list of roles and the logins that have the roles assigned to them. The syntax of **sp_helpsrvrolemember** is as follows:

```
sp_helpsrvrolemember [[@srvrolename =] 'role']
```

The **sp_srvrolepermission** returns a list of roles and the permissions that have been assigned to the roles. The syntax of **sp_srvrolepermission** is as follows:

```
sp_srvrolepermission [[@srvrolename =] 'role']
```

Database Roles

SQL Server also provides the capability of having roles that are database dependent. That is, a login can have different roles depending on the database that the login is using. There are three types of database roles: fixed database, user-defined, and application.

Fixed Database Roles

The fixed database roles are standard roles that are provided by SQL Server to perform basic database jobs. Table 4.2 lists the fixed database roles.

User-Defined Database Roles

Besides providing the standard fixed database roles, SQL Server 7 allows you to create and delete user-defined database roles. The stored procedure **sp_addrole** is used to add user-defined database roles. The syntax of **sp_addrole** is as follows:

```
sp_addrole [@rolename =] 'role' [,[@ownername =] 'owner']
```

Vital Table 4.2   Fixed database roles.

Role	Role Type	Description
db_owner	Database owners	Performs activity of all other database roles and other maintenance activities
db_accessadmin	Database access administrators	Adds and removes database users
db_securityadmin	Database security administrators	Manages database roles and statements and object permissions
db_ddladmin	Database DDL administrators	Adds, modifies, and drops objects
db_backupoperator	Database backup operators	Backs up the database
db_datareader	Database data readers	Views all data from every table in the database
db_datawriter	Database data writers	Adds, changes, and deletes data from every table in the database
db_denydatareader	Database deny data readers	Refuses access to read data
db_denydatawriter	Database deny data writers	Refuses access to write data

To remove user-defined database roles, you use the **sp_droprole** stored procedure. The syntax of **sp_droprole** is as follows:

```
sp_droprole [@rolename=] 'role'
```

You can drop only user-defined database roles with **sp_droprole**. If the role has members, you cannot drop the role. A role that owns objects cannot be removed.

> *Note: If you need to remove a role that owns an object, either drop the object or use the **sp_changeobjectowner** stored procedure to change the owner of the object. The syntax of **sp_changeobjectowner** is as follows:*
>
> ```
> sp_changeobjectowner {@objname = ] 'objectowner.object',
>     [@newowner = ] = 'owner'
> ```

By default, users are not members of any user-defined database roles. To assign users to a role, you use the **sp_addrolemember** stored procedure. To assign a user to a role, you must either have a **db_securityadmin** or **db_owner** role or you must be the role owner.

The syntax of **sp_addrolemember** is as follows:

```
sp_addrolemember [@rolename =] 'role',
   [@membername =] 'security_account'
```

You can assign a user-defined database role to a SQL Server database user, to a SQL Server role, or to any Windows NT user or group that has been granted access to the database with the **sp_grantdbaccess** stored procedure.

By assigning one user-defined role to another user-defined role, you can set up a hierarchical chain of permissions. In this chain, you first define your roles; then, you can assign the higher-level roles to be a member of the lower-level roles. Listing 4.1 illustrates a three-level role chain. The levels in this chain are clerk, auditor, and manager.

Listing 4.1   Setting up a hierarchical role chain.

```
-- step 1 is to add all of the roles
exec sp_addrole 'clerk'
go
exec sp_addrole 'auditor'
go
exec sp_addrole 'manager'
go

-- step 2: assign the higher-level role to be a member
--         of the lower-level role
exec sp_addrolemember 'auditor','clerk'
go
exec sp_addrolemember 'manager','auditor'
go
```

After setting up the hierarchical role chain, you can add users to the roles and grant permissions to the roles. The roles higher in the chain will have the permissions of the roles lower in the chain, along with any permissions explicitly assigned to them. Users are removed from user-defined roles with the **sp_droprolemember** stored procedure. The syntax of **sp_droprolemember** is as follows:

```
sp_droprolemember [@rolename =] 'role',
   [@membername =] 'security_account'
```

The Public Role

In every database, there is a special role called *public*. Every database user is a member of the public role. The public role cannot be removed, nor can you assign users, groups, or roles to the public role. You assign default permissions to the public role; then, every user in the database automatically gets those permissions.

Application Roles

Besides user-defined database roles, SQL Server allows you to add application roles. Unlike other roles, application roles do not have members. To gain the permissions of an application role, you must specifically activate the role.

Application roles are created with the **sp_addapprole** stored procedure. The syntax of **sp_addapprole** is as follows:

```
sp_addapprole [@rolename =] 'role',
   [@password =] 'password'
```

When creating an application role, you must supply a password for the role. The user will employ the password when activating the application role.

Application roles are activated with the **sp_setapprole** stored procedure. To deactivate an application role, you must first disconnect from SQL Server. The syntax of **sp_setapprole** is as follows:

```
sp_setapprole [@rolename =] 'name' ,
   [@password =] {Encrypt N 'password'} | 'password'
   [,[@encrypt =] 'encrypt_style']
```

 When an application role is activated, all the current permissions are lost for the connection. Additionally, the application role permissions are applied to the connection. If the connection needs to access other databases, the connection will use the guest user account in the other databases.

Application roles are removed with the **sp_dropapprole** stored procedure. The syntax of **sp_dropapprole** is as follows:

```
sp_dropapprole [@rolename =] 'role'
```

You can drop only application database roles with **sp_dropapprole**. If the role has active users, you cannot drop the role. A role that owns objects cannot be removed. If you need to remove a role that owns an object, either drop the object or use the **sp_changeobjectowner** stored procedure to change the owner of the object.

Viewing Information About Database Roles

SQL Server provides two stored procedures for viewing information about database roles, application roles, and role members for the current database.

The stored procedure **sp_helprole** displays fixed database roles, user-defined database roles, and application roles for the current database. The syntax of **sp_helprole** is as follows:

```
sp_helprole [[@rolename = ] 'role'
```

The stored procedure **sp_helprolemember** displays members of fixed database and user-defined database roles. The syntax of **sp_helprolemember** is as follows:

```
sp_helprolemember [[@rolename = ] 'database role'
```

Permissions

An object is owned by the user who created it, and initially only the object owner can access the object. The **GRANT, DENY,** and **REVOKE** commands are used by the object owner to control other users' access to the object. The object owner can control the permissions listed in Table 4.3.

In addition to controlling permissions on objects, you can also control permissions on statements. The following statements can be granted, revoked, and denied:

➤ CREATE DATABASE

➤ CREATE DEFAULT

➤ CREATE PROCEDURE

➤ CREATE RULE

➤ CREATE TABLE

➤ CREATE VIEW

Table 4.3 Object permissions.	
Command	**Description**
SELECT	Allows a user to read the table or view
INSERT	Allows a user to add data to a table or view
UPDATE	Allows a user to modify data in a table or view
DELETE	Allows data to be removed from a table or view
EXECUTE	Allows a stored procedure to be executed
REFERENCES	Allows a user to refer to a table or view in a **WHERE** clause
ALL	Grants all permissions

➤ BACKUP DATABASE

➤ BACKUP LOG

➤ ALL (all of the preceding SQL statements)

Only the dbo has permission to control security on the previous statements.

Granting Permissions

The **GRANT** statement is used to assign permissions to a role or a user. The syntax of the **GRANT** statement is different for granting permissions on database objects than it is for granting permissions on statements. Listing 4.2 contains the syntax of the **GRANT** statement.

Listing 4.2   Syntax of the GRANT statement.

```
/* table level */
GRANT {ALL [PRIVILEGES] | permission[,...n]}
  { [(column[,...n])] ON {table | view}
    | ON {table | view}[(column[,...n])]
    | ON {stored_procedure | extended_procedure}
  }
  TO security_account[,...n]
  [WITH GRANT OPTION]
  [AS {group | role}]

/* statement level */
GRANT {ALL | statement[,...n]}
  TO security_account[,...n]
```

The security account is the user, role, NT user, or NT group that you want to grant permissions to. The **WITH GRANT OPTION** allows the user to grant the permissions to other users. If you use the **AS** *group* or *role* option, then the role must be used when executing the statement granted. The following example illustrates the use of the **GRANT** statement:

```
/*allow John to insert and update author rows */
grant insert, update on authors to John
```

Denying Access To Objects

The **DENY** statement is used to specifically deny a user or group access to objects. The **DENY** statement prevents the specific security account from inheriting the permissions through NT groups or SQL Server roles. The syntax of the **DENY** statement is shown in Listing 4.3.

Listing 4.3   Syntax of the DENY statement.

```
/* statement permissions */
DENY{ALL | statement[,...n]}
   TO security_account[,...n]

/*Object permissions */
DENY {ALL [PRIVILEGES] | permission[,...n]}
   {
   [(column[,...n])] ON {table | view}
   | ON {table | view}[(column[,...n])]
   | ON {stored_procedure | extended_procedure}
   }
  TO security_account[,...n]
  [CASCADE]
```

By default, if the security account to which you are denying permissions has granted the permissions to other accounts, the other accounts retain their permissions on the object. The **CASCADE** option causes the deny to pass on to security accounts that the permissions were granted by the account that is being denied.

Revoking Permissions

The **REVOKE** statement removes any permissions that were granted or denied. Like the **GRANT** and **DENY** statements, the **REVOKE** statement has a different syntax for statement permissions than for object permissions. The syntax of **REVOKE** is shown in Listing 4.4.

Listing 4.4   Syntax of the REVOKE statement.

```
/* statement permission */
REVOKE {ALL | statement[,...n]}
   FROM security_account[,...n]

/*Object permissions */
REVOKE [GRANT OPTION FOR]
   {ALL [PRIVILEGES] | permission[,...n]}
   {
   [(column[,...n])] ON {table | view}
   | ON {table | view}[(column[,...n])]
   | {stored_procedure | extended_procedure}
   }
  {TO | FROM}
   security_account [,...n]
  [CASCADE]
  [AS {group | role}]
```

Viewing Permissions

SQL Server provides the **sp_helprotect** stored procedure to check permissions on objects, users, grantors, and permission areas. The syntax of **sp_helprotect** is as follows:

```
sp_helprotect [[@name =] 'object_statement']
   [,[@username =] 'security_account']
   [,[@grantorname =] 'grantor']
   [,[@permissionarea =] 'type']
```

If you use any of the parameters of **sp_helprotect**, the rows displayed by **sp_helprotect** will be limited to the rows that match the criteria of the parameters. The **@permissionarea** parameter allows you to specify to display object permissions ('o'), statement permissions ('s'), or both object and statement permissions ('o' and 's' in any order).

SQL Server also provides the **sp_table_privileges** stored procedure to display a list of permissions for tables. The syntax of **sp_table_privileges** is as follows:

```
sp_table_privileges [@table_name_pattern =] 'table_name_pattern'
   [,[@table_owner_pattern =] 'table_owner_pattern']
   [,[@table_qualifier =] 'database_name']
```

The stored procedure **sp_table_privileges** displays information that meets the criteria of the parameters. Both **@table_name_pattern** and **@table_owner_pattern** support wildcard matching.

Notes On Permissions

The following information holds true for **GRANT, REVOKE,** and **DENY**:

➤ By default, only the object owner has access to the object.

➤ Column names can be specified in permission lists, so you can grant, deny, or revoke permission on only parts of a table.

➤ If a permission is denied at any level (user, group, or role), the denial takes precedence over any permissions that have been granted.

➤ If a permission is denied and you then grant the same permission at the same level, the grant will cancel the denial. If the object is stilled denied at another level, the denial at the other level will still apply.

➤ A dbo cannot maintain permissions on another's table, unless the dbo uses the **SETUSER** statement.

➤ It is easier to first grant broad permissions and then limit the permissions.

➤ The Create Database privilege can be granted only in the master database.

Permissions Chains

Views and stored procedures provide another security mechanism. In a permission chain, either one user or multiple users can own all the objects.

If the same user who owns the underlying objects owns the view or stored procedure, then SQL Server will not check permissions on the underlying objects. In this scenario, if you have permission to **SELECT** from a view, you do not need to be granted **SELECT** on the underlying tables.

If the view or stored procedure is owned by users different from those owning the underlying objects, then SQL Server will check permissions on the underlying objects. In this scenario, if you have permission to **SELECT** from a view, you need to be granted **SELECT** on the underlying tables.

Note: To use views effectively, it is recommended to have objects owned by a single owner, who should usually be a dbo.

Limitations On Logins, Users, Roles, And Passwords

SQL server places some limitations on login names, user names, role names, and passwords. The limitations are as follows:

➤ Logins, users, roles, and passwords can be from 1 through 128 characters.

➤ Logins, users, roles, and passwords cannot contain backslashes.

➤ Logins, users, and roles must not be keywords.

➤ Logins, users, and roles must not be a special login or user name.

Practice Questions

Question 1

> Which of the following stored procedures will assign an application role to a user?
>
> ○ a. sp_addappmember
>
> ○ b. sp_addrolemember
>
> ○ c. sp_addsrvrolemember
>
> ○ d. None of the above.

The correct answer is d. You do not specifically assign application roles to users. To use an application role, the user must issue the **sp_setapprole** stored procedure.

Question 2

> If user Joe owns a table named Sales and Jane creates a view named smallsales (without using the With Check view option), what SQL statement can user Bailey do if the following grants were performed on the table and view? [Check all the correct answers]
>
> ```
> -- Joe performs these grants:
> grant insert on sales to public
> grant select, delete, update on sales to Jane
>
> -- Jane then performs these grants on her view:
> grant insert, update on smallsales to Bailey
> ```
>
> ❏ a. Bailey can perform a SELECT on the smallsales view.
>
> ❏ b. Bailey can perform an INSERT on the smallsales view.
>
> ❏ c. Bailey can perform a DELETE on the smallsales view.
>
> ❏ d. Bailey can perform an UPDATE on the smallsales view.
>
> ❏ e. None of the above.

The correct answer is b. Because the view isn't owned by the same user who owns the underlying object, permissions are checked against the view and the underlying object. Bailey has permissions to insert data using the smallsales view. Bailey also has permissions (through the public role) to insert data into the table Sales. Answer a is incorrect; Bailey has permissions to **SELECT** data from the table Sales, but not from the smallsales view. Answer c is incorrect; Bailey has permissions to **DELETE** data from the table Sales, but not from the smallsales view. Answer d is incorrect; Bailey has **UPDATE** permissions on the smallsales view, but Bailey doesn't have permissions to update the table Sales. Answer e is incorrect because the correct answer is provided.

Question 3

Which of the following SQL batches will allow the SQL Server login Connor to be a user in the database MyDB and a member of the user-defined database role BigGuy? [Check all the correct answers]

❑ a.
```
sp_adduser @DB='MyDB',@loginame = 'connor',
     @grpname = 'BigGuy'
```

❑ b.
```
use MyDB
go
sp_grantdbaccess @loginname = 'connor',
     @rolename = 'BigGuy'
```

❑ c.
```
use MyDB
go
sp_adduser @loginame = 'connor',
     @grpname = 'BigGuy'
```

❑ d.
```
use MyDB
go
sp_grantdbaccess @loginname = 'connor'
exec sp_addrolemember 'BigGuy','connor'
```

The correct answers are c and d. Answer a is incorrect because there is no **@DB** parameter for the **sp_adduser** stored procedure. Answer b is incorrect because there is no **@rolename** parameter for the **sp_grantdbaccess** stored procedure.

Question 4

If Paula is a member of the user-defined database groups Sales and Accounting, which of the following SQL batches will allow her to have SELECT permissions on the table MyStuff? [Check all the correct answers]

❑ a.
```
grant all on MyStuff to sales
```

❑ b.
```
grant all on MyStuff to accounting
revoke select on MyStuff to dfp3
```

❑ c.
```
revoke select on MyStuff to dfp3
grant select on MyStuff to sales
```

❑ d.
```
grant all on d2 to sales
deny select on d2 to accounting
```

❑ e.
```
deny select on d2 to accounting
grant all on d2 to sales
```

The correct answers are a and c. Answer a is correct because a **GRANT ALL** will give the role Sales permissions to perform a **SELECT**. Answer c is correct; **REVOKE** and **GRANT** depend on the order in which they are performed. If a **REVOKE** is performed before the **GRANT**, the **GRANT** will take place. Answer b is incorrect; **REVOKE** and **GRANT** depend on the order in which they are performed. If a **REVOKE** is performed after the **GRANT**, the **REVOKE** will take place. Answers d and e are incorrect; a **DENY** always takes precedence over a **GRANT**.

Question 5

> Which of the following stored procedures will add a new server-wide role?
>
> ○ a. sp_addrole
>
> ○ b. sp_addsrvrole
>
> ○ c. sp_newsrvrole
>
> ○ d. sp_addapprole
>
> ○ e. None of the above

The correct answer is e. You cannot add new server roles. Answer a is incorrect because the **sp_addrole** stored procedure adds a new user-defined database role. Answers b and c are incorrect because neither of these two stored procedures exists. Answer d is incorrect because **sp_addapprole** creates a new database-level application role.

Question 6

> Which of the following is true about the stored sp_defaultdb procedure? [Check all the correct answers.]
>
> ❑ a. The default database must exist when the sp_defaultdb stored procedure is executed.
>
> ❑ b. The sp_defaultdb stored procedure can change the default database for any SQL Server login.
>
> ❑ c. If you use sp_defaultdb for a SQL Server login, Windows NT user or Windows NT group that has not been granted access to the database, the user or group will automatically be granted access to the database.
>
> ❑ d. The sp_defaultdb stored procedure can change the default database for any Window NT user or group that has been granted access to SQL Server.
>
> ❑ e. Members of the SQL Server sysadmin fixed server role can change the default database for other users.

The correct answers are a, b, d, and e. The only incorrect answer is c; **sp_defaultdb** doesn't make the login, NT user, or NT group a user of the database.

Need To Know More?

 Amo, William C. *Transact- SQL* (IDG Books Worldwide, Foster City, CA, 1998, ISBN 0-7645-8048-5). Chapter 3 provides an overview of SQL Server security.

 Coffman, Gayle. *SQL Server 7: The Complete Reference* (Osborne/McGraw-Hill, Berkley, CA, 1999, ISBN 0-07-882494-X). Chapter 5 covers integrating SQL Server with NT security. Chapter 21 provides a complete TSQL reference on the command to control security.

 McGehee, Brad and Matthew Shepker. *Using Microsoft SQL Server 7.0* (QUE, Indianapolis, IN, 1998, ISBN 0-7897-1628-3). Chapters 11, 12, and 13 provide a thorough discussion of SQL Server security.

 MS SQL Server Books Online.

 Search the TechNet CD-ROM (or its online version, through **www.microsoft.com**).

 www.microsoft.com/sql This site contains up-to-date information on using SQL Server.

Databases And Files

Terms you'll need to understand:

√ File and group layouts

√ Tables

√ Transaction log

√ Virtual log file

Techniques you'll need to master:

√ Creating databases

√ Altering databases

√ Creating file groups

√ Altering file groups

√ Planning files and file groups

√ Configuring databases

Database Overview

One of the basic structures in SQL Server is the database. The database provides the context in which data is stored and controlled.

Besides the four system databases (discussed in Chapter 2), SQL Server can have up to 32,767 databases. All SQL Server database objects revolve around the use, access, and integrity of the tables.

A database is all of the following:

➤ A collection of tables that relate to one another

➤ A linked set of allocations in SQL Server storage

➤ The unit of data for backup

➤ Two or more files

➤ An important unit of data for security and control

Database Files

A database contains 2 through 32,767 database files. A file has two names—a logical name and a physical name. The logical name follows standard SQL Server object-naming conventions. Physical files can be any local or networked files. The files can automatically grow larger.

A database file can be used by only one database.

Databases can contain three types of files: primary files, secondary files, and log files. Every database must have at least one primary file and one log file. Table 5.1 describes the uses of these three file types. SQL Server doesn't enforce the file-name extensions shown in Table 5.1, but we recommend that you follow this convention.

Database File Groups

A file group is a way of linking a set of files. A file can belong to only one group. (Log files, however, cannot belong to any group.) A file group is used to spread I/O across multiple disks for tables placed in a group. If a file group contains more than one file, I/O to that group is spread across the files in the group. A database can contain up to 256 file groups.

Table 5.1	Types of database files.		
File Type	**Extension**	**Use**	**Number Per Database**
Primary file	.mdf	Stores database startup information and data	At least one or more per database.
Secondary file	.ndf	Spreads I/O out across multiple disks	Optional. A database doesn't have to contain secondary data files.
Log file	.ldf	As a write-ahead log, keeps track of changes made in data before the data is written to the data files	At least one per database.

Every database has a primary file group named PRIMARY. This group contains the primary data file and all data files that are not specifically assigned to another file group.

Data can be assigned to any file group. All data that isn't assigned to a group is placed in the default file group. One file group can be configured as the default file group at any given time.

File And File Group Issues

A file or file group can be used in only one database. A file can be a member of only one file group. You must have separate files for data and for log information. The data and log files cannot both be in the same file group. Log files are never part of any file group.

A maximum of 256 file groups are allowed in a database.

Most of the time, your database will meet your performance requirements with a single data file and a single log file. If you plan to use multiple files, however, use the primary file only for system tables and objects. Then, create at least one secondary file for storing user data and objects.

To maximize the performance of your database, follow these guidelines:

➤ Make sure that files or file groups are created on as many different local physical disks as are available. (You should not use network drives for your database. If you do use network drives, your system performance can become significantly slower than if you only use local drives.)

➤ Place into different file groups objects that compete heavily for space.

➤ Place into different file groups different tables used in the same queries. Doing this will improve performance due to parallel disk I/O searching for joined data.

➤ Place heavily accessed tables and the nonclustered indexes belonging to those tables on different file groups. Doing this will improve performance due to parallel I/O if the files are located on different physical disks.

➤ Do not place the log file(s) on the same physical disk with the other files and file groups or with any files used for anything besides SQL Server.

Devices

In SQL Server, it is possible to create devices before you create the database. You can do so with the **DISK INIT** command. The SQL Server 7 database limitations are still in place, even if you create devices with the **DISK INIT** command. You should not use the **DISK INIT** command. Listing 5.1 shows the syntax of the **DISK INIT** command for backward-compatible use only.

Listing 5.1   Syntax of the DISK INIT command.

```
DISK INIT
     NAME = 'logical_name',
     PHYSNAME = 'physical_name',
     VDEVNO = virtual_device_number,
     SIZE = number_of_2K_blocks
     [, VSTART = virtual_address]
```

The device will then show up in the **sysdevices** table in the master database. This table will also contain any dump devices and the devices for the master database, the model database, and the tempdb database.

The Transaction Log

The transaction log contains a serial record of all changes that occur in a database. The primary purpose of this log is to recover transactions. When a server is restarted, all uncommitted transactions are rolled back, and the changes will be undone. This process makes sure that the data in the database is the same as it was before the uncommitted transactions. All committed transactions are rolled forward, updating the database to contain all the data changes.

The transaction log is made up of multiple virtual log files. A *virtual log file* is a segment of the log file. When a transaction log is truncated, the truncation removes all the records in one or more virtual log files. A log file contains at least two virtual log files. The minimum size for a virtual log file is 256K. SQL Server will create more virtual files as the log files grow. The number and size of these virtual files depends on the size of the growth increment for the log file. Larger growth increments will cause the virtual file to be larger.

Planning A Database

Planning your database layout is an important part of administrating databases, files, and file groups. A poorly laid out database will not perform as well as one that has a good layout.

 We recommend that you initially create your database files so that they will hold all the data you expect the database to hold when it is fully populated.

If you allow your database files to grow, you need to place a limit on how large a file can grow to make sure that the files will not fill the disk. To reduce file fragmentation and to keep files from competing for space as they grow, you should place files on different physical disks.

Use as many physical disks as possible. Place database objects with a lot of activity in different file groups. For tables with a lot of activity, have multiple files in their file groups.

Creating Databases

Databases are created with the **CREATE DATABASE** command. Anyone with the SQL Server Administrator role or anyone to whom the sa has specifically given permissions can create a database. Listing 5.2 shows the syntax for the **CREATE DATABASE** command.

Listing 5.2   Syntax of the **CREATE DATABASE** command.

```
CREATE DATABASE db_name
    [ ON [PRIMARY] ([ NAME = logical_file_name, ]
            FILENAME = 'os_file_name'
            [, SIZE = size]
            [, MAXSIZE = { max_size | UNLIMITED } ]
            [, FILEGROWTH = growth_increment [MB|KB|%] )
```

```
        | {FILEGROUP filegroup_name FILEDEFINITIONS}
        [,...n] ]
[LOG ON {[ NAME = logical_file_name, ]
        FILENAME = 'os_file_name'
        [, SIZE = size]
        [, MAXSIZE = { max_size | UNLIMITED } ]
        [, FILEGROWTH = growth_increment]  } [,...n]
   [FOR LOAD | FOR ATTACH]
```

You can use the **CREATE DATABASE** command to attach a new database to devices created with the **DISK INIT** command. We recommend that you use the **CREATE DATABASE** command to create the files and assign them to the database.

When you create a database and if you do not specify both a primary file and a log file, SQL Server will create the missing file (or files). The physical files will be located in the default data-file location and will be named *database_name*.mdf for the primary file and *database_name*_log.ldf for the log file.

If you don't specify a file size, the primary file will be the same size as the primary file in the model database. The log file and any secondary data files will be 1MB. The size can be larger if the model database has information that causes the new database to need more space. Although it's optional to specify files and sizes, in practice, you will always want to specify them.

SQL Server creates a database in two steps. First, SQL Server copies the model database into the new database. Second, SQL Server initializes all unused pages.

The following list describes the **CREATE DATABASE** parameters:

➤ **PRIMARY** Specifies the file as a primary device or a member of the PRIMARY file group. When you create tables and indexes, the primary file group is used if you do not specify another file group.

➤ **NAME** Specifies the logical file name. It defaults to the physical file name specified with the **FILENAME** parameter.

➤ **FILENAME** Provides the fully qualified disk file name.

➤ **SIZE** Indicates the initial size of the file. The minimum size for a log file is 512K.

➤ **MAXSIZE** Specifies the largest size to which the file can grow.

➤ **UNLIMITED** Enables the file to grow to an unlimited size.

➤ **FILEGROWTH** Specifies the increment of growth in megabytes (MB), kilobytes (K), or percent (%). Growth defaults to 10%. If you do not specify file growth to be in megabytes, kilobytes, or percentage, the increment will default to megabytes.

➤ **FOR LOAD** Provides backward compatibility.

➤ **FOR ATTACH** Specifies that the database file already exists.

The user who creates the database owns it. All database configuration options are copied from the model database, unless the database is created with the **FOR ATTACH** option. In this case, the database configuration options are read in from the existing database files. Listing 5.3 shows examples of the **CREATE DATABASE** command.

Listing 5.3   Examples of the **CREATE DATABASE** command.

```
/* database with default size on default files */
CREATE DATABASE test1

/* database size is 2MB for data and default size for log*/
CREATE DATABASE test2
    ON (FILENAME ='c:\d1.mdf', SIZE = 2 , NAME = 'd1')

/* database is 20MB, with a 10MB primary and one Filegroup
** and log 10MB */
CREATE DATABASE test3
ON PRIMARY (FILENAME ='c:\test3.mdf',
            SIZE = 10 , NAME = 'd1'),
FILEGROUP g1 (FILENAME ='c:\g1.mdf',
            SIZE = 10 , NAME = 'g1')
LOG ON (FILENAME ='c:\test3.ldf',
            SIZE = 10 , NAME = 'log1')
```

 If you don't specify a transaction log file, one will be automatically created that is either 25 percent of the size of the primary file or 512K, whichever is larger.

Altering Databases

Because a SQL Server 7 database can automatically grow, there isn't as much need to alter a database as in previous versions. You may still want to add files and file groups, shrink a database, change a database owner, change a database name, or reconfigure an existing file or file group. The syntax for these commands are discussed in the following sections. When the database is in multiuser mode, you can do everything except rename a database.

Removing A Database

Databases are removed with the **DROP DATABASE** command. The syntax for the **DROP DATABASE** command is as follows:

```
DROP DATABASE database_name[, n]
```

You can drop one or more databases. When you remove a database, the files used by it are deleted. If the database is in use, you cannot drop the database. After you drop a database, the database and its files cannot be used.

Changing A Database Owner

You can change the database owner with the **sp_changedbowner** command. You can change the database owner to any login that is not currently a user of the database. If the current dbo (database owner) has aliases, you can specify whether you want the aliases to be assigned to the new dbo.

The syntax of the change database owner command is as follows:

```
sp_changedbowner [@loginame =] 'login' [,[@map =] drop_alias_flag]
```

Only users with system administration permissions can change a database owner.

 You cannot change the owner of the system databases.

When you change a database's owner, you must first be in the database you want to change. The following example shows the use of the **sp_changedbowner** procedure:

```
USE MyDb
go
sp_changedbowner @loginame='NewDBO'
go
```

Renaming Databases

If you want to change the name of a database, SQL Server provides the **sp_renamedb** stored procedure. The syntax of the procedure used to rename a database is as follows:

```
sp_renamedb "old_name","new_name"
```

Only someone with the system administrator role can rename a database. To change a name, you must first put the database into single-user mode (see the "Configuring Databases" section later in this chapter). Make sure that you put the database back into multiuser mode after you are done. Listing 5.4 shows how to use the **sp_renamedb** procedure.

Listing 5.4   Using the sp_renamedb procedure.

```
use master
go
exec sp_dboption MyDB,'single','true'
go
exec sp_renamedb MyDB,'MyNewDB'
go
exec sp_dboption MyNewDB,'single','false'
go
```

Altering Databases

The **ALTER DATABASE** command allows you to change the definition and the size of a database. Listing 5.5 shows the syntax of the **ALTER DATABASE** command.

Listing 5.5   Syntax of the ALTER DATABASE command.

```
ALTER DATABASE database
  { ADD FILE <filespec> [,...n] [TO FILEGROUP filegroup_name]
  | ADD LOG FILE <filespec> [,...n]
  | REMOVE FILE logical_file_name
  | ADD FILEGROUP filegroup_name
  | REMOVE FILEGROUP filegroup_name
  | MODIFY FILE <filespec>
  | MODIFY FILEGROUP filegroup_name filegroup_property
  }

<filespec> ::=
  (NAME = 'logical_file_name'
  [, FILENAME = 'os_file_name' ]
  [, SIZE = size]
  [, MAXSIZE = { max_size | UNLIMITED } ]
  [, FILEGROWTH = growth_increment] )
```

The **ALTER DATABASE** command allows you to add a file to an existing file group or add a new log file. If you are adding a new data file and you do not specify a file group, the file will be added to the primary file group.

You can remove empty files. However, there must always be at least one file in the primary file group and one log file in the database. When you remove a file, the physical file is deleted.

You can add new file groups. When you add a new file group, no file is automatically added to it. You must add these files.

You can use the **ALTER DATABASE** command to remove a file group. If any files are in the file group, however, they must be empty, or you cannot remove the file group. You cannot remove the primary file group.

When using **ALTER DATABASE** to modify files, you must specify the logical name of the file you are modifying. You can change the rest of the options in the file specification, but you can change only one option in a single **ALTER DATABASE** command. If you change the size of a file, the new size must be at least as large as the current file size.

When modifying a file group, you can set the following properties:

➤ **READONLY** Specifies that the file group is read-only. Use of this property prevents objects in the file group from being modified. The primary file group cannot be made read-only. Only users who have exclusive access to the database can mark a file group as read-only.

➤ **READWRITE** Reverses the **READONLY** property. Updates are allowed to the objects in the file group. Only users who have exclusive access to the database can mark a file group as read-write.

➤ **DEFAULT** Specifies that the file group is the default file group for the database. When you set the default property for a file group, the default property is removed from the previous default file group. When you create a database, the primary file group is set as the default file group. If no file group is specified in the **CREATE TABLE, ALTER TABLE,** or **CREATE INDEX** statements, new tables and indexes are created in the default file group.

It isn't possible to move a file from one file group to another file group. If you need to do this, you must first remove the file and then add it to the new file group.

Listing 5.6 shows examples of the **ALTER DATABASE** command.

Listing 5.6   Examples of the **ALTER DATABASE** command.

```
/* the following example will add a new data file,
pubs_data2.ndf  size = 50m to a new group grp2 */
```

```
ALTER DATABASE pubs ADD FILEGROUP grp2

ALTER DATABASE pubs ADD FILE ( NAME = 'PubsFile2',
    FILENAME = 'c:\temp\pubsdata2.ndf',
    SIZE = 50 ) TO FILEGROUP grp2

/* the following example will remove the group grp2
which was added in the last example from the pubs database*/
ALTER DATABASE pubs REMOVE FILE PubsFile2

ALTER DATABASE pubs REMOVE FILEGROUP grp2
```

Manually Shrinking Databases

To shrink a database, you run the **DBCC SHRINKDATABASE** command. The syntax of the **SHRINKDATABASE** command is as follows:

```
DBCC SHRINKDATABASE
( database_name [, target_percent]
[, {NOTRUNCATE | TRUNCATEONLY}]
)
```

When shrinking a database, you can specify an optional percentage, which is the amount of free space you would like to leave in the database. The **NOTRUNCATE** option overrides the default behavior and leaves the free space in the operating-system files after shrinking the file. The **TRUNCATEONLY** option causes any unused space in the data files to be released to the operating system and shrinks the files to the last allocated extent. No attempt is made to move rows to unallocated pages. When the **TRUNCATEONLY** option is used, the *target_percent* option is ignored. The **NOTRUNCATE** option will not shrink a file smaller than the minimum file size.

The **DBCC SHRINKFILE** command will not shrink a file past the minimum size needed to store the data in the file. If you use the **NOTRUNCATE** option with the *target_percent* option, the only effect is that used pages will move to the front of the file. A database cannot be made smaller than the **model** database.

To shrink a database file, you run the **DBCC SHRINKFILE** command in the database that contains the file you want to shrink. The syntax of the **SHRINKFILE** command is as follows:

```
DBCC SHRINKFILE
( {file_name | file_id }
{ [, target_size]
| [, {EMPTYFILE | NOTRUNCATE | TRUNCATEONLY}]
}
)
```

Before you can shrink a file, you must use the database that contains the file. You can shrink a file by using either its file name or its file ID. When you shrink a file, data is normally moved to the pages at the front of the file.

The target size is an integer that specifies how large you want the file to be. If you do not specify a size, the file will be shrunk as much as possible. When the file size reaches the amount of space needed to store the data, the file will not shrink further.

The **EMPTYFILE** option will move all the data from the emptied file to other files in the file group. SQL Server will no longer allow data to be placed in the file. This prepares the file for being removed with the **ALTER DATABASE** statement.

The **NOTRUNCATE** option releases unused space, but it will not move data rows. When the **NOTRUNCATE** option is used, the *target_size* option is ignored.

Configuring Databases

With SQL Server, multiple options can be configured at a database level. You use the **sp_dboption** stored procedure to set the options. The syntax of the **sb_dboption** procedure is as follows:

```
sp_dboption ['database'] [, 'option_name'] [, 'on' | 'off']
```

If you don't specify a database, **sp_configure** will list all the settable options. Table 5.2 shows the valid options.

The only option you can set for the master database is **TRUNC. LOG ON CHKPT**. When you create a new database, the options that are currently set in the model database are the options that will be turned on in the new database.

> If you want specific options in all your new databases, set the options on the **model** database.

Only the dbo or someone with the system administrator role can set database options.

> When you set a configuration value, it doesn't take effect until the database is checkpointed. Unlike previous versions of SQL Server, however, SQL Server 7 automatically checkpoints the database for you.

Table 5.2   Database configuration options.

Option	Description
ANSI NULL DEFAULT	When on, if you do not specify **NOT NULL** for a column when creating or altering a table, the column will use the SQL-92 rules to determine whether a column allows **NULL** values.
ANSI NULLS	When on, all comparisons to a **NULL** value evaluate to **UNKNOWN**. When **FALSE** and not using **UNICODE** values, **NULL = NULL** value evaluates to **TRUE**.
ANSI WARNINGS	When on, errors or warnings are issued when conditions such as "divide by zero" occur.
AUTOCLOSE	When on, the database is shut down cleanly, and its resources are freed after the last user exits.
AUTOSHRINK	When on, the database files are candidates for automatic periodic shrinking.
CONCAT NULL YIELDS NULL	When on, if either operand in a concatenation operation is **NULL**, the result is **NULL**.
CURSOR CLOSE ON COMMIT	When on, any cursors that are open when a transaction is committed or rolled back are closed. When off, such cursors remain open when a transaction is committed. When off, rolling back a transaction closes any cursors except those defined as **INSENSITIVE** or **STATIC**.
DBO USE ONLY	When on, only the database owner can use the database.
DEFAULT TO LOCAL CURSOR	When on, cursor declarations default to **LOCAL**.
MERGE PUBLISH	When on, the database can be published for a merge replication.
OFFLINE	When on, the database is offline and cannot be used by anyone.
PUBLISHER	When on, the database can be published for replication.
QUOTED IDENTIFIER	When on, double quotation-characters mark (") can be used to surround delimited identifiers.
READ ONLY	When on, users can only read data in the database; they cannot modify it.
RECURSIVE TRIGGERS	When on, enables triggers to cause the same trigger to fire as a result of its data modifications.

(continued)

Table 5.2	Database configuration options *(continued)*.
Option	**Description**
SELECT INTO/BULKCOPY	When on, the **SELECT INTO** statement, unlogged **WRITETEXT**, unlogged **UPDATETEXT**, and fast bulk copies are allowed.
SINGLE USER	When on, only one user at a time can access the database.
SUBSCRIBED	When on, the database can be subscribed for publication.
TORN PAGE DETECTION	When on, incomplete pages can be detected.
TRUNC. LOG ON CHKPT.	When on, the database is truncated every time a checkpoint occurs in the database. An automatic checkpoint occurs whenever the log becomes more than 70 percent full, or SQL Server estimates that it will take longer than the "recovery interval" to recover the database. Other conditions that can cause a checkpoint are when the **CHECKPOINT** command is issued, the SQL Server is stopped, the **sp_dboption** procedure is used, or a **BACKUP LOG** statement is issued.

Viewing Database Information

SQL Server provides three standard catalog procedures for viewing information about databases, files, and file groups: **sp_helpdb**, **sp_helpfile**, and **sp_helpfilegroup**.

The catalog procedure **sp_helpdb** displays information about databases and about how the database is configured. The syntax of the **sp_helpdb** stored procedure is as follows:

```
sp_helpdb [database_name]
```

If you do not provide the name of the database about which to retrieve information, you get a one-line report about every database. If you run **sp_helpdb** with a database name, it produces a more detailed report than when you don't specify a database name. This report will contain the information from **sp_helpdb** and the same information as the report produced by **sp_helpfile**.

The **sp_helpfile** stored procedure is used to list information about files attached to the current database. The syntax of **sp_helpfile** is as follows:

```
sp_helpfile [[@filename = ] 'name']
```

If you don't specify a file name, you will get information about all files in the database.

The **sp_helpfilegroup** stored procedure is used to list information about file groups in the current database. The syntax of **sp_helpfilegroup** is as follows:

```
sp_helpfilegroup  [[@filegroupname = ] 'name']
```

If you don't supply the name, you get information about every file group. If you pass on the file group name, **sp_helpfilegroup** also runs **sp_helpfile** on every file in the group.

 If you want information about the PRIMARY file group, you must enclose **PRIMARY** in quotes, because it is a reserved word.

Practice Questions

Question 1

> If you want to remove a file from a database, which of the following statements are true? [Check all the correct answers]
>
> ❑ a. You must be in the database from which you want to remove the file.
>
> ❑ b. You must run the DBCC SHRINKFILE command to make sure that the file is empty.
>
> ❑ c. You cannot remove the file if its file group has data in it.
>
> ❑ d. You run the DBCC REMOVEFILE command to remove the file from the database.
>
> ❑ e. The OS file still will have the data in it after the file is removed from the database.
>
> ❑ f. The database must be in single-user mode.
>
> ❑ g. None of the above.

Answer g is correct. Answer a is incorrect because you don't have to be in the database to run the **ALTER DATABASE** command. Answer b is incorrect. Although the file must not have any data in it, you don't have to shrink a file before removing it. Answer c is incorrect. You can remove a file if other files in its file group still contain data. Answer d is incorrect because there is no **DBCC REMOVEFILE** command. Answer e is incorrect because after you remove a database file, the operating system file will be deleted. Answer f is incorrect. You can alter a database when the database is in multiuser mode.

Question 2

> Which of the following will create a database called MyDB with
> an initial size of 50MB for the database files?
>
> ○ a. CREATE DATABASE MyDB datasize = 40, logsize = 10
>
> ○ b. CREATE DATABASE MyDB on File1 = 40 log on file2 = 10
>
> ○ c. CREATE DATABASE MyDB on NAME = 'File1', size = 40
>   log on name = file2, size = 10
>
> ○ d. CREATE DATABASE MyDB on(NAME = 'File1', size = 40)
>   log on(name = file2, size = 10)
>
> ○ e. CREATE DATABASE MyDB on (NAME = 'File1', size = 40
>   log on name = file2, size = 10)

The only answer that is syntactically correct is d. Answer a is missing the **on**
and **log on** keywords. Answer b follows the pre-SQL Server 7 syntax. Answer
c is missing parentheses. Answer e has the parentheses in the wrong place.

Question 3

> To find information about all files used in the current database,
> you would use which of the following SQL statements?
>
> ○ a. sp_helpgroup
>
> ○ b   sp_helpdb
>
> ○ c. sp_helpfile
>
> ○ d. sp_listfiles

The correct answer is c. Answer a, **sp_helpgroup**, without a file name, will list
only groups. Answer b, **sp_helpdb**, without a name, will list only the one-line
database report. The stored procedure **sp_listfiles** doesn't exist, which makes
answer d incorrect.

Question 4

How do you stop users from modifying data in a database? [Check all the correct answers]

❏ a. Set the NOWRITE database configuration option.

❏ b. Set the READONLY file option for every file in the database.

❏ c. Set the READONLY file group option for every file in the database.

❏ d. Set the READONLY database configuration option.

❏ e. It cannot be done.

The correct answers are c and d. There is no **NOWRITE** database configuration option, so answer a is incorrect. There is no **READONLY** file option, so answer b is incorrect. Because answers c and d are correct, answer e is incorrect.

Question 5

The online database option performs which of the following? [Check all the correct answers]

❏ a. It makes the database read-only.

❏ b. It is used to make the database available for users.

❏ c. It is used to stop users from being able to access a database.

❏ d. It makes a complete file group read-only.

❏ e. None of the above.

The correct answer is e. Answers a, b, c, and d are incorrect because there are no online database options. The correct option is **OFFLINE**, and the **OFFLINE** option allows you to mark a database as being available or unavailable for use.

Need To Know More?

Amo, William C., *Transact—SQL* (Foster City, CA, IDG Books Worldwide, 1998, ISBN 0-7645-8048-5). Chapter 5 covers data definition language.

Coffman, Gayle, *SQL Server 7: The Complete Reference* (Berkley, CA, Osborne/McGraw-Hill, 1999, ISBN 0-07-882494-X). Chapter 21 provides a complete TSQL reference.

McGehee, Brad and Shepker, Matthew: *Using Microsoft SQL Server 7.0* (Indianapolis, IN, QUE, 1998, ISBN 0-7897-1628-3). Chapter 8 covers planning databases and managing databases

MS SQL Server Books Online.

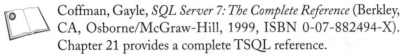

Search the TechNet CD-ROM (or its online version, through **www.microsoft.com**).

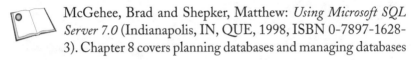

www.microsoft.com/sql has up to date information on using SQL Server.

Transferring Data

Terms you'll need to understand:

√ Value list

√ Bulk Copy Program

√ The bcp optimizer hint

√ Import

√ Export

√ Transformation

√ Data Transformation Service

Techniques you'll need to master:

√ Using the **INSERT** statement

√ Inserting data into identity columns

√ Inserting default values into columns

√ Using the **SELECT INTO** statement

√ Using the bcp program

√ Using the **BULK INSERT** statement

√ Importing and exporting selected data

√ Using the Data Transformation Service

√ Using the dtswiz program

After creating a database, you need a way to transfer data to and from it. SQL Server provides several ways to import, or load, data into a database. You can also use some of these options to export, or move, data from a database. This chapter discusses several options: the **INSERT** statement, the **SELECT** statement, the **BULK INSERT** statement, the bcp program, and the Data Transformation Service.

The INSERT Statement

The **INSERT** statement is used to add data to an existing table in a database. The **INSERT** statement has four forms. In two forms, you specify the values for a single row. The other two forms can move multiple rows, based on a **SELECT** statement or a stored procedure.

The syntax of the **INSERT** statement is as follows:

```
INSERT [INTO] {table|view}
{ {[(column_list)] VALUES ({DEFAULT | constant_expression }[,...n])
  | select_statement
  | execute_statement
  }
  | DEFAULT VALUES
}
```

No matter which form of **INSERT** you use, you must follow some basic rules:

➤ The **INSERT** statement appends rows to a table. Unless a trigger exists that will then modify existing rows, an **INSERT** statement cannot modify existing data.

➤ Derived columns cannot be inserted or specified in a column list. If you do an **INSERT** without specifying a column list, all the columns in the table that are not derived columns are considered to be in the column list. A *column list* is a comma-separated list of columns enclosed in parentheses. This list doesn't have to be in the same order as the columns in the table.

➤ All non-null columns that don't have a default value or a value provided in some other way must be supplied in the **INSERT** statement's column list.

➤ If you don't specify a column list, the values must be listed in the order of the columns in the table. The values specified must match the order and data types of the column list or (if you do not supply a column list) the order of the columns in the table.

You cannot normally insert a value into an identity column. To insert a value into an identity column, you must have the **IDENTITY_INSERT** property turned on for the table, as shown here:

```
SET IDENTITY_INSERT [database.[owner.]]{table} {ON | OFF}
```

When the **IDENTITY_INSERT** option is turned on for a table, you can insert a value into the identity column. If you do not specify the identity column, the identity column will get the next identity value. If you explicitly assign a value to the identity column, that value will be used. If the value assigned is greater than the current identity value, the identity counter will start counting at the new value.

Remember that an identity column doesn't guarantee that the column is unique.

Unless they have default values, columns with the **UNIQUEIDENTIFIER** property do not automatically get values assigned to them. The value you insert is a 36-digit hexadecimal value in the format xxxxxxxx-xxxx-xxxx-xxxx-xxxxxxxxxxxx. The dashes are mandatory. You can use the **NEWID()** function to generate a unique global ID to assign to the column.

When inserting into **CHAR, VARCHAR,** or **VARBINARY** data types, the actual value inserted depends on the **ANSI_PADDING** option in effect when the table is created, as follows:

➤ If this option is set to **OFF, CHAR** values are padded to the column width, **VARCHAR** values remove trailing spaces, strings that contain only spaces are set to a single space, and **VARBINARY** values have trailing zeros removed.

➤ If this option is set to **ON, CHAR** columns are padded, and **VARCHAR** and **VARCHAR** columns are neither truncated nor padded.

The SQL Server's default value for **ANSI_PADDING** is **OFF**. However, the Microsoft SQL Server ODBC driver and the MS SQL Server OLE DB provider both turn it on when connecting to SQL Server. Microsoft recommends that you always turn on this option.

After performing an **INSERT**, the function **@@ROWCOUNT** will return the number of rows inserted. This number will be some non-negative number equal to the number of rows inserted. Having zero rows inserted for an insert using a **SELECT** statement or a stored procedure doesn't mean that an error occurred; it could mean that the **SELECT** statement or stored procedure returned no rows.

Inserting A Single Row

The most common use of an **INSERT** statement is to add a single row to a table. Normally, to specify a single-row insert, you use the **VALUES** keyword. Let's look at some examples. The following examples show how to insert rows into a table:

```
INSERT MyTable VALUES ('a',1234)
```

The preceding example illustrates how to insert into a table with out specifying a column list. Here is another way to use the **VALUES** keyword in an **INSERT** statement:

```
INSERT MyTable (a) VALUES ('ccc')
```

The preceding example illustrates the use of a column list to limit what columns you are specifying values to be inserted. The next code snippet combines the **DEFAULT** and **VALUES** keywords in an **INSERT** statement:

```
INSERT MyTable DEFAULT VALUES
```

The preceding example illustrates how to use the **DEFAULT** keyword. In this example, because the **DEFAULT** keyword is placed before the **VALUES** keyword, every column in the table will be set to its default value.

 When using the **DEFAULT** keyword before the **VALUES** keyword, every column must have a default value or allow nulls.

The next example illustrates the use of the **DEFAULT** keyword after the **VALUES**.

```
INSERT MyTable VALUES (DEFAULT,5)
```

In the preceding example, in which the **DEFAULT** keyword appears after the **VALUES** keyword, only the column in the column list corresponding to the **DEFAULT** keyword position in the value list will have its default value assigned.

The next example illustrates the use of functions in the value list:

```
INSERT MyTable VALUES (user_name(),@@ROWCOUNT)
```

For every column in the column list, you must specify some scalar expression to generate its value. This expression can be a constant, any scalar function, and any expression that contains constants and scalar functions or the **DEFAULT** keyword. You cannot specify a subquery, columns, or an aggregate function in the **VALUES** clause. Either the value inserted must implicitly convert to the column's data type, or you must perform an explicit conversion.

There are two ways the **DEFAULT** keyword can be used in an **INSERT** statement:

➤ If you use the **DEFAULT** keyword *in* the values list, the **DEFAULT** keyword applies to the corresponding column in the column list.

➤ If you use the **DEFAULT** keyword *before* the values list, it applies to every non-derived column in the table, and you cannot have a column list.

If a default value is assigned to the column, that value will be used. If you haven't assigned a default value to the column, a null value will be inserted. If the column doesn't allow nulls, an error is generated. If the column is a **TIMESTAMP** data type, the next timestamp value will be assigned to it. You cannot use **DEFAULT** in a value list with an identity column, but you can use the **DEFAULT** keyword before the **VALUE** keyword with an identity column.

The following examples show how to use the **DEFAULT** keyword with an identity column:

Table as follows:

```
CREATE TABLE Test ( Col1 NUMERIC(10) IDENTITY,
        Col2 VARCHAR(32) DEFAULT 'Test' NOT NULL)
```

This insert is valid:

```
INSERT Test DEFAULT VALUES
```

The first insert will add a row with the next value for Col1 and 'Test' for Col2.

This insert is not valid:

```
INSERT Test VALUES ( DEFAULT,DEFAULT)
```

The second insert will fail, even if the table is configured to allow inserts into identity columns.

Using A **SELECT** Statement To Insert Rows

You can use **INSERT** with most valid **SELECT** statements to add multiple rows to a table. The **SELECT** statement cannot use the **COMPUTE** or **COMPUTE BY** clauses.

 You can insert data into a table with a **SELECT** statement retrieving data from the table you are inserting rows into; but, you have to make sure that you do not violate any unique indexes.

If **ROWCOUNT** is set to anything except zero, then the insert will stop when the **ROWCOUNT** number of rows is reached.

It's possible for a **SELECT** statement to not return any rows. This occurrence is not an error. If any inserted row violates a constraint on the table, the whole insert will fail. Here's an example of inserting with a **SELECT** statement:

```
INSERT MyTable ( a, b )  SELECT c,SUM(d) FROM MyTable2 GROUP BY c
```

Using A Stored Procedure To Insert Rows

You can use a stored procedure to add multiple rows to a table. You can use any stored procedure that returns data by using a **SELECT** statement or a **READTEXT** statement. You can also use this procedure to update and to insert rows into other tables.

The procedure can be in any database on the local server or on a remote server, or the procedure can be an extended stored procedure. It can retrieve multiple results and perform more than one **SELECT** statement. The data retrieved must match the data type and the number of columns from the column list. If the procedure uses **READTEXT** to retrieve data, it is limited to 1,024K in each **READTEXT**.

If **ROWCOUNT** is set to anything except zero, the insert will stop when the **ROWCOUNT** number of rows is reached.

It's possible for the stored procedure to not return any rows. This is not an error. If any inserted row violates a constraint on the table, the whole insert will fail. Here's an example of using a stored procedure to insert rows:

```
INSERT MyTable ( a, b ) EXECUTE SomeValidProcedure
```

In this example, **SomeValidProcedure** must return one or more result sets containing two columns of compatible data types to **a** and **b**.

The SELECT INTO Statement

You can use the INTO clause of the SELECT statement to create a table and insert data all in one step. For this option to work, the database option SELECT/INTO must be turned on, or you cannot create tables in the database.

 Usually, **SELECT INTO** isn't used in production databases. If it is used, it tends to be used to create a temporary table.

The syntax of a SELECT statement using SELECT INTO is as follows:

```
SELECT select_list INTO table_name [from_clause] [where_clause]
[groupby_clause] [having_clause] [orderby_clause]
```

The SELECT statement with the INTO clause will make a new table that matches the SELECT results. This new table will have columns that match the columns in the select list. With the SELECT statement, you can use all clauses except for the COMPUTE and COMPUTE BY clauses.

All columns in the select list must have a unique non-null name. If two columns have the same column name, you must give one of them a column alias. Any expressions or functions must be given a column alias. Finally, you cannot perform SELECT INTO inside of a transaction.

 The **SELECT INTO** statement will fail if the table being created already exists.

You can use the WHERE and HAVING clauses to limit the number of rows inserted. If the SELECT statement returns no rows, then a blank table is created.

 Often, you will see a table created with a **SELECT INTO** statement using **1=2** in the **WHERE** clause to create an empty table.

Identity properties are inherited unless one of the following conditions is true:

➤ The SELECT statement contains a join, an aggregate function

➤ A GROUP BY clause, a union, or multiple identity columns in the select list

➤ The column is used in an expression. Computed columns will become regular noncomputed columns in the new table. Constraints and indexes are not created in the new table.

 To perform the **SELECT INTO** procedure, you must have table-creation privileges in the target database, and you must have data-retrieval privileges in the tables you are selecting from, or the procedure will fail.

Here's an example of a **SELECT** statement with the **INTO** clause:

```
SELECT * INTO TestTable FROM authors
```

The preceding SELECT statement will copy all rows and columns from the table named "authors" into a new table called "TestTable."

 The table being selected into does not have to be in the current database. You can use any fully qualified table name that does not already exist. The table can also be a temporary table.

The BULK INSERT Statement

SQL Server 7 provides a new way to load data into a table from a file. You can use the **BULK INSERT** statement, as shown in Listing 6.1. This statement behaves like the command-line bcp program, which is discussed later in this chapter.

 The major difference between the bcp program and the **BULK INSERT** statement is that the **BULK INSERT** statement can only load data; it cannot export data from SQL Server to a data file.

Listing 6.1 Syntax of the BULK INSERT statement.

```
BULK INSERT [['database_name'.]['owner'].]
            {'table_name' FROM data_file}
[WITH (
   [ BATCHSIZE = batch_size]
   [[,] CHECK_CONSTRAINTS]
   [[,] CODEPAGE = ACP | OEM | RAW | code_page]
   [[,] DATAFILETYPE =
        {'char' | 'native'| 'widechar' | 'widenative'}]
   [[,] FIELDTERMINATOR = 'field_terminator']
   [[,] FIRSTROW = first_row]
   [[,] FORMATFILE = 'format_file_path']
```

```
  [[,] KEEPIDENTITY]
  [[,] KEEPNULLS]
  [[,] LASTROW  = last_row]
  [[,] MAXERRORS  = max_errors]
  [[,] ORDER ({column [ASC | DESC]} [, ...n])]
  [[,] ROWTERMINATOR  = 'row_terminator']
  [[,] TABLOCK]
)
]
```

The only parts of the statement that must be specified are the table that will have rows inserted into it and the data file. If you do not specify a database name, the statement will default to the current database. If you do not specify an owner, the statement will default to the current user. If you do not own the table and do not specify the table owner, the statement will try to insert rows into a table owned by the dbo.

To use the **BULK INSERT** statement to insert rows into a table that is owned by someone else, you must have the db_owner role or the sysadmin role. Otherwise, the **BULK INSERT** will fail.

Data_file is the full path name of the file to load. The file can be from any kind of disk. The path is based on the computer that's running SQL Server; it isn't the path on your local computer. To load a data file from your local computer, you should specify the network name of your local computer.

When you use the **BULK INSERT** statement to access data files that are physically located on other computers, you should first create a named share on the other computer. You can use the administrator hidden share, a share that is the drive letter followed by a dollar sign ($), but security will inevitably shut it down at some point in larger companies.

Any other parameters can show up in the test. Most of these parameters are simple in the tasks they do. If you have multiple parameters, remember to separate them with a comma. It's important to remember that parentheses are needed around everything after the **WITH** keyword.

BATCHSIZE specifies the number of rows to send to the server in a batch. By default, all rows are sent in a single transaction. If the **BULK INSERT** aborts, the current batch will be rolled back. All previous batches will be rolled forward. Because batch size affects the amount of data written to the transaction log, setting the **BATCHSIZE** number can significantly improve load performance.

CHECK_CONSTRAINTS tells SQL Server to check all constraints on the table. Without this parameter, you can use BULK INSERT to load data that you cannot normally insert due to referential integrity or other constraints.

CODEPAGE specifies which character code page to use for data in the data file. This parameter affects only character columns, and it affects them only if there are characters with ASCII values less than 32 or greater than 126. **ACP** specifies that the file contains the ANSI/Microsoft Windows code page ISO 1252. **OEM** specifies that the file contains the OEM code page. **RAW** specifies that you do not perform character conversion; this option loads data the fastest. Any other value specifies a specific code page.

DATEFILETYPE specifies what the data file looks like. **CHAR** is the default type. It's used for files that have all the data stored in character format with a tab character between fields and a newline character at the end of each row. **NATIVE** specifies that the file contains SQL Server data types. **NATIVE** is used for files exported from SQL Server by the bcp utility. **WIDECHAR** is used if the file contains UNICODE characters. Otherwise, it behaves in the same way **CHAR**. **WIDENATIVE** specifies that the file contains SQL Server data types, but any character fields are stored as UNICODE characters.

For data files that are **CHAR** and **WIDECHAR**, you can change the field and row terminators. The **FIELDTERMINATOR** option allows you to pick a different field terminator, and the **ROWTERMINATOR** option allows you to pick a different row terminator. The terminator can be any string that is one or more characters long.

For all data-file types, you can specify a **FORMATFILE**. This file allows you to have a wider variety of data files. Here are a few of the options: You can have fixed-length fields, you can have different terminators for each field, and you can skip over columns.

If you want to load only part of a file, you can use **FIRSTROW** and **LASTROW** to specify the first and last rows to load. You do not have to specify both options. If **FIRSTROW** is greater than the number of rows in the file, then no rows are inserted and no errors are generated. If **LASTROW** is greater than the number of rows in the file, then the **BULK INSERT** stops at the end of the file and will generate no errors. **FIRSTROW** should be less than or equal to **LASTROW**; if it is not, **LASTROW** is ignored.

If the table has an identity column, SQL Server does not load the value for the identity column from the file. If you want the value in the file to be loaded, you must specify the **KEEPIDENTITY** option.

The **KEEPNULL** option causes defaults to be ignored for columns that are not loaded. A null value is placed in any of the columns that are not loaded.

Normally, the **BULK INSERT** procedure stops after 10 errors occur. The **MAXERRORS** option allows you to specify how many errors can occur before the procedure will stop.

If the data file is sorted in the clustered index order, then using the **ORDER** option speeds up the **BULK INSERT**. If the data turns out to be unsorted, SQL Server will ignore this option. If you manually sort the data file, but the SQL Server sort order would sort it differently, SQL Server treats the data file as being unsorted.

The following lines of code show an example of a **BULK INSERT**:

```
BULK INSERT pubs.dbo.authors FROM 'c:\data\authors.blk'
WITH FIELDTERMINATOR ='||', LASTROW = 300
```

This **BULK INSERT** statement will insert up to the first 300 rows from the data file. The file will have data in character format. Each field uses two pipes '||' as a separator. Also, each record will have a newline character at the end of the row.

SQL Server can perform a fast, unlogged form of **BULK INSERT** under the following conditions:

➤ The database option **SELECT INTO/BULKCOPY** is set to **TRUE**.

➤ The table has no triggers.

➤ The table is not being replicated.

Any bulk copy into SQL Server that doesn't meet these conditions is logged.

The bcp Program

The Bulk Copy Program utility (bcp.exe or bcp) is used to import data into and export data from a SQL Server database table. The bcp program can read and write files in a variety of formats. When copying data *from* a file, bcp appends data to an existing database table; when copying data *to* a file, bcp overwrites any previous contents of the file. Version 7 of bcp uses ODBC to connect to the server.

When you load data into a table, the table must already exist in the database, and you must have insert and select permissions on the table. The number of fields in the file and the order of the fields do not have to match the columns in the table. If they do not match, however, you must use a format file. The data types in the file must be compatible with the column data types.

Many parameters can be used to control bcp behavior. Listing 6.2 shows the syntax of the bcp program.

Listing 6.2   Syntax of the bcp program

```
bcp [{[database_name.][owner].]table_name | "query"}
    {in | out | format | queryout} data_file
    [-m max_errors] [-f format_file] [-e err_file]
    [-F first_row] [-L last_row] [-b batch_size]
    [-n] [-c] [-w] [-N] [-6] [-q] [-C code_page]
    [-t field_term] [-r row_term]
    [-i input_file] [-o output_file] [-a packet_size]
    [-S server_name] [-U login_id] [-P password]
    [-T] [-v] [-k] [-E] [-h "hint [,...n]"]
```

The parameters for bcp behave the same as the equivalent parameters for a **BULK INSERT** statement. If a parameter contains any special characters, the parameter must be in quotes.

The first parameter of the bcp program is either the qualified table name or a query to execute that will generate data. You must specify a query when using the **QUERYOUT** option, and you must specify a table when you use the **IN**, **OUT**, or **FORMAT** option. If you use a query, it can be any **SELECT** statement or stored procedure that returns one result set. If you use a stored procedure that returns more than one result set, the first result set will be copied to the file.

IN|OUT|FORMAT|QUERYOUT specifies the action of bcp. If you specify the **FORMAT** option, the bcp utility will create a format file and will not import or export data. You must specify the -f parameter if you use the format option. If the format option is used, and neither -n, -c, -w, -6, nor -N is specified, bcp prompts for format information.

The remaining parameters are as follows:

➤ You can use the -m parameter to limit the number of errors that can occur. Any row that has an error is ignored. The default value for this option is 10 errors.

➤ You can specify a format file with the -f option. The format file gives bcp finer control over how the data being imported or exported looks. If you specify the format file without specifying that bcp is doing a format action, that format file must exist.

➤ You can use the -e option to specify an error file. All error messages and the row that caused the error are written to the error file.

➤ You can use the -F and -L options to specify the first row and last row to bulk copy. The default is to copy from the first row to the last row.

➤ You can use the -b parameter to specify the batch size or the number of rows to bulk copy in a batch. The default is the whole file. Each batch is in its own transaction. If the bulk copy aborts for any reason, all rows inserted from the current batch are rolled back. You cannot use this parameter with the **-h** "**ROWS_PER_BATCH** = *bb*" option.

➤ The **-n** parameter causes bulk copy to use the native (database) data types of the data.

➤ The **-c** parameter causes bulk copy to convert everything to a character data type. This option uses **CHAR** as the storage type, no prefixes, \t (tab character) as the field separator, and \n (newline character) as the row terminator.

➤ The **-w** parameter causes bulk copy to convert everything to an Unicode data type. This option uses **CHAR** as the storage type, no prefixes, \t (tab character) as the field separator, and \n (newline character) as the row terminator. This parameter cannot be used with SQL Server 6.5 or earlier.

➤ The **-N** parameter causes bulk copy to use the native (database) data types of the data for non-character data, and to use Unicode characters for character data. This option offers a higher-performance alternative to the **-w** option and is intended for transferring data from one SQL Server to another by using a data file. This parameter cannot be used with SQL Server 6.5 or earlier.

➤ The **-6** parameter causes bulk copy to use SQL Server 6 or 6.5 data types. This option is used with the **-c** and **-n** options to load data that was generated by previous versions of bcp.

➤ The **-q** parameter specifies that the table name contains special characters. When you use this option, you must enclose the full table name in double quotes (").

➤ The **-C** parameter specifies a code page to use for character data. This parameter affects columns with character values greater than 127 or less than 32.

➤ The **-t** parameter specifies the field terminator. The default is \t (tab character).

➤ The **-r** parameter specifies the row terminator. The default is \n (newline character).

➤ The **-i** parameter specifies the name of an input response file. This file provides the responses to questions for each field when performing a bulk copy and when not using -n, -c, -w, -6, -N, or an input file.

➤ The **-o** parameter specifies the name of a file that receives output from bcp. This parameter doesn't affect where the data is stored.

➤ The -a parameter specifies the network packet size. This option can range from 4,096 through 65,535 bytes; the default is 4,096. Increased packet size can enhance performance of bulk copy operations. If a larger packet is requested but cannot be granted, the default is used.

➤ The -S parameter specifies which SQL Server to connect to on the network (some servers may run more than one instance of SQL Server). The default is the local server. This option is required when you execute bcp from a remote computer on the network.

➤ The -U parameter is used to specify the login ID used to connect to SQL Server. The parameter will default to the current user.

➤ The -P parameter is used to specify the password for the login ID. If this option is not used and the -T parameter is not specified, bcp prompts for a password. If you use this option at the end of the parameter list with no password following it, bcp uses the default password (**NULL**).

➤ The -T parameter specifies that bcp connects to SQL Server with a trusted connection, using the security credentials of the network user. No SQL Server login or password is required.

➤ The -v parameter reports the version number and copyright information of the bcp program and then exits.

➤ The -k parameter causes empty columns to be null during bulk copy inserts, instead of having the default values applied to the columns inserted.

➤ The -E parameter is used to specify that identity columns are present in the file being imported. If -E is not given, the file being imported should not contain values for these columns, because SQL Server automatically assigns unique values. If -E is specified, SQL Server takes the values for the identity columns from the data file.

➤ The -h parameter is used to specify hints that the optimizer uses during a bulk copy of data. You cannot use the -h parameter when using the **QUERYOUT** parameter. Table 6.1 lists the bcp hints.

The following examples illustrate the use of the bcp program. The first example copies all the rows from the author table in the pubs database to the file authors.dat:

```
bcp pubs..author out authors.dat -Usa -c
```

Data is stored in character format. The bcp program connects as the user sa and prompts you for the password.

Vital Table 6.1	The bcp optimizer hints.
Hint	**Definition**
ORDER (column [ASC | DESC] [,n])	Sort order of the data in the data file.
ROWS_PER_BATCH = bb	Number of rows of data per batch. Do not use with the **-b** parameter.
KILOBYTES_PER_BATCH = cc	Number of kilobytes of data per batch.
TABLOCK	A table-level lock is acquired for the duration of the bulk copy operation.
CHECK_CONSTRAINTS	Causes SQL Server to check table constraints during data loads.

The following example copies data from the file moreauthors.dat into the author table in the pubs database:

```
bcp pubs..author in moreauthors.dat -Usa -P sapw -f fmt.file -S S2
```

The bcp program connects as sa, using the supplied password sapw, to the server S2. The format file fmt.file will describe the format of the data.

The next example copies data returned from executing the stored procedure **sp_who** into the file sp.dat:

```
bcp "exec sp_who" queryout sp.dat  -c -F 3 -L 5
```

The data is in character format, and rows three, four, and five are saved. You will connect as the current user that is logged into the network. Finally, bcp prompts you for a password.

The following example copies data into the authors table in your default database:

```
bcp authors in mauthors -c -h "TABLOCK, ROWS_PER_BATCH=10"
```

Because a password wasn't supplied, bcp prompts you for a password. The data in the file is in character format, and the optimizer hints **TABLOCK** and **ROWS_PER_BATCH** will be used.

Running bcp

When you use the **-n** or **-c** option to copy data into or out of a file, bcp prompts you for only your password, unless you supply the **-P** option. If you don't supply either the **-n** or **-c** options, bcp prompts for information for each field in the table. Each prompt displays a default value, in brackets, which you can accept by pressing a carriage return. The prompts include the following:

➤ The file storage type, which can be a character or any valid SQL Server data type

➤ The prefix length, which is an integer indicating the length in bytes of the following data

➤ The storage length of the data in the file

➤ The field terminator, which can be any character string

After you answer the questions for each field, the bcp utility asks if you want to save the format information in a file.

You can perform multiple bulk copies into a table simultaneously. This can be done only if all requirements for non-logged bulk copy are met (the database **SELECT INTO/BULKCOPY** option is turned on, the table has no triggers, and the table is not being replicated) and the table has no indexes.

The Data Trasformation Service

The Data Transformation Service (DTS) imports, exports, and transforms data between multiple heterogeneous data sources. You can use DTS with any data source that can be accessed with OLE DB. If an OLE DB driver isn't provided for the data source, you can use Microsoft's OLE DB for ODBC to access data.

The Data Transformation Service uses the DTS wizard to create a Data Transformation Package (DTP). You can run the DTP to transform data. You can call DTS directly from the SQL Server Enterprise Manager, run the dtswiz.exe program, or call the DTS Distributed Management Object (DMO).

DTS Components

DTS consists of four components. These components are DTS Import Wizard, DTS Export Wizard, DTS Package Designer, and the DTS COM programming interfaces.

The DTS Import Wizard

The DTS Import Wizard walks you through the steps for importing data into a SQL Server database. These steps are as follows:

1. Start the DTS wizard, and click on Next.

2. In the new Wizard window, choose the data source that contains the data you want to import. Enter any necessary parameters to make the connection; these parameters will depend on the data source. Click on Next.

3. In the Wizard window, choose the data destination. Enter all necessary parameters to make the connection. Then, click on Next.

4. On the next screen, choose the Copy Tables option to pick individual tables to copy or Use Query option to write a SQL Statement to define the data to copy. Then, click on Next.

5. If you picked the Copy Tables option, you see a screen that allows you to select the tables to copy. If you picked the Use Queries option, you need to either write the query in the next screen or use the Query Builder (click on the Query Builder button to open the Query Builder) to write the query for you. Then, click on Next.

6. Indicate whether you want to run the package, save the package, create a replication package, or schedule the package. Then, click on next. If you opt to run the package, you will see the package status window. If you save the package, you will be asked to supply the package's name, description, and server information.

7. In the final window, click on Finish to perform the options you selected.

The DTS Export Wizard

The DTS Export Wizard walks you through the steps for exporting data from a SQL Server database. The steps are as follows:

1. Start the DTS wizard, and click on Next.

2. On the next screen, choose the data source that contains the data you want to export, and enter any necessary parameters to make the connection. Click on Next.

3. In the new Wizard window, choose the data destination, and enter all necessary parameters to make the connection. Click on Next.

4. On this screen, choose the Copy Tables or Use Query option, and click on Next.

5. If you picked the Copy Tables option, you see a screen that allows you to select the tables to copy. If you picked the Use Queries option, you need to either write the query in the next screen or use the Query Builder (click on the Query Builder button) to write the query. Then, click on Next.

6. Indicate whether you want to run the package, save the package, create a replication package, or schedule the package. If you run the package, you will see the package status window. Then, click on Next. If you save the package, you will be asked to supply the package's name, description, and server information. Then, click on Next.

7. In the final Wizard window, click on Finish to run the package you just created.

The DTS Package Designer

The DTS Package Designer allows you to graphically design a DTS package. A DTS package is a set of steps to perform when transforming data. In the simplest form, a DTS package contains one import or export step defined by the DTS Import Wizard or the DTS Export Wizard. You can create a package as part of an import or export, or you can create a package separately. This wizard enables you to save the DTS package in the SQL Server msdb database, the Microsoft Repository, or a COM-structured storage file. You can also schedule the DTS package for later execution.

The DTS COM Programming Interfaces

A DTS COM interface is used to create and execute DTS packages. A DTS COM interface allows you to create custom applications using DTS packages and DTS Data Pump objects. You can access the COM interfaces through any programming language that supports OLE animation.

Transforming Data

An important DTS feature is the capability to transform data. When DTS transforms data, a set of operations is defined to be run on the data at the destination. DTS allows new values to be calculated based upon one or more source fields. This transformation can perform complex data validation, scrubbing, and enhancement during import and export.

DTS moves schemas and data between data sources. Other database objects—such as triggers, stored procedures, rules, defaults, constraints, and user-defined data types—are not converted. When using the DTS Import and Export Wizards, you can specify column mappings and transformation information.

Column Mappings

The Column Mappings tab in the Column Mappings And Transformation dialog box (see Figure 6.1) allows you to define the structure of the table you are sending data to and define the mapping between columns. You can configure DTS to create the destination tables, dropping and re-creating any of the tables that exist. If you don't create the destination table, you can delete all data in the existing table or append data to the existing table.

The Column Mappings screen allows you to change the source field that is mapped to a given destination field. You can also change other properties of

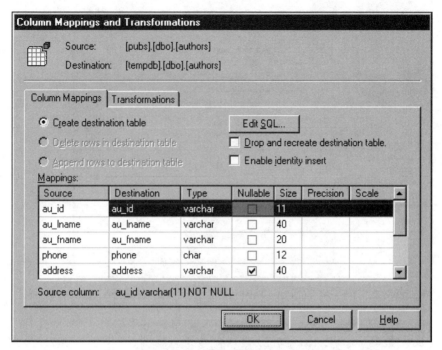

Figure 6.1   The DTS Column Mappings tab of the Column Mappings And Transformation dialog box.

the field, such as the data type, whether the field allows nulls, and the size, scale, and precision of the output field. If you use the Edit SQL option, the Create Table SQL Statement dialog box opens, as shown in Figure 6.2. You can specify custom SQL statements for the destination table.

Transformations

The Transformations tab in the Column Mappings And Transformation dialog box (see Figure 6.3) allows you either to copy the source columns directly to the destination columns or to run a script to perform the data transformation.

If you choose to copy the data directly, you can use the Advanced options to control the transformations. The Advanced Transformation Properties screen allows you to set the flags listed in Table 6.2. To display the Advanced Transportation properties screen, click on the Advanced button in the in the Column Mappings And Transformation dialog box.

For most data transformations, the flags will provide all the functionality you need. To perform transformations of greater complexity, use the Transfer Information option on the Transformations screen. You can specify a script to

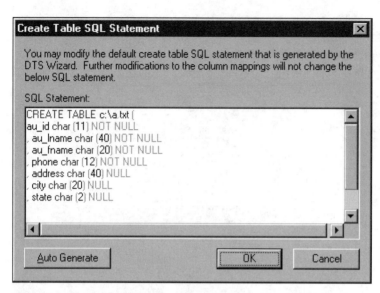

Figure 6.2 The DTS Create Table SQL Statement dialog box.

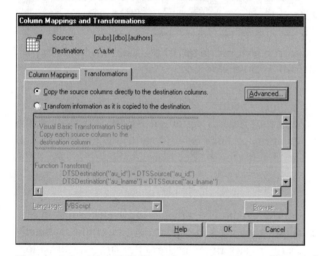

Figure 6.3 The DTS Transformations tab of the Column Mappings And Transformation dialog box.

run in Java Script, Perl Script, or Visual Basic Script. DTS will generate a default script of each type. These scripts can perform complex data transformations. Listing 6.3 shows a sample data transformation script.

Table 6.2   Data Transformation flags from the Advanced Transformation Properties screen.

Flag	Effect
Default Transformation Flags— all possible conversions are allowed	Allows data type conversions that do not lose data; allows data type promotion and **NULL** conversions.
Require exact match between source and destination	Specifies that columns must have the same data type, size, precision, scale, and nullability in both source and destination tables. This is the strictest transformation.
Custom Transformation Flags	Allows you to choose any one of the following data type transformations: promotion, demotion, or **NULL** conversion.
Allow data type promotion	Allows numeric data types to be converted to larger numeric data types. For example, a tinyint can be converted to an integer.
Allow data type demotion	Allows numeric data types to be converted to smaller numeric data types. For example, an integer can be converted to a tinyint. If the number being converted is larger than the destination field will allow, an overflow error will be generated.
Allow NULL conversion	Allows a source column that doesn't permit **NULL** to be converted to a destination column that permits **NULL**s.

Listing 6.3   A Visual Basic data transformation script.

```
'*******************************************************************
'  Visual Basic Transformation Script
'  Copy each source column to the
'  destination column
'*******************************************************************

Function Transform()
        DTSDestination("au_id") = DTSSource("au_id")
        DTSDestination("au_lname") = DTSSource("au_lname")
        DTSDestination("au_fname") = DTSSource("au_fname")
        DTSDestination("phone") = DTSSource("phone")
        DTSDestination("address") = DTSSource("address")
        DTSDestination("city") = DTSSource("city")
        DTSDestination("state") = DTSSource("state")
        DTSDestination("zip") = DTSSource("zip")
```

```
        DTSDestination("contract") = DTSSource("contract")
        Transform = 1
End Function
```

The dtswiz Utility

The dtswiz utility is a standalone program that allows you to run the Data Transformation Services from the command line. When running dtswiz, you can specify options to bypass the prompts on the DTS Import, Export, and Data Transformation screens.

The syntax for dtswiz is as follows:

```
dtswiz [/f filename] [/i | /x] [/r provider_name]
[/s server_name] [/u login_id] [/p password] [/n]
[/d database_name] [/y]
```

The following list describes the available dtswiz parameters:

➤ **/f** Allows you to specify a COM-structured file to store the DTS package created by the wizards.

➤ **/i** Specifies that you are performing an import to a SQL Server database table.

➤ **/x** Specifies that you are performing an export from a SQL Server database table.

➤ **/r** The name of the provider that is used to connect to the data source when importing, or to the destination when exporting.

➤ **/s** The SQL Server where data is to be exported from or imported to. To go from a SQL Server to another SQL Server, one source must be configured as an ODBC data source, with the server name, login, password, and database declared in the ODBC configuration.

➤ **/u** Specifies the SQL Server login to use when connecting.

➤ **/p** The password for the SQL Server login.

➤ **/n** Specifies that this is a trusted connection and that the /u and /p parameters will not be used.

➤ **/d** Specifies the SQL Server database to use.

➤ **/y** Specifies that the dtswiz utility should hide the system tables and system databases.

Practice Questions

Question 1

> Which of the following statements are true about the bulk insert create option?
>
> ○ a. It creates a table in the user's current database.
>
> ○ b. It creates the values for any identity columns.
>
> ○ c. It fails if the table does not already exist.
>
> ○ d. All of the above.
>
> ○ e. None of the above.

The correct answer is c. No create option exists for the **BULK INSERT** statement.

Question 2

> Using the pubs database (see this book's appendix), which of the following statements about this insert statement are true? [Check all the correct answers]
>
> ```
> insert discounts ( stor_id, lowqty, discount,
>      discounttype )
>    values  (6380, 10, 20,'MyDiscount')
> ```
>
> ❑ a. It will insert one row into the table discount if the stor_id 6380 exists in the stores table.
>
> ❑ b. The insert will fail because stor_id is a character column, and you are trying to insert an integer into it.
>
> ❑ c. The column highqty will be set to NULL.
>
> ❑ d. If a discounttype 'MyDiscount' already exists, the row will not be added.
>
> ❑ e. None of the above.

The correct answers are a and c. Answer b is false; SQL Server automatically converts an integer to a character. Because no unique indexes, constraints, or triggers enforcing uniqueness exist, answer d is false. Answer e is incorrect, because answers a and c satisfy the questions requirements.

Question 3

> Which of the statements are true about the following SQL state-
> ments? [Check all the correct answers]
>
> ```
> select * into #pubs1 from authors where au_id >
>     '123-45-6789'
> select * into #pubs1 from authors where
>     au_fname like 'A%'
> ```
>
> ❑ a. A table is created in the current database.
>
> ❑ b. A table is created in tembdb.
>
> ❑ c. It works only if the 'Select Create' database option is
> turned on.
>
> ❑ d. The table created will have the rows only from the first
> select statement.
>
> ❑ e. None of the above.

The correct answer is e. All the other answers are false, because when the
second **SELECT INTO** statement is compiled, the #pubs1 table will already
exist. This will stop the whole batch from running. If you want to load data
from two separate **SELECT** statements into a new table, you need to do one
of the following SQL batches:

```
select * into #pubs1 from authors where au_id > '123-45-6789'
insert #pubs1 select * from authors where au_fname like 'A%'
```

or

```
select * into #pubs1 from authors where au_id > '123-45-6789'
union
select * into #pubs1 from authors where au_fname like 'A%'
```

Question 4

> Which of the following statements are true about this bcp statement? [Check all the correct answers]
>
> ```
> bcp c in  -Uaaaaaa -P xyccc
> ```
>
> ❑ a. It will try to connect to a local server.
> ❑ b. It will fail because the database name is missing.
> ❑ c. It will connect to the user's aaaaaa default database.
> ❑ d. It will prompt the user for information about the file's format.
> ❑ e. None of the above.

The correct answer is e. The first parameter after the direction -Uaaaaaaa, will be treated as the input file name. If the file is valid, this statement will try to connect to the local server as the current user, with the password of xyccc. If the file doesn't exist, an error message is generated.

Question 5

> Which of the following programming languages can the DTS data transformation GUI use to directly transform data? [Check all the correct answers]
>
> ❑ a. Perl
> ❑ b. C
> ❑ c. Visual Basic
> ❑ d. Java
> ❑ e. Visual C++

The correct answers are a, c, and d. Perl, Visual Basic, and Java are supported by the DTS data transformation GUI. The other languages, C and Visual C++, are not directly supported by the DTS data transformation GUI; therefore, answers b and e are incorrect.

Question 6

> Which dtswiz parameter can be used to specify the login to use when connecting to an SQL Server? [Check all the correct answers]
>
> ❑ a. -n
>
> ❑ b. -u
>
> ❑ c. -l
>
> ❑ d. U
>
> ❑ e. None of the above.

The correct answer is e. All **dtswiz** parameters start with a slash (/), not with a dash (-). Answers a, b, and c are incorrect, because they all start with a dash (-). Answer d is incorrect, because it lacked a slash.

Question 7

> Which option is used to configure bcp to redirect errors to a file?
>
> ○ a   -e
>
> ○ b   -o
>
> ○ c   -m
>
> ○ d. -f
>
> ○ e. None of the above.

The correct answer is a. You specify -e *file_name* to redirect bcp errors to a file. Answer b is incorrect, because the **-o** parameter redirects standard output, not errors. Answer c is incorrect, because the **-m** parameter limits the number of errors bcp can hit without aborting. Answer d is incorrect, because the -f parameter specifies the first row to import or export.

Need To Know More?

 Amo, William C.: *Transact- SQL.* (Foster City, CA, IDG Books Worldwide, 1998, ISBN 0-7645-8048-5). Chapter 2 covers the bcp utility.

 McGehee, Brad and Shepker, Matthew, *Using Microsoft SQL Server 7.0.* (Indianapolis, IN, Que Corporation, 1998, ISBN 0-7897-1628-3). Chapter 16 covers DTS, BCP and the BULK INSERT statement.

 MS SQL Server Books Online.

 Search the TechNet CD-ROM (or its online version at **www. microsoft.com**).

 www.microsoft.com/sql has current information on using SQL Server.

Backing Up
Databases

Terms you'll need to understand:

√ Backup

√ Backup files and sets

√ Differential database backup

√ Dump

√ Dump database

√ Dump device

√ Dump transaction

√ Restore

√ Recovery

√ Transaction log

Techniques you'll need to master:

√ Backing up databases and transaction logs

√ Creating a backup strategy

√ Creating dump devices

We back up a database because bad things happen to nice people. Three basic things can go wrong with your data, requiring you to use your backup to restore data that was lost. The following list describes the three ways you can lose data:

➤ The physical device(s) on which your database resides can crash. If this happens, you will have to replace the physical device(s) before you can restore the data.

➤ The DBMS (Microsoft SQL Server) can corrupt data due to server bugs.

➤ Users can inadvertently (or maliciously) drop or delete data that still belongs in the database.

In any of these cases, the working database is no longer functional or accessible, and you must restore it from your backup. Besides these disasters, backups are sometimes also created to migrate data or database structures from one server to another.

But how do we get the backup in the first place? What is an appropriate backup strategy? This chapter covers these questions.

Types Of Backups

There are two types of backups. The first kind of backup is a copy of *every used page* in the entire database. This method used to be called a "database dump" but is now called simply a "backup." The second kind of backup is a copy of *every modification* to the database since the entire database was last backed up. This method used to be called a "transaction log dump" but is now called a "backup of the transaction log."

Backup Devices

The first thing you need to decide when getting ready to back up a database is which device type you want to back up *to*. You can back up to a file, to a named pipe, or to any tape device that NT can be made aware of.

Adding A Dump Device

After you've decided which device you want to use for your backup, you must define the device to SQL Server. You do this with the **sp_addumpdevice** stored procedure. (Note the number of "d"s in the stored procedure.) Listing 7.1 shows the syntax for the **sp_addumpdevice** stored procedure.

Listing 7.1 The syntax of sp_addumpdevice.

```
sp_addumpdevice {'device_type', 'logical_name', 'physical_name'}
[, {
```

```
{controller_type
|
'device_status'}
}
]
```

Arguments

Here are the arguments to the **sp_addumpdevice** stored procedure:

➤ '*device_type*' Specifies the type of backup device. The *device_type* is **varchar(10)**, with no default, and can be one of the following values:

➤ **disk** Adds a hard-disk file as a backup device.

➤ **pipe** Adds a named pipe.

➤ **tape** Adds any tape devices supported by Microsoft Windows NT. If you specify **tape** for the device value, **noskip** is the default.

➤ '*logical_name*' Specifies the name of the backup device you will use in the BACKUP and RESTORE statements. The *logical_name* is **sysname**; it cannot be NULL, and it has no default value. This is how you identify the name of the device at backup time.

➤ '*physical_name*' Specifies the location of the backup device. Physical names must include a full path and must follow either the rules for operating-system file names or universal naming conventions for network devices. The *physical_name* is **nvarchar(260)**; it cannot be NULL, and it has no default value.

If you are adding a tape device, this parameter must be the physical name assigned to the local tape device by Windows NT—for example, \\.\TAPE0 for the first tape device on the computer. The tape device must be attached to the server computer; it cannot be used remotely. Enclose in quotation marks names that contain nonalphanumeric characters.

➤ *controller_type* This parameter is not required when you create backup devices. However, if it's used in scripts, you can still supply this parameter, but SQL Server ignores it. Specify either *controller_type* or *device_status*, but not both. The *controller_type* is **smallint**, with a default of NULL, and it can be one of the following values:

➤ **2** Use with a device_type of **disk**.

➤ **5** Use with a device_type of **tape**.

➤ **6** Use with a device_type of **pipe**.

➤ '*device_status*' Specifies whether ANSI tape labels are read (**noskip**) or ignored (**skip**). Specify either *controller_type* or *device_status* but not both. The *device_status* is **varchar(40)**, with a default value of **noskip**.

Note: Permissions must be defined correctly on the target device, or you will be unable to define and use the dump device.

Also, you should be in the master database to create the device, because the device is a server-wide resource and will add a row to the sysdevices table in master.

Listing 7.2 shows a sample statement using the **sp_addumpdevice** stored procedure.

Listing 7.2   An example of sp_addumpdevice syntax.

```
USE master
EXEC sp_addumpdevice 'disk', 'newdumpdev', 'c:\dump\newdump.dat'
```

After you have defined a dump device, you can use the defined device as a target for an actual backup.

The BACKUP Command

Now that we have defined the device, it's time to copy the database to the dump device. To do this, you use the **BACKUP** command (see Listings 7.3 through 7.5).

Note: You do not need to memorize all of the following syntax; it is included here for the sake of completeness. It is sufficient to know that you can back up a database or its transaction log. Following Listings 7.3 through 7.5, you will find a list of arguments to remember.

Listing 7.3   Syntax of the BACKUP DATABASE command.

```
BACKUP DATABASE {database_name | @database_name_var}
TO <backup_device> [, ...n]
[WITH
[BLOCKSIZE = {blocksize | @blocksize_variable}]
[[,] DESCRIPTION = {text | @text_variable}]
[[,] DIFFERENTIAL]
[[,] EXPIREDATE = {date | @date_var}
| RETAINDAYS = {days | @days_var}]
[[,] FORMAT | NOFORMAT]
[[,] {INIT | NOINIT}]
```

```
[[,] MEDIADESCRIPTION = {text | @text_variable}]
[[,] MEDIANAME = {media_name | @media_name_variable}]
[[,] [NAME = {backup_set_name | @backup_set_name_var}]
[[,] {NOSKIP | SKIP}]
[[,] {NOUNLOAD | UNLOAD}]
[[,] [RESTART]
[[,] STATS [= percentage]]
]
```

Listing 7.4   Syntax of the **BACKUP DATABASE** command, used to back up specific files or file groups.

```
BACKUP DATABASE {database_name | @database_name_var}
<file_or_filegroup> [, ...m]
TO <backup_device> [, ...n]
[WITH
[BLOCKSIZE = {blocksize | @blocksize_variable}]
[[,] DESCRIPTION = {text | @text_variable}]
[[,] EXPIREDATE = {date | @date_var}
| RETAINDAYS = {days | @days_var}]
[[,] FORMAT | NOFORMAT]
[[,] {INIT | NOINIT}]
[[,] MEDIADESCRIPTION = {text | @text_variable}]
[[,] MEDIANAME = {media_name | @media_name_variable}]
[[,] [NAME = {backup_set_name | @backup_set_name_var}]
[[,] {NOSKIP | SKIP}]
[[,] {NOUNLOAD | UNLOAD}]
[[,] [RESTART]
[[, ] STATS [= percentage]]
]
```

Listing 7.5   Syntax of the **BACKUP LOG** command, used to back up a transaction log.

```
BACKUP LOG {database_name | @database_name_var}
{
[WITH
{ NO_LOG | TRUNCATE_ONLY }]
}
|
{
TO <backup_device> [, ...n]
[WITH
[BLOCKSIZE = {blocksize | @blocksize_variable}]
[[,] DESCRIPTION = {text | @text_variable}]
[[,] EXPIREDATE = {date | @date_var}
```

```
| RETAINDAYS = {days | @days_var}]
[[,] FORMAT | NOFORMAT]
[[,] {INIT | NOINIT}]
[[,] MEDIADESCRIPTION = {text | @text_variable}]
[[,] MEDIANAME = {media_name | @media_name_variable}]
[[,] [NAME = {backup_set_name | @backup_set_name_var}]
[[,] NO_TRUNCATE]
[[,] {NOSKIP | SKIP}]
[[,] {NOUNLOAD | UNLOAD}]
[[,] [RESTART]
[[,] STATS [= percentage]]
]
}
<backup_device> :: =
{
{backup_device_name | @backup_device_name_var}
|
{DISK | TAPE | PIPE} =
{'temp_backup_device' | @temp_backup_device_var}
}
<file_or_filegroup> :: =
{
FILE = {logical_file_name | @logical_file_name_var}
|
FILEGROUP = {logical_filegroup_name | @logical_filegroup_name_var}
}
```

Arguments

Here are the arguments for the **BACKUP** command:

➤ **DATABASE** Specifies the complete backup of the database. If a list of
files and file groups is specified, then only those files and file groups are
backed up.

*Note: During a full database backup or differential backup, SQL Server
backs up enough of the log to produce an internally consistent database
when the database is restored.*

➤ {*database_name* | *@database_name_var*} Specifies the database from
which the log, partial database, or complete database is being backed up.
If supplied as a variable (*@database_name_var*), this name can be specified either as a string constant (*@database_name_var* = *database name*) or
as a variable of character-string data type, except for the ntext or text
data types.

➤ *<backup_device>* Specifies the permanent or temporary backup device to use for the backup operation. Can be one or more of the following:

➤ *{backup_device_name}* | *{@backup_device_name_var}* Specifies the logical name of the backup device(s) (created by **sp_addumpdevice**) to which the database is backed up. (The logical name must follow the rules for identifiers.) If supplied as a variable (*@backup_device_name_var*), the backup device name can be specified either as a string constant (*@backup_device_name_var* = *backup device name*) or as a variable of character-string data type, except for the ntext or text data types.

➤ { DISK | TAPE | PIPE } = *'temp_backup_device'* | *@temp_backup_device_var* Allows backups to be created on the named disk, tape, or pipe device. When you use a temporary disk as your backup device, the temporary disk-backup file must not exist before you specify the **BACKUP** statement. When you use a tape backup device, specify **WITH FORMAT** to ensure that the backup device is a valid Microsoft tape format data set.

 Use the **FORMAT** command carefully, because it overwrites all contents on the current tape.

With disk and tape, specify the complete path and file name—for example, DISK = 'c:\mssql7\backup\mybackup.dat' or TAPE = \\.\TAPE0. With pipe, specify the name of the named pipe that will be used by the client application. If supplied as a variable (*@temp_backup_name_var*), the name of the temporary backup device can be specified as a string constant or as a variable of character-string data type, except for the ntext or text data types.

Pipe files were added to SQL Server 7 to allow third-party vendors a flexible and powerful way to connect their own software. For typical Transact-SQL use, pipe files are not used.

 When specifying multiple files, you can mix logical file names (or variables) and temporary file names (or variables). However, all devices must be of the same type (disk, tape, or pipe).

➤ *n* Serves as a placeholder, indicating that multiple backup devices can be specified. The maximum number of backup devices is 32.

➤ **BLOCKSIZE** = {*blocksize* | *@blocksize_variable*} Specifies the physical block size in bytes.

For **DISK, BLOCKSIZE** is ignored.

For tape media, **BLOCKSIZE** applies only if the tape is being overwritten by using **FORMAT**. When you use tape media, the backup operation selects an appropriate block size. Explicitly stating a block size overrides the backup operation's selection of a block size.

For **PIPE**, the backup operation uses 65,536 bytes unless **BLOCKSIZE** is specified.

➤ **DESCRIPTION** = {*text* | *@text_variable*} Specifies the free-form text describing the backup set. Can be a maximum of 255 characters.

➤ **DIFFERENTIAL** Specifies that the database backup should consist of only the portions of the database that have changed since the last full backup. A differential database backup usually takes up less space than full database backup. Use the **DIFFERENTIAL** option so that all individual log backups since the last full-database backup do not need to be applied.

The **DIFFERENTIAL** option is specified for full database backups only.

Note: During a full database backup or a differential database backup, SQL Server backs up enough of the log to produce a consistent database when the database is restored.

➤ **EXPIREDATE** = {*date* | *@date_var*} Specifies the date when the backup set expires and can be overwritten. If supplied as a variable (*@date_var*), this date can be specified as a string constant (*@date_var* = *date*), as a variable of character-string data type (except for the *ntext* or text data types), or as a **smalldatetime** or **datetime** variable, in which case, it must follow the configured **datetime** format for the system. This option is used for **DISK** and **TAPE** devices only and is effective only when specified with all backup sets on the media.

➤ **RETAINDAYS** = {*days* | *@days_var*} Specifies the number of days that must elapse before the backup media set can be overwritten. If supplied as a variable (*@days_var*), it must be specified as an integer. This option is used for disk and tape devices only and is effective only when specified with **INIT**. Specifying **SKIP** overrides this option.

If **EXPIREDATE** or **RETAINDAYS** is not specified, expiration is determined by the media-retention configuration setting of **sp_configure**. These options only prevent SQL Server from overwriting a *file*. Tapes can still be erased with other methods, and disk files can still be deleted through the operating system.

➤ FORMAT Specifies that the media header should be written on all volumes used for this backup operation and rewrites the backup device. Any existing media header is overwritten. The FORMAT option also invalidates the entire media contents, ignoring any existing password.

When FORMAT is specified, the backup operation implies SKIP and INIT, and SKIP and INIT do not need to be explicitly stated.

➤ NOFORMAT Specifies that the media header should not be written on all volumes used for this backup operation and does not rewrite the backup device unless INIT is specified.

➤ INIT Specifies that the backup set should be the first file on the disk or tape device and preserves the media header. If INIT is specified, any existing data on that device is overwritten.

The backup media are not overwritten if either of the following conditions is met:

➤ All backup sets on the media have not yet expired. For more information, see the EXPIREDATE and RETAINDAYS options.

➤ The backup-set name given in the BACKUP statement, if provided, doesn't match the name on the backup media. For more information, see the NAME option.

Note: If the backup media are password-protected or encrypted, SQL Server does not write to the media. To overwrite media that are either password-protected or encrypted, specify the WITH FORMAT option.

Use the SKIP option to override the following checks:

➤ NOINIT Specifies that the backup set is appended to the current DISK or TAPE device. NOINIT is the default.

➤ MEDIADESCRIPTION = {*text* | *@text_variable*} Specifies the free-form text description, maximum of 255 characters, describing the media set.

➤ MEDIANAME = {*media_name* | *@media_name_variable*} Specifies the media name, a maximum of 128 characters, for the entire set of backup media. If **MEDIANAME** is specified, it must match the media name previously specified for the backup volume(s). If the media name is not specified or if the **SKIP** option is specified, there is no verification check of the media name.

Note: If **FORMAT** *is specified,* **MEDIANAME** *specifies the media name that is written. In addition, tapes shared between SQL Server database backups and Microsoft Windows NT backups must have a nonnull* **MEDIANAME**.

➤ **NAME** = {*backup_set_name* | *@backup_set_var*} Specifies the name of the backup set. Names are limited to 128 characters. If **NAME** is not specified, it is blank.

➤ **NOSKIP** Instructs the **BACKUP** statement to check the expiration date and the name of all backup sets on the media before allowing them to be overwritten.

➤ **SKIP** Disables the checking of the backup-set expiration and name. (This checking is usually performed by the **BACKUP** statement to prevent overwrites of backup sets.)

➤ **NOUNLOAD** Specifies that the tape is not unloaded automatically from the tape drive after a backup. **NOUNLOAD** remains set until **UNLOAD** is specified. This option is used only for tape devices.

➤ **UNLOAD** Specifies that the tape is automatically rewound and unloaded when the backup is finished. **UNLOAD** is set by default when a new user session is started. It remains set until that user specifies **NOUNLOAD**. This option is used only for tape devices.

➤ **RESTART** Specifies that SQL Server restarts a backup operation that was interrupted. The **RESTART** option saves time, because it restarts the backup operation at the point at which it was interrupted. To **RESTART** a specific backup operation that was interrupted, repeat the entire **BACKUP** statement, and add the **RESTART** option. Using the **RESTART** option is not required but can save time.

➤ **STATS** [= *percentage*] Displays a message every time another percentage completes and is used to gauge progress. If percentage is omitted, SQL Server displays a message after every 10 percent is completed.

➤ *<file_or_filegroup>* Specifies the logical names of the files or file groups to include in the database backup. Multiple files or file groups can be specified.

➤ FILE = {*logical_file_name* | *@logical_file_name_var*} Names one or more files to be included in the database backup.

➤ FILEGROUP = {*logical_filegroup_name* | *@logical_filegroup_name_var*} Names one or more file groups to be included in the database backup.

Note: Back up a file when the database size and performance requirements make a full database backup impractical. (This option is a component of DATABASE BACKUP.) To separately back up the transaction log, use BACKUP LOG.

To recover a database by using file and file group backups, you must use BACKUP LOG to create a separate backup of the transaction log.

File and file group backups are disallowed if trunc. log on chkpt. is enabled for the database. If trunc. log on chkpt. is enabled, the log has been truncated, and the log backups needed to restore individual files and file groups are not available.

The **BACKUP** statement requires that you back up as one unit all file groups affected by a **CREATE INDEX** statement since the last file group backup was made:

➤ If an index is created on a file group, the entire file group must be backed up in a single backup operation.

➤ If an index is created on a file group different from the one that the table resides in, both file groups (the file group that contains the table and the file group containing the new index) must be backed up.

➤ If more than one index is created on a file group different from the file group in which the table resides, then all file groups must be backed up immediately to accommodate these differing file groups.

The **BACKUP** statement detects all these file-group situations and communicates to the backup user the minimum number of file groups that must be backed up.

➤ *m* Serves as a placeholder, indicating that multiple files and file groups can be specified. There is no maximum number of files or file groups.

➤ LOG Specifies a backup of the transaction log only. The log is backed up from the last successfully executed **LOG** backup to the current end of the log. By default, SQL Server truncates the log up to the beginning of the active portion of the log, which contains the oldest open transaction.

Note: If backing up the log does not appear to truncate most of the log, you might have a very old open transaction in the log. Log space can be monitored with DBCC SQLPERF (LOGSPACE).

➤ **NO_LOG | TRUNCATE_ONLY** Removes the inactive part of the log without making a backup of it, and truncates the log. This option frees space. You do not need to specify a backup device because the log backup is not saved.

Note: After backing up a log by using the TRUNCATE_ONLY option or the NO_LOG option, you should immediately make a backup of the database by using BACKUP DATABASE. You must back up the log (using BACKUP LOG) until a full database backup (using BACKUP DATABASE) is performed.

After you use either **NO_LOG** or **TRUNCATE_ONLY** to back up the log, the changes recorded in the log cannot be recovered. For recovery purposes, you should immediately execute the **BACKUP DATABASE** statement.

➤ **NO_TRUNCATE** Backs up the log without truncating it. Also backs up the log if the database becomes damaged, is marked suspect, or has not been recovered.

Database backups can be performed on a database while it is up, running, and live. Additionally, dumps can append to existing dump sets, so dumps of databases and their transaction logs can exist on the same physical device in the same physical file location.

Here are a few things you *cannot* do to a database while it is being dumped:

➤ Run file-management operations, such as the **ALTER DATABASE** statement with either the **ADD FILE** or the **REMOVE FILE** options. However, **INSERT, UPDATE,** or **DELETE** statements are allowed during a backup operation.

➤ Use **SHRINK** database or **SHRINK** file.

➤ Use **CREATE INDEX**.

➤ Run nonlogged operations, such as a bulk load, **SELECT INTO, WRITETEXT,** and **UPDATETEXT.** The database option **SELECT INTO/BULKCOPY** must be enabled for these operations to be nonlogged.

If a backup is started when one of the preceding operations is in progress, the backup will abort. If a backup is running and one of these operations is attempted, the operation will fail. In other words, the task that starts first has precedence.

> *Note: There are tables in the msdb database that store information about the backups.*

Differential Database Backup

This is a new term for an old act. When you back up the transaction log, you make a copy of changes in the database (the differential between the last dump and the current state of the database). Look out for this term.

Choosing A Backup Strategy

Your backup strategy will depend on the size of your database, how often it is updated, and how much money you have to spend. Typically, if you have a small database, you will periodically back up the full database. If you have a large database, you will typically dump the database, then periodically back up the transaction log (which contains changes made since the last database backup). This will be driven by how long the backup takes, and how much of the database changes.

Your choice of backup device will be based on several factors: where you will be storing the backup set, how quickly you need to get to it, and how you will get it off site.

Practice Questions

Question 1

How often should you issue the dump database command?

○ a. Daily.

○ b. Weekly.

○ c. Monthly.

○ d. Annually.

○ e. It depends on the size of the database and the frequency of database changes.

○ f. Never.

The correct answer is e. The **DUMP** command will be going away in future versions, so you should use the **BACKUP** command instead.

Question 2

When do you need to back up the transaction log? [Check all the correct answers]

❑ a. Never

❑ b. When it starts to get too big.

❑ c. When the database gets too big.

❑ d. Weekly.

❑ e. When you need to recover the space it is taking up.

The correct answers are b and e. The transaction-log backup cleans up the space in the log and makes copies of all transactions. Answers a, c, and d are incorrect because the correct answers are given.

Question 3

Where is information pertaining to the backup stored? Check all the correct answers]

❏ a. In the master database.

❏ b. In a flat file.

❏ c. In the msdb database.

❏ d. In the NT Registry.

❏ e. None of the above.

The correct answers are a and c. Answer a is correct because master contains information on the device. Answer c is correct because MSDB contains information on other dump characteristics.

Question 4

What should you do before backing up a database?

○ a. Decide how often to back it up.

○ b. Decide where you are backing it up to.

○ c. Define the device on which you are backing it up.

○ d. Determine dump frequency.

○ e. All of the above.

The correct answer is e. All of the answers describe good practices, requirements, or both.

Question 5

What can you do while a database is being backed up? Check all the correct answers]

❑ a. All normal processing.

❑ b. Anything that doesn't affect the log.

❑ c. Queries only.

❑ d. All transactions, except non-logged operations.

❑ e. Absolutely nothing. All users are blocked during a backup.

The correct answer is d. Backups are relatively unintrusive.

Need To Know More?

 Coffman, Gayle, *SQL Server 7: The Complete Reference*. (Berkley, CA, Osborne/McGraw-Hill, 1999, ISBN 0-07-882494-X). Chapter 15 covers backing up databases, and Chapter 21 provides a complete TSQL reference.

 McGehee, Brad and Shepker, Matthew, *Using Microsoft SQL Server 7.0*. (Indianapolis, IN, Que Corporation, 1998, ISBN 0-7897-1628-3). Chapter 14 covers developing a backup strategy and how to perform backups.

 MS SQL Server Books Online.

 Search the TechNet CD-ROM (or its online version, through **www.microsoft.com**).

 www.microsoft.com/sql has current information on using SQL Server.

Restoring
Databases

Terms you'll need to understand:

- ✓ Backup files and sets
- ✓ Recovery
- ✓ Restore
- ✓ Standby server
- ✓ Transaction log

Techniques you'll need to master:

- ✓ Identifying the contents of an existing backup
- ✓ Restoring databases, transaction logs, files, and filegroups from a backup
- ✓ Restoring from different kinds of backup media
- ✓ Restoring to a standby server
- ✓ Using variations of the **RESTORE** command to verify the integrity of a backup
- ✓ Identifying system tables relevant to the process of restoringx

How you restore your database depends on how you backed it up. If you backed up only the database, you need to restore only the database. If you backed up the database and its transaction logs, you need to restore the corresponding transaction logs as well as the database. Backing up and restoring transaction logs will be simplest if you have stored them in a single file.

This chapter covers restoring databases, transaction logs, files, and filegroups.

The RESTORE Command

You restore databases and transaction logs with the **RESTORE** command. (You can also use the older **LOAD** command, but this command will eventually be discarded.)

> *Note: Restoring is actually a destructive process. If you restore a database from a backup into an existing database, that entire database will be overwritten. The backed-up database becomes the current one, in exactly the state it was in when it was backed up. Any partial transactions in the database when it was backed up will be rolled back.*

When the restoration is complete, the server automatically runs recovery. This recovery synchronizes the log with the data to ensure that any information that may have been in cache (instead of on disk) when the database was backed up is properly reflected in the database before users can access the data.

You can restore the database with the syntax shown in Listing 8.1. You can restore the individual files or file groups with the syntax shown in Listing 8.2. You can restore a transaction log with the syntax shown in Listing 8.3.

Listing 8.1   Syntax used to restore a complete database.

```
RESTORE DATABASE {database_name | @database_name_var}
[FROM <backup_device> [, ... n]]
[WITH
[DBO_ONLY]
[[,] FILE = file_number]
[[,] MEDIANAME = {media_name | @media_name_variable}]
[[,] MOVE 'logical_file_name' TO 'operating_system_file_name']
[,...p]
[[,] {NORECOVERY | RECOVERY | STANDBY = undo_file_name}]
[[,] {NOUNLOAD | UNLOAD}]
[[,] REPLACE]
[[,] RESTART]
[[,] STATS [= percentage]]
]
```

Listing 8.2   Syntax used to restore specific files or filegroups.

```
RESTORE DATABASE {database_name | @database_name_var}
<file_or_filegroup> [, ...m]
[FROM <backup_device> [, ...n]]
[WITH
[DBO_ONLY]
[[,] FILE = file_number]
[[,] MEDIANAME = {media_name | @media_name_variable}]
[[,] NORECOVERY]
[[,] {NOUNLOAD | UNLOAD}]
[[,] REPLACE]
[[,] RESTART]
[[,] STATS [= percentage]]
]
```

Listing 8.3   Syntax used to restore a transaction log.

```
RESTORE LOG {database_name | @database_name_var}
[FROM <backup_device> [, ...n]]
[WITH
[DBO_ONLY]
[[,] FILE = file_number]
[[,] MEDIANAME = {media_name | @media_name_variable}]
[[,] {NORECOVERY | RECOVERY | STANDBY = undo_file_name}]
[[,] {NOUNLOAD | UNLOAD}]
[[,] RESTART]
[[,] STATS [= percentage]]
[[,] STOPAT = {date_time | @date_time_var}]
]

<backup_device> :: =
{
{'backup_device_name' | @backup_device_name_var}
| {DISK | TAPE | PIPE} =
{'temp_backup_device' | @temp_backup_device_var}
}
<file_or_filegroup> :: =
{
FILE = {logical_file_name | @logical_file_name_var}
|
FILEGROUP = {logical_filegroup_name | @logical_filegroup_name_var}
}
```

You can simply point the **RESTORE** command at the dump, or you can pass it arguments to control the actions of the restore process.

Arguments

The **RESTORE** command uses the arguments described in this section:

➤ **DATABASE** Specifies that the complete database will be restored from a backup. If you list files and/or filegroups, then only those files and groups of files will be restored.

➤ {*database_name* | *@database_name_var*} Specifies the database that the log or the complete database will be restored into. If supplied as a variable (*@database_name_var*), the database name can be specified either as a string constant (*@database_name_var* = *database name*) or as a variable of character-string data type, except for the ntext or text data types.

➤ **FROM** Specifies the devices from which the backup will be restored. If you don't use the **FROM** clause, the restore of a backup does not take place. Instead, the database is recovered. You can omit the **FROM** clause to attempt recovery of a non-suspect database that has been restored with the **NORECOVERY** option, or to switch over to a standby server. If you omit the **FROM** clause, then you must specify **NORECOVERY**, **RECOVERY**, or **STANDBY**.

➤ <backup_device> Specifies the backup device(s) to use for the restore operation. It can be either a device name or a variable containing the name of the backup device.

➤ {'*backup_device_name*' | *@backup_device_name_var*} Specifies the logical name of the backup device(s)—created by **sp_addumpdevice**—from which the database is restored. (Logical names must follow the rules for identifiers.) The maximum number of backup devices in a single **RESTORE** statement is 32. If supplied as a variable (*@backup_device_name_var*), the backup-device name can be specified either as a string constant (*@backup_device_name_var* = *backup_device_name*) or as a variable of character-string data type, except for the ntext or text data types. The backup device can be a disk, tape, or pipe.

➤ {DISK | TAPE | PIPE} = '*temp_backup*_device' | *@temp_backup_device_var* Restores from the named disk, tape, or pipe device. If specified as a variable (*@temp_backup_device_var*), the device name can be specified either as a string constant (*@temp_backup_device_var* = '*temp_backup_device*') or as a variable of character-string data type, except for the ntext or text data types. The device types work in the following way:

　　➤ The device types of *disk* and *tape* should be specified with the complete path and file name of the device. For example, DISK = 'c:\mssql7\ backup\mybackup.dat' or TAPE = \\.\TAPE0.

➤ A device type of *pipe* should specify the named pipe that will be used by the client application.

Pipe devices have been added to allow third-party vendors a flexible and powerful way to connect their own software. For typical Transact-SQL use, the pipe device is not used.

If you are using either a network server with a UNC name or a redirected drive letter, specify a device type of disk.

➤ *n* Serves as a placeholder indicating that multiple backup devices and temporary backup devices can be specified. The maximum number of backup devices or temporary backup devices is 32.

➤ DBO_ONLY Restricts access for the newly restored database to only the DBO. Causes the **dbo use only** option of **sp_dboption** to be set to **true**. This database option restricts access to the database owner after the restore operation; the restriction stays in effect until you set the option to **false** by executing **sp_dboption**. If the DBO_ONLY option is not specified, the setting of the **dbo use only** database option may or may not change. Use DBO_ONLY with the RECOVERY option.

Note: Using DBO-ONLY will become a standard practice at many sites. It allows a dba/dbo to peruse the database before the users pounce on it.

➤ FILE = *file_number* Identifies the backup set to be restored. For example, a *file_number* of 1 indicates the first backup set on the backup medium, and a *file_number* of 2 indicates the second backup set.

➤ MEDIANAME = {*media_name* | *@media_name_variable*} Specifies the media name for the entire backup set. If provided, the media name must match the media name on the backup volume(s); otherwise, the restore operation terminates. If no media name is given in the RE-STORE statement, then the check for a matching media name on the backup volume(s) is not performed.

Note: Consistently using media names in BACKUP and RESTORE operations provides an extra safety check for the media selected for the restore operation.

➤ MOVE '*logical_file_name*' TO '*operating_system_file_name*' Specifies that the given *logical_file_name* should be moved to *operating_system_file_name*. By default, the *logical_file_name* is restored to its original location. If either the **BACKUP** command or the **RESTORE** command is used to copy a database to the same or a different server, the **MOVE** option might be needed to relocate the database files and to avoid collisions with existing files. Each logical file in the database can be specified in a different **MOVE** statement.

➤ *p* Serves as a placeholder indicating that more than one logical file can be moved by specifying multiple **MOVE** statements.

➤ **NORECOVERY** Instructs the restore operation to *not* roll back any uncommitted transactions. Either the **NORECOVERY** option or the **STANDBY** option *must* be specified if another transaction log needs to be applied to the current database (this would be the application of a transaction log backup). If neither **NORECOVERY, RECOVERY,** nor **STANDBY** is specified, **RECOVERY** is the default.

SQL Server requires that the **WITH NORECOVERY** option be used on all but the final **RESTORE** statement when you restore a database backup and multiple transaction logs or when you need multiple **RE-STORE** statements. A good example of this: when a differential database backup follows a full database backup.

*Note: When you specify the **NORECOVERY** option, the database is not usable in this intermediate, non-recovered state.*

When used with a file or filegroup restore operation, **NORECOVERY** forces the database to remain in load state after the restore operation. This state is useful when either of the following two conditions exists:

➤ A restore script is being run, and the log needs to be applied to the database.

➤ A sequence of file restores is used, and the database does not need to be usable between two of the restore operations.

➤ **RECOVERY** Rolls back any uncommitted transactions. After the recovery process, the database is ready for use. However, **RECOVERY** should not be specified when another transaction log must be applied to the database. If neither **NORECOVERY, RECOVERY,** nor **STANDBY** is specified, **RECOVERY** is the default. If **RECOVERY** is specified, the database version is updated for databases and transaction logs.

➤ **STANDBY** = *undo_file_name* Specifies the undo file name so that the recovery can be undone. This file has no size limit. If neither

NORECOVERY, RECOVERY, nor **STANDBY** is specified, **RECOVERY** is the default.

➤ **STANDBY** allows a database to be brought up for read-only access between transaction-log restores. **STANDBY** can be used with either warm backup-server situations or special recovery situations when it is useful to check the database between log restores.

If the specified *undo_file_name* does not exist, SQL Server creates it. If the file exists, SQL Server overwrites it, unless the file contains current undo information for a database.

 If not enough free disk space remains on the drive containing the specified *undo_file_name,* the restore operation aborts.

➤ **NOUNLOAD** Specifies that the tape will not be unloaded automatically from the tape drive after a restore operation. **NOUNLOAD** remains set until **UNLOAD** is specified. The **NOUNLOAD** option is used only for tape devices. If a non-tape device is being used for the restore operation, this option is ignored.

➤ **UNLOAD** Specifies that the tape is automatically rewound and unloaded when the restore operation is finished. **UNLOAD** is set by default when a new user session is started. It remains set until that user specifies **NOUNLOAD**. The **UNLOAD** option is used only for tape devices. If a non-tape device is being used for the restore operation, this option is ignored.

➤ **REPLACE** Specifies that SQL Server should create the specified database and its related files even if another database already exists with the same name. In such a case, the existing database is first destroyed. When the **REPLACE** option is not specified, a safety check occurs (which prevents the accidental overwriting of a different database). The safety check ensures that the **RESTORE DATABASE** statement will not restore the database to the current server if both of the following conditions are true:

  ➤ The database named in the **RESTORE** statement already exists on the current server.

  ➤ Either the database name is different from the database name recorded in the backup set, or the set of files in the database is different from the set of files in the backup. Differences in file size are ignored.

When used with a file or filegroup restore operation, **REPLACE** allows overwriting an existing file. This overwriting is useful only when you're trying to restore a file on a disk that is replacing a failed disk.

➤ **RESTART** Specifies that SQL Server should restart the restore operation that was interrupted. The **RESTART** option saves time because it will restart the restore operation at the point at which it was interrupted. To **RESTART** a specific restore operation that was interrupted, you repeat the entire **RESTORE** statement and add the **RESTART** option. Using the **RESTART** option is not required but can save time.

Note: This option can be used only for restores directed from tape media and for restores that span multiple tape volumes.

➤ **STATS** [= *percentage*] Displays a message every time another percentage completes and is used to gauge progress. By default, SQL Server displays a message after every 10 percent is completed.

➤ **<file_or_filegroup>** Specifies the names of the logical files or filegroups to be included in the database restore. Multiple files or filegroups can be specified.

➤ **FILE** = {*logical_file_name* | *@logical_file_name_var*} Names one or more files to be included in the database restore.

➤ **FILEGROUP** = {*logical_filegroup_name* | *@logical_filegroup_name_var*} Names one or more filegroups to be included in the database restore.

When using this option, you must apply the log to the database files immediately after the last file or filegroup restore operation. This step is necessary to roll the files forward to be consistent with the rest of the database. If all files being restored have not been modified since they were last backed up, then no log needs to be applied. The **RESTORE** statement informs the user of this situation.

➤ *m* Serves as a placeholder, indicating that multiple files and filegroups can be specified. There is no maximum number of files or filegroups.

➤ **LOG** Specifies that a transaction log backup is to be applied to this database. Logs must be applied in sequential order. SQL Server checks the backed-up log to ensure that the transactions are being loaded into the correct database and in the correct sequence. In order to apply multiple transaction logs, use the **NORECOVERY** option on all restore operations except the last.

➤ STOPAT = *date_time* | *@date_time_var*   Specifies that the database be restored to the state it was in as of the specified date and time. If a variable is used for **STOPAT**, the variable must be one of the following data types: varchar, char, smalldatetime, or datetime. Only log records written before the specified date and time are applied to the database.

This option provides point-in-time recovery.

Limitations Of Restoring A Database

You can only recover a database under certain specific conditions. Limitations follow:

➤ The database that is being restored must not be in use. One common mistake is to create and then "use" the database. When you try to restore, you get an error because you are in the database you are trying to restore.

➤ Sort orders don't necessarily have to match (from backup to restore). However, having them match is a good idea because you want all your indexes to work, and you'll have much work to do if you don't have matching sort orders.

➤ A restore is not especially fast. You need to be sure that, no matter how much your database grows, it doesn't grow beyond your recovery window.

Restoring To A Standby Server

Microsoft describes a standby server as a server that is maintained by backing up the database, and subsequently transaction logs, from a primary server and periodically restoring transaction logs to the "standby" server. If your primary server goes down, your application can switch to the standby server.

 Restoring to a standby server isn't a particularly new strategy, and you will want to understand the term.

Other RESTORE Options

The **RESTORE** command has several other uses, mostly associated with verifying and identifying backup files. It is not required that you verify backup files, but it's an important practice to periodically determine that what has been backed up can actually be restored. It's a very unpleasant surprise when you lose a database, try to restore it, and find that the restored data is bad.

There is no substitute for simply restoring the database into a different database on the server, and then accessing the data and/or running *database consistency checker* (dbcc) commands.

In addition to restoring databases and transaction logs, you can use variations of the **RESTORE** command to do the following:

➤ Get a list of files in the backup set (**RESTORE FILELISTONLY**)

➤ Get the header information for all backup sets on a particular backup device (**RESTORE HEADERONLY**)

➤ Get information about the backup media identified by the given backup device (**RESTORE LABELONLY**)

➤ Verify the completeness of the backup without restoring the backup (**RESTORE VERIFYONLY**)

The following sections discuss these options.

RESTORE FILELISTONLY

The **RESTORE FILELISTONLY** command returns a result set with a list of the database and log files contained in the backup set. In this way, you can identify the contents of a dump if you failed to label your tapes properly. Listing 8.4 shows the syntax for the RESTORE FILELISTONLY command.

Listing 8.4   Syntax for the RESTORE FILELISTONLY command.

```
RESTORE FILELISTONLY
FROM <backup_device>
[WITH
[FILE = file_number]
[[, ] {NOUNLOAD | UNLOAD}]
]

<backup_device> :: =
{
{'backup_device_name' | @backup_device_namevar}
| {DISK | TAPE | PIPE} =
{'temp_backup_device' | @temp_backup_device_var}
}
```

RESTORE HEADERONLY

The **RESTORE HEADERONLY** command retrieves all the backup header information for all backup sets on a particular backup device. Executing **RESTORE HEADERONLY** results in a result set.

The **RESTORE HEADERONLY** command allows you to look at basic dump information for each backup on the backup media. It gives you basic information, such as the name of the database, the backup's version, and its expiration date. This operation can take a while to complete on a large backup device because the server will scan the entire device as it looks for additional headers. Listing 8.5 shows the syntax for the **RESTORE HEADERONLY** cammand.

Listing 8.5   Syntax for the **RESTORE HEADERONLY** command.

```
RESTORE HEADERONLY
FROM <backup_device>
[WITH {NOUNLOAD | UNLOAD}]

<backup_device> :: =
{
{'backup_device_name' | @backup_device_name_var}
| {DISK | TAPE | PIPE} =
{'temp_backup_device' | @temp_backup_device_var}
}
```

RESTORE LABELONLY

The **RESTORE LABELONLY** command returns a result set that contains information about the backup media identified by the given <backup_device>, as opposed to the contents of the backup itself. Listing 8.6 shows the syntax for the **RESTORE LABELONLY** command.

Listing 8.6   Syntax for the **RESTORE LABELONLY** command.

```
RESTORE LABELONLY
FROM <backup_device>

<backup_device> :: =
{
{'backup_device_name' | @backup_device_name_var}
| {DISK | TAPE | PIPE} =
{'temp_backup_device' | @temp_backup_device_var}
}
```

RESTORE VERIFYONLY

The **RESTORE VERIFYONLY** command verifies the backup, but doesn't restore the backup. Rather, this command checks to see that the backup set is complete and that all volumes are readable. However, **RESTORE**

VERIFYONLY does *not* attempt to verify the structure of the data contained in the backup volumes. (Remember, you should perform a full restore to ensure that you can restore the data when you need it.) If the backup is valid, Microsoft SQL Server returns the message, "The backup set is valid." Listing 8.7 shows the syntax for the **RESTORE VERIFYONLY** command.

Listing 8.7 Syntax for the **RESTORE VERIFYONLY** command.

```
RESTORE VERIFYONLY
FROM <backup_device> [,...n]
[WITH
[FILE = file_number]
[[,] {NOUNLOAD | UNLOAD}]
[[,] LOADHISTORY]
]
```

Relevant System Tables

You should be aware that the msdb database contains system tables that track restore activity. These system tables are described in the following list:

➤ **restorefile** Contains one row for each restored file, including files restored indirectly by filegroup name.

➤ **restorefilegroup** Contains one row for each restored filegroup.

➤ **restorehistory** Contains one row for each restore operation.

Practice Questions

Question 1

When would you restore a database? [Check all the correct answers]

- ❏ a. Daily
- ❏ b. Weekly
- ❏ c. When it is required because a disaster ruined an existing database
- ❏ d. During a database migration
- ❏ e. When prompted to do so by SQL Server

The correct answers are c and d. You restore only when it is necessary.

Question 2

What constitutes a full restore of a database to its backed-up state? [Check all the correct answers]

- ❏ a. RESTORE FILELISTONLY
- ❏ b. RESTORE HEADERONLY
- ❏ c. RESTORE LABELONLY
- ❏ d. RESTORE VERIFYONLY
- ❏ e. None of the above

Answer e is correct. Answers a, b, c, and d are RESTORE options used to scan a backup, not restore the data.

Question 3

> Which of the following statements are true? [Check all the correct answers]
>
> ❏ a. You can restore only from a full database dump.
> ❏ b. Restoring requires a database that is not in use.
> ❏ c. The msdb database contains data about the backups.
> ❏ d. You can read the dumped headers without actually restoring the full backup.
> ❏ e. The backup command can be used interchangeably with the load command.

All answers are correct.

Question 4

> Which of the following lists the contents of the dumps on a device?
>
> ○ a. RESTORE FILELISTONLY
> ○ b. RESTORE HEADERONLY
> ○ c. RESTORE LABELONLY
> ○ d. RESTORE VERIFYONLY
> ○ e. None of the above

Answer b is correct.

Question 5

> How do you determine information about the backup media?
>
> ○ a. RESTORE FILELISTONLY
> ○ b. RESTORE HEADERONLY
> ○ c. RESTORE LABELONLY
> ○ d. RESTORE VERIFYONLY
> ○ e. None of the above

Answer c is correct.

Need To Know More?

 Coffman, Gayle: *SQL Server 7: The Complete Reference*. (Berkley, CA, Osborne/McGraw-Hill, 1999, ISBN 0-07-882494-X). Chapter 21 provides a complete TSQL reference.

 McGehee, Brad and Shepker, Matthew: *Using Microsoft SQL Server 7.0*. (Indianapolis, IN, QUE, 1998, ISBN 0-7897-1628-3). Chapter 15 covers how to restore user databases and system databases.

 Browse MS SQL Server Books Online.

 Search the TechNet CD-ROM (or its online version, through **www.microsoft.com**)

 The **www.microsoft.com/sql** Web site has up-to-date information on using SQL Server.

Monitoring
The Server

Terms you'll need to understand:

➤ Optimizer

➤ Statistics

➤ Error log

➤ DBCC

➤ Deadlock

Techniques you'll need to master:

➤ Using the **SHOWPLAN** command to check queries

➤ Updating statistics on tables and indexes

➤ Monitoring the error log

➤ Using the **sp_who** stored procedure to determine who is logged on and how many connections are in use

➤ Using the **sp_lock** stored procedure to detect locking contention problems

➤ Using **sp_who** and **sp_lock** together

➤ Using the **sp_spaceused** stored procedure to get information about a database's disk-space usage

➤ Using the **sp_monitor** stored procedure to display information about SQL Server's monitoring of itself

➤ Using the Database Consistency Checker (DBCC) to verify the allocation of data and system tables

➤ Diagnosing and resolving locking problems

➤ Using SQL Server Profiler to monitor certain predefined events

After SQL Server and its applications are up and running, the next step is to ensure that they stay that way. The server must be administered so that it will run well. Microsoft provides several tools to help administrators ensure that their servers run as efficiently as possible. These tools include the following:

➤ **SHOWPLAN** command

➤ **UPDATE STATISTICS** command

➤ Error log

➤ **sp_who** stored procedure

➤ **sp_lock** stored procedure

➤ **sp_spaceused** stored procedure

➤ **sp_monitor** stored procedure

➤ Database Consistency Checker (DBCC)

➤ **SET DEADLOCK PRIORITY** command

➤ SQL Server Profiler

This chapter discusses these tools.

The SHOWPLAN Command

One way to verify the performance of SQL Server is to make sure that your queries are performed as you intend. You can determine whether indexes are being used, for example, or whether SQL Server performs a complete scan of a table. The **SHOWPLAN** command is an excellent tool for both improving query design and making queries as efficient as possible.

You can also use **SHOWPLAN** to estimate the I/O cost of a query before you run it. Doing this can prevent a badly developed query (one that produces a Cartesian product or returns too many rows) from being executed before it is corrected. If a query begins to run more slowly than usual, you can use SHOWPLAN to determine whether or not the server is running the queries with the appropriate index choices.

SQL Server 7 provides the following two versions of **SHOWPLAN**:

➤ **SET SHOWPLAN_TEXT**

➤ **SET SHOWPLAN_ALL**

A graphical version of **SHOWPLAN** also exists in the SQL Query Analyzer.

SHOWPLAN_TEXT

The **SHOWPLAN_TEXT** command, which displays results as text, provides information about how SQL Server will approach a particular query. The **SHOWPLAN** command will not display results unless the option is set on, by way of a command in isql, SQL Query Analyzer, or another script editor, as illustrated by the syntax and sample output in Listings 9.1 and 9.2.

Listing 9.1   Syntax of the SET SHOWPLAN_TEXT command.

```
SET SHOWPLAN_TEXT [ON|OFF]
```

Listing 9.2   Query and results for SET SHOWPLAN_TEXT.

```
StmtText
---------------------------------------------------
select * from titles
where title_id = 'BU1111'

(1 row(s) affected)

StmtText
---------------------------------------------------------------------
  |--Clustered Index Seek(pubs..titles.UPKCL_titleidind,
     SEEK:(titles.title_id=@1) ORDERED)
```

SHOWPLAN_ALL

Like **SHOWPLAN_TEXT**, the **SHOWPLAN_ALL** command provides detailed information about proposed query and what will occur when the query is run. However, **SHOWPLAN_ALL** is designed for use during runtime execution. The output of **SHOWPLAN_ALL** is provided in the form of a table. While the **SHOWPLAN_ALL** option is **ON**, no queries will be executed for the session. All queries for the session will be analyzed until the **SHOWPLAN_ALL** option is turned off. Listing 9.3 shows the syntax for the **SHOWPLAN_ALL** command.

Listing 9.3   Syntax of the SHOWPLAN_ALL command.

```
SET SHOWPLAN_ALL [ON|OFF]
```

The columns in the **SHOWPLAN_ALL** output are described in the following list:

➤ **StmtText** Contains the original SQL query analyzed by **SHOWPLAN**. This column also contains **PLAN_ROWS,** which contain descriptions of the server's approach to the query.

➤ **StmtId** Indicates the number of the statement in the current batch. If the batch has multiple statements, the number will exceed 1.

➤ **NodeId** Displays the ID of the node in the current query.

➤ **Parent** Displays the Node ID of the parent step.

➤ **PhysicalOp** Describes the physical implementation used to execute the query. This is used only for **PLAN_ROWS.**

➤ **LogicalOp** Describes the logical implementation used to execute the query. This is used only for **PLAN_ROWS.**

➤ **Argument** Displays more detailed information about the query operation, based on the operators in the query.

➤ **DefinedValues** Displays the list of values that will be used by the query. This list will include columns specified in the **SELECT** or **WHERE** clauses. It is used only for **PLAN_ROWS.**

➤ **EstimateRows** The number of output rows estimated by SQL Server for the **PLAN_ROWS.**

➤ **EstimateIO** The estimated I/O to be performed based on the **PLAN_ROWS.**

➤ **EstimateCPU** Estimated CPU cost for the **PLAN_ROWS.**

➤ **AvgRowSize** Estimated size of the return row.

➤ **TotalSubtreeCost** Estimated cost of the query. This is a cumulative value.

➤ **OutputList** List of columns to be output by the query.

➤ **Warnings** List of warning messages for the query.

➤ **Type** Node type for the query. This value can describe the type of query (such as **SELECT, INSERT, DELETE,** or **EXECUTE**) or, for **PLAN_ROWS,** will display "**PLAN_ROW**".

The **UPDATE STATISTICS** Command

SQL Server uses a cost-based optimizer in the resolution of its queries. This optimizer estimates how much I/O will need to be performed to produce a result. The optimizer also looks at alternative approaches to solving a query, including deciding whether or not to use an index and which order to access the tables in a multitable query. These plans are displayed via the **SHOWPLAN_TEXT** and **SHOWPLAN_ALL** commands. However, for these estimates to be produced, the optimizer requires information that describes the data and its distribution. This descriptive information is stored in the statistics pages when an index is created. In an actively changing table, this information might become outdated. With outdated information in the statistics tables, the optimizer might not optimize queries properly because the statistics could produce inaccurate estimates.

To keep the optimizer running at peak efficiency, the statistics for a table and its indexes should be updated regularly. In the past, system administrators performed this as a scheduled task. For SQL Server 7, statistics are automatically updated on a periodic basis. SQL Server updates the statistics based on a random sample of data from the table and performs this sampling at periods, based on the size of the table and the table's rate of growth.

SQL Server also provides a method for altering how the statistics are updated. If the standard sampling of the table doesn't produce the desired query performance or if the wrong query plans are produced when **SHOWPLAN** is used, the **UPDATE STATISTICS** command (see Listing 9.4) can be used to manually redefine how statistics kept for a table and its indexes.

Listing 9.4 Syntax of the UPDATE STATISTICS command.

```
UPDATE STATISTICS {table_name}
[index_name | (index_or_column_list
[, ...n])
]
[WITH
[[FULLSCAN]| SAMPLE number {PERCENT | ROWS}]]
[[,] [ALL | COLUMNS | INDEX]
[[,] NORECOMPUTE]
]
```

The following list defines key portions of the preceding code:

➤ **FULLSCAN** Using the **FULLSCAN** option, SQL Server performs a full scan of the index or the table when gathering statistics. The statistics are based on the complete sample of all the data over the entire table.

➤ **SAMPLE** Performing a **FULLSCAN** on a table or index can be time and resource intensive. As an alternative to scanning the entire table or index, choose a sample size. Rather than forcing SQL Server to base its statistics on the complete table, you can instruct SQL Server to build new statistics pages based on a sample of the data from the table. The sample size can be entered as a percent or as a defined number of rows.

➤ **ALL | COLUMNS | INDEX** By default, the UPDATE STATISTICS command affects only the statistics for indexes. However, statistics can also be maintained for columns as well as both indexes and columns.

➤ **NORECOMPUTE** This command disables the capability to perform automatic updates for statistics by way of the **sp_autostats** stored procedure.

sp_updatestats

In previous versions of SQL Server, all tables required an individual **UPDATE STATISTICS** statement. In SQL Server 7, the **sp_updatestats** stored procedure runs the **UPDATE STATISTICS** command for all user tables in the current database. This procedure is restricted to users with the SA_ROLE and to database owners.

sp_autostats

When updating statistics was a system administrator's scheduled task in previous versions of SQL Server, the system administrators explicitly issued **UPDATE STATISTICS** commands. With the automatic updating of statistics provided by SQL Server 7, it may become necessary to shut off this feature with certain tables. For example, lookup tables that do not change over a period need not be updated. The **sp_autostats** stored procedure provided in Listing 9.5 allows the deactivation of the automatic updating of statistics for a specified table. The default for updating statistics for the indexes is to take a random sample from the smallest non-clustered index. The **sp_autostats** procedure can also be used to specify that automatic statistics updates are performed on specific indexes. This can be useful for indexes that are used on many common queries but are not chosen by SQL Server for automatic update.

Listing 9.5   Syntax for sp_autostats.

```
sp_autostats 'table_name' [,'ON'|'OFF']['index_name']
```

The Error Log

SQL Server often produces messages about system-level events. These messages may indicate a problem or a potential problem. These messages are placed in the MS SQL error log. Error logs are archived in the MSSQL7\logs directory. The error logs contain messages about any unexpected failures in the server as well as standard messages about the startup and maintenance tasks on the server.

It is important to monitor the error log regularly to ensure that any unexpected errors are detected by their error-log messages and dealt with. Listing 9.6 provides an example of a SQL error log file.

Listing 9.6   A sample error log.

```
98/11/19 10:24:20.94 kernel  Microsoft SQL Server  7.00 - 7.00.517
    (Intel X86)
      Jun 19 1998 17:06:54
      Copyright (c) 1988-1998 Microsoft Corporation
      Enterprise version on Windows NT

98/11/19 10:24:21.07 kernel   Copyright
    (C) 1988-1997 Microsoft Corporation.
98/11/19 10:24:21.07 kernel   All rights reserved.
98/11/19 10:24:21.07 kernel   Logging SQL Server messages
    in file 'F:\MSSQL7\log\ERRORLOG'.
98/11/19 10:24:21.37 kernel   initconfig:
    Number of user connections limited to 32767.
98/11/19 10:24:21.52 kernel
    SQL Server starting at priority class 'normal'(1 CPU detected).
98/11/19 10:24:21.66 kernel
    User Mode Scheduler configured for thread processing
98/11/19 10:24:23.27 server   Directory Size: 3356
98/11/19 10:24:23.32 spid1    Using dynamic lock allocation.
    [2500] Lock Blocks, [5000] Lock Owner Blocks
98/11/19 10:24:23.33 kernel
Attempting to initialize Distributed Transaction Coordinator.
98/11/19 10:24:24.73 spid1    Starting up database 'master'.
98/11/19 10:24:24.73 spid1
    Opening file F:\MSSQL7\data\master.mdf.
98/11/19 10:24:24.76 spid1
    Opening file F:\MSSQL7\data\mastlog.ldf.
98/11/19 10:24:25.22 spid1
    Loading SQL Server's  Unicode collation.
98/11/19 10:24:26.82 spid1
    Loading SQL Server's  non-Unicode sort order and character set.
98/11/19 10:24:27.13 spid1    Starting up database 'model'.
98/11/19 10:24:27.13 spid1    Opening file F:\MSSQL7\DATA\model.mdf.
```

```
98/11/19 10:24:27.23 spid1
    Opening file F:\MSSQL7\DATA\modellog.ldf.
98/11/19 10:24:27.44 spid1     Clearing tempdb database.
98/11/19 10:24:27.49 spid1
    Creating file F:\MSSQL7\DATA\TEMPDB.MDF.
98/11/19 10:24:27.66 spid1     Closing file
    F:\MSSQL7\DATA\TEMPDB.MDF.
98/11/19 10:24:27.68 spid1
    Creating file F:\MSSQL7\DATA\TEMPLOG.LDF.
98/11/19 10:24:27.77 spid1
    Closing file F:\MSSQL7\DATA\TEMPLOG.LDF.
98/11/19 10:24:27.82 spid1     Opening file
    F:\MSSQL7\DATA\TEMPDB.MDF.
98/11/19 10:24:27.86 spid1
    Opening file F:\MSSQL7\DATA\TEMPLOG.LDF.
98/11/19 10:24:28.96 spid1     Closing file
    F:\MSSQL7\DATA\TEMPDB.MDF.
98/11/19 10:24:29.02 spid1
    Closing file F:\MSSQL7\DATA\TEMPLOG.LDF.
98/11/19 10:24:29.08 spid1     Starting up database 'tempdb'.
98/11/19 10:24:29.08 spid1     Opening file
    F:\MSSQL7\DATA\TEMPDB.MDF.
98/11/19 10:24:29.17 spid1
    Opening file F:\MSSQL7\DATA\TEMPLOG.LDF.
98/11/19 10:24:29.55 spid1     Server name is 'TENCHI'.
98/11/19 10:24:29.56 kernel
    Using 'SQLEVN70.DLL' version '7.00.517'.
98/11/19 10:24:29.57 kernel
    Using 'OPENDS60.DLL' version '7.00.00.0517'.
98/11/19 10:24:29.57 spid6     Starting up database 'msdb'.
98/11/19 10:24:29.58 spid6
    Opening file F:\MSSQL7\DATA\msdbdata.mdf.
98/11/19 10:24:29.58 spid7     Starting up database 'pubs'.
98/11/19 10:24:29.59 spid7     Opening file F:\MSSQL7\data\pubs.mdf.
98/11/19 10:24:29.63 spid8     Starting up database 'Northwind'.
98/11/19 10:24:29.63 spid8
    Opening file F:\MSSQL7\DATA\northwnd.mdf.
98/11/19 10:24:29.64 ods       Using 'SSNMPN70.DLL' version '7.0.517'
    to listen on '\\.\pipe\sql\query'.
98/11/19 10:24:29.64 ods       Using 'SSMSSO70.DLL' version '7.0.517'
    to listen on '1433'.
98/11/19 10:24:29.65 ods       Using 'SSMSRP70.DLL' version '7.0.517'
    to listen on 'TENCHI'.
98/11/19 10:24:30.10 spid7
    Opening file F:\MSSQL7\data\pubs_log.LDF.
98/11/19 10:24:30.16 spid6
    Opening file F:\MSSQL7\DATA\msdblog.ldf.
```

```
98/11/19 10:24:30.17 spid8
    Opening file F:\MSSQL7\DATA\northwnd.ldf.
98/11/19 10:24:32.14 spid1    Recovery complete.
98/11/19 10:24:32.15 spid1    SQL Server's Unicode collation is:
98/11/19 10:24:32.15 spid1         'English' (ID = 1033).
98/11/19 10:24:32.15 spid1         comparison style = 196609.
98/11/19 10:24:32.15 spid1    SQL Server's non-Unicode sort order
                              is:
98/11/19 10:24:32.15 spid1         'nocase_iso' (ID = 52).
98/11/19 10:24:32.16 spid1
    SQL Server's non-Unicode character set is:
98/11/19 10:24:32.16 spid1         'iso_1' (ID = 1).
```

The sp_who Stored Procedure

You can use the **sp_who** stored procedure to determine who is logged on to SQL Server and how many connections are being used on the server at any given time. Listing 9.7 shows a sample output of the **sp_who** stored procedure.

Listing 9.7   Sample output of sp_who.

Spid	status	loginame	hostname	blk	dbname	cmd
1	sleeping	sa		0	master	SIGNAL HANDLER
2	sleeping	sa		0	pubs	LOCK MONITOR
3	sleeping	sa		0	pubs	LAZY WRITER
4	sleeping	sa		0	pubs	LOG WRITER
5	sleeping	sa		0	pubs	CHECKPOINT SLEEP
6	background	sa		0	pubs	AWAITING COMMAND
7	sleeping	NT AUTHORITY\SYSTEM	TENCHI	0	master	AWAITING COMMAND
8	sleeping	NT AUTHORITY\SYSTEM	TENCHI	0	master	AWAITING COMMAND
9	sleeping	user1	KIYONE	10	pubs	UPDATE
1	runnable	user2	KIYONE	0	pubs	SELECT

In Listing 9.7, process 9 is being blocked by process 10. User1 (who is running process 9) must wait until the resources being held by process 10 are released. The **sp_who** stored procedure can be used with the **sp_lock** stored procedure to verify which object is causing the blockage and which kind of lock is being used.

The **sp_who** stored procedure outputs the following columns:

➤ **Spid** System process ID.

➤ **Status** Process status.

- ➤ **Loginame** Login of user who is running the process.

- ➤ **Hostname** Host name or system name that is calling the process.

- ➤ **Blk** Process ID that is preventing completion of the current process.

- ➤ **Dbname** Name of database used in the process.

- ➤ **Cmd** Type of SQL Server command that is executing the process.

 Microsoft also provides an undocumented **sp_who2** stored procedure that performs the same basic function as **sp_who**. This stored procedure also provides information about the connection's CPU time, the amount of disk I/O, the calling program name, and the time the last batch was sent.

The sp_lock Stored Procedure

The **sp_lock** stored procedure polls the **syslocks** table to gather information on the locks in use by the server. Running this procedure at peak usage times on the server can help determine the number of locks configured for the server. This number is set dynamically by default. SQL Server will reserve two percent of the memory allocated for maintaining locks. This procedure can be used to help detect any locking contention problems. Listing 9.8 provides a sample output for **sp_lock**.

Listing 9.8 Sample output of sp_lock.

spid	dbid	ObjId	IndId	Type	Resource	Mode	Status
1	1	0	0	DB		S	GRANT
6	1	0	0	DB		S	GRANT
7	1	0	0	DB		S	GRANT
8	1	0	0	DB		S	GRANT
9	1	0	0	DB		S	GRANT
9	2	0	0	DB		S	GRANT
9	5	0	0	DB		S	GRANT
9	5	261575970	1	PAG	1:103	IS	GRANT
9	1	117575457	0	TAB		IS	GRANT
9	5	261575970	0	TAB		IS	GRANT
9	5	261575970	1	KEY	(42b753b5aa62)	IS-S	GRANT
9	5	261575970	1	KEY	(45b852b7aa62)	IS-S	GRANT
10	5	0	0	DB		S	GRANT
10	5	261575970	1	PAG	1:103	IS	GRANT
10	5	261575970	0	TAB		IS	GRANT
10	5	261575970	1	KEY	(42b753b5aa62)	IS-S	GRANT
10	5	261575970	1	KEY	(45bc55b3aa64)	IS-S	GRANT

The **sp_lock** stored procedure can be used with the **sp_who** stored procedure to determine who has been granted locks and whether the locks are blocking the processes of other users.

The output of the **sp_lock** stored procedure includes columns for the following:

➤ **Spid** System process ID.

➤ **Dbid** Database ID.

➤ **ObjID** Object ID.

➤ **IndID** Index ID.

➤ **Type** Lock type. Describes the level of locking. Valid types include Table (TAB), Page (PG), KEY (KEY), and Database (DB).

➤ **Resource** Information stored in the syslockinfo.restext.

➤ **Mode** Lock mode. Valid modes include Shared (S), Update (U), Exclusive (X), Intent Shared (IS), Intent Exclusive (IX), and Shared with Intent Exclusive (SIX).

➤ **Status** Lock request status, including GRANT, WAIT, and CONVERT.

The sp_spaceused Stored Procedure

The **sp_spaceused** stored procedure displays the amount of disk space reserved and used by the database. If a table name is specified, then the procedure provides information about how much space has been reserved and used by the table. Gathering this data over time can help you gauge how fast a table and its indexes are growing versus the amount of space reserved for them by the database. This stored procedure is granted to the public group so any user can execute it. Listing 9.9 shows the syntax of **sp_spaceused**.

Listing 9.9   Syntax of sp_spaceused.

```
sp_spaceused ['tablename']
```

Listing 9.10   Sample output of sp_spaceused.

```
Sp_spaceused
database_name   database_size      unallocated space
-------------   ---------------    ----------------
pubs            219.31 MB          25.15 MB
```

```
(1 row(s) affected)
reserved              data                  index_size          unused
------------------    ------------------    ----------------    ------
198824 KB             195888 KB             2664 KB             272 KB

Sp_spaceused 'titles'
Name      rows     reserved    data     index_size          unused
--------  -------- ----------  -------- ----------------    -----
titles    18       24 KB       8 KB     32 KB               -16 KB
```

The sp_monitor Stored Procedure

SQL Server is designed to monitor itself. The results of this monitoring are available via the **sp_monitor** stored procedure. This procedure returns values describing the amount of work that SQL Server has performed since the last time the **sp_monitor** procedure was executed. This output as illustrated by Listing 9.11, which provides information about how many seconds the CPU spent processing queries, performing I/O, or sitting idle. The output provides a count of how many reads were conducted as well as how many writes to disk were performed. It also provides a count of how many network packets were received and the number of network packets sent.

Listing 9.11   Sample output of sp_monitor.

```
Sp_monitor
last_run                      current_run                    seconds
--------------------------    --------------------------    ----------
1998-11-19 21:51:01.200       1998-11-19 21:58:42.943        461

(1 row(s) affected)

cpu_busy                      io_busy                       idle
----------------------        -------------------------     ---------------
424(4)-0%                     1(0)-0%                       39940(442)-95%

(1 row(s) affected)

packets_received              packets_sent                  packet_errors
----------------------        -----------------------       ----------------
8358(94)                      4178(47)                      0(0)

(1 row(s) affected)

total_read            total_write        total_errors       connections
----------------      -----------------  ----------------   -----------
576(0)                288(2)             0(0)               14(0)
```

Many of the output values are returned in the following formats:

```
Number1(Number2)
```

or

```
Number1(Number2) - Number3%
```

Number1 is the value with respect to the start of the server. Number2 is the value with respect to the last execution of **sp_monitor**. Number3 is a percentage of the total.

Based on values in Listing 9.11, the **cpu_busy** values are 424(4)-0%. This means that the CPU was busy performing query processing for 424 seconds since the server was started and only 4 seconds since the last time sp_monitor was run. The percentage of the total counted time is **0%**.

> *Note: In theory, the sum of the percentages for **cpu_busy** and for **idle** should add up to **100%**. This does not always happen, however.*

The **sp_monitor** returned values are as follows:

➤ **last_run** The date and time **sp_monitor** was last run.

➤ **current_run** The date and time of the current execution of sp_monitor.

➤ **seconds** The number of seconds elapsed between **last_run** and **current_run**.

➤ **cpu_busy** The number of seconds that the server CPU has been doing work relating to SQL Server.

➤ **io_busy** The number of seconds that SQL Server has spent performing I/O operations.

➤ **idle** The number of seconds that SQL Server has been idle.

➤ **packets_received** The number of network packets read by SQL Server.

➤ **packets_sent** The number of network packets sent by SQL Server.

➤ **packet_errors** The number of errors occurring while sending or receiving network packets.

➤ **total_read** The number of physical disk reads made by SQL Server.

➤ **total_write** The number of physical disk writes made by SQL Server.

➤ **total_errors** The number of errors occurring during a physical disk read or write.

➤ **connections** The number of login attempts made to SQL Server.

The Database Consistency Checker (DBCC)

The Database Consistency Checker (DBCC) is not a process—it is a series of commands that can be used to verify the allocation of data and system tables. This verification can be used to detect potential disk allocation problems before they escalate into corrupt databases. Some of the available commands that can be used for monitoring and maintaining a database are described in the following list:

➤ **DBCC checkdb** Checks all the tables in the database. If errors are encountered, the command can be run again with the **REPAIR_ALLOW_DATA_LOSS, REPAIR_FAST,** or **REPAIR_REBUILD** option to fix the problems.

➤ **DBCC checktable** Checks the consistency of a specific table. If errors are found, the command can be run again with the **REPAIR_ALLOW_DATA_LOSS, REPAIR_FAST,** or **REPAIR_REBUILD** option to fix the problems.

➤ **DBCC checkcatalog** Checks the consistency of the system tables.

➤ **DBCC checkalloc** Checks the consistency of the page allocations. If errors are found, the command can be run again with the **REPAIR_ALLOW_DATA_LOSS, REPAIR_FAST,** or **REPAIR_REBUILD** option to fix the problems.

➤ **DBCC sqlperf (LOGSPACE)** Displays information about the use of space by the database transaction logs.

➤ **DBCC perfmon** Displays performance-related information for SQL Server.

Detecting And Resolving Locking Problems

Whenever SQL Server retrieves data for reading or modification, the server locks the data. This prevents others from changing the data while it is being read, or it can prevent others from reading or altering data while another user is changing it. It's possible, however, that more than one user at a time will try to lock the same piece of information. This situation, called *locking contention*, can be a performance drain on a server. To determine which locks are being used, run the **sp_lock** and **sp_who** stored procedures (see Listing 9.12). The combined procedures can help determine whether any processes are being blocked, and by whom.

Listing 9.12   Sample output of sp_lock and sp_who.

```
sp_lock
spid   dbid   ObjId        IndId   Type  Resource        Mode    Status
------ ------ -----------  ------  ----  --------------  ------  ------
1      1      0            0       DB                    S       GRANT
6      1      0            0       DB                    S       GRANT
7      1      0            0       DB                    S       GRANT
8      1      0            0       DB                    S       GRANT
9      1      0            0       DB                    S       GRANT
9      2      0            0       DB                    S       GRANT
9      5      0            0       DB                    S       GRANT
9      5      261575970    1       PAG   1:103           IS      GRANT
9      1      117575457    0       TAB                   IS      GRANT
9      5      261575970    0       TAB                   IS      GRANT
9      5      261575970    1       KEY   (42b753b5aa62)  IS-S    GRANT
9      5      261575970    1       KEY   (45b852b7aa62)  IS-S    GRANT
10     5      0            0       DB                    S       GRANT
10     5      261575970    1       PAG   1:103           IS      GRANT
10     5      261575970    0       TAB                   IS      GRANT
10     5      261575970    1       KEY   (42b753b5aa62)  IS-S    GRANT
10     5      261575970    1       KEY   (45bc55b3aa64)  IS-S    GRANT
```

```
sp_who
Spid status    loginame              hostname blk dbname cmd
---- --------  --------------------  -------- --- ------ ------------
1    sleeping  sa                             0   master SIGNAL
                                                         HANDLER
2    sleeping  sa                             0   pubs   LOCK MONITOR
3    sleeping  sa                             0   pubs   LAZY WRITER
4    sleeping  sa                             0   pubs   LOG WRITER
5    sleeping  sa                             0   pubs   CHECKPOINT
                                                         SLEEP
6    backgrnd  sa                             0   pubs   AWAITING
                                                         COMMAND
7    sleeping  NT AUTHORITY\SYSTEM TENCHI     0   master AWAITING
                                                         COMMAND
8    sleeping  NT AUTHORITY\SYSTEM TENCHI     0   master AWAITING
                                                         COMMAND
9    sleeping  user1                 KIYONE   10  pubs   UPDATE
10   runnable  user2                 KIYONE   0   pubs   SELECT
```

In Listing 9.12, process 9 is being blocked by process 10. User1 (who is running process 9) must wait until the resources being held by process 10 are released. The **sp_lock** output reveals page locks on object number 261575970 by processes 9 and 10.

Deadlocking

A *deadlock,* or deadly embrace, is a situation in which two processes block each other. Each process has resources that the other needs but can't lock onto those resources until the opposing process releases them. However, the opposing process cannot release the resources until it gets the pages it needs. Neither side can relinquish the pages, so the processes get stuck (see Figure 9.1).

SQL Server detects deadlocks by looking for circular chains of lock requests. If a deadlock is found, one of the two locking processes is declared a *deadlock victim* and is aborted. The other locking process then moves to completion. The victim receives an Error 1205, along with a message from the server,

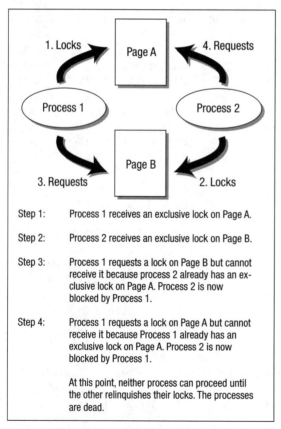

Step 1: Process 1 receives an exclusive lock on Page A.

Step 2: Process 2 receives an exclusive lock on Page B.

Step 3: Process 1 requests a lock on Page B but cannot receive it because process 2 already has an exclusive lock on Page A. Process 2 is now blocked by Process 1.

Step 4: Process 1 requests a lock on Page A but cannot receive it because Process 1 already has an exclusive lock on Page A. Process 2 is now blocked by Process 1.

At this point, neither process can proceed until the other relinquishes their locks. The processes are dead.

Figure 9.1 Deadlock diagram.

announcing that the process is the victim of a deadlock and the transaction should be run again. If this occurs in a stored procedure, the return code will be –3. Applications developed for SQL Server should be designed to react to these error codes.

By default, SQL Server chooses the least "expensive" transaction as the victim. However, you can use the **SET DEADLOCK_PRIORITY LOW** command to designate a particular session as a victim. This forces the session to be chosen as the victim whenever it is involved in a deadlock. Setting **DEADLOCK_ PRIORITY** to **NORMAL** resets the deadlock response. The **SET DEADLOCK PRIORITY** syntax is described in Listing 9.13.

Listing 9.13   Syntax of the SET DEADLOCK PRIORITY command.

```
SET DEADLOCK_PRIORITY {[LOW]|[NORMAL]}
```

You cannot eliminate deadlocks, but you can take actions to minimize their occurrence. These actions are as follows:

➤ Have processes access tables in the same sequence. In the previous example, the deadlock might have been avoided if both processes accessed Page A first.

➤ Avoid user interaction within transactions. The less time a transaction is open, the less time the locks are held, leading to less locking contention, which can lead in turn to fewer deadlocks.

➤ Commit transactions as soon as possible. Doing this also releases the locks as soon as possible, allowing the newly released pages to be locked by other users.

➤ Avoid the use of the holdlock, if possible. The holdlock allows for a shared lock to remain in place until a transaction is committed. (The default is to release a lock as soon as the read is completed.) An extended lock can create a locking contention problem because no one will be able to gain exclusive access to the page until the last shared lock is released.

SQL Server Profiler

Microsoft includes with SQL Server 7 a product named SQL Server Profiler. This monitoring tool allows an administrator to monitor the instances of predefined events, such as login attempts, connections, and disconnections to the server; the execution of TSQL batches; and the monitoring of deadlocks. The

Administrator can be provided with information about when the monitored events occurred, when the event ceased, which applications or users started those events, and what the calling code was. This allows the administrator to gather information about the types of events that exist on a server and act accordingly.

The program can create trace files or create tables in a database for data storage on the server. If the tables are stored on the server, Profiler can replay the stored queries to assist in the analysis of problem queries.

Monitoring With Windows NT Performance Monitor

Included with Windows NT is a graphical tool, Windows NT Preformance Monitor, that can be used to monitor SQL Server Activity. Along with monitoring Windows NT activity, this tool can display and monitor various SQL Server Activity. Some of the information that can be monitored is:

➤ Disk activity

➤ Processor utilization

➤ Memory usage

➤ Buffer Cache hit ratio

➤ User connections

➤ Locks

➤ Replication information

➤ SQL statement statistics

Practice Questions

Question 1

What does the blk column in the sp_who output display?

○ a. The user_id of the blocking process.

○ b. The process_id of the blocking process.

○ c. The process_ id of the process being blocked.

○ d. The user_id of the process being blocked.

○ e. Nothing.

The correct answer is b. The other answers are incorrect because the blk column in the output of the **sp_who** stored procedure displays the **process_id** of the blocking process.

Question 2

What kinds of information are output by sp_monitor? [Check all the correct answers]

❑ a. The number of seconds the CPU spends on I/O.

❑ b. The number of connections on the servers.

❑ c. The number of rows modified.

❑ d. The number of physical disk writes.

❑ e. The number of physical disk reads.

The correct answers are a, d, and e. Answer b is incorrect because the number of connections isn't counted; rather, the number of logins since the last run of **sp_monitor** is counted. Answer c is incorrect because the **sp_monitor** doesn't display any information on the number of rows modified.

Question 3

What method can you use to avoid a deadlock?

○ a. Avoid the use of holdlock.

○ b. Avoid user interaction in transactions.

○ c. Commit transactions as quickly as possible.

○ d. Access the same tables in the same order.

○ e. All of the above.

The correct answer is e. All of the answers provide methods that can be used to avoid deadlocking.

Question 4

What is the purpose of sp_updatestats?

○ a. To activate the automatic updating of statistics for a table in the database.

○ b. To activate the automatic updating of statistics for an index in the database.

○ c. To update the statistics on all the tables in a database.

○ d. To update the statistics on a specific table in the database.

○ e. To update the statistics on a specific index in the database.

Answer c is the only correct answer.

Question 5

What does the SET SHOWPLAN_ALL option do? [Check all the correct answers]

☐ a. Disables execution of batches sent to the SQL server.

☐ b. Returns an estimated I/O cost for the query.

☐ c. Returns an estimated CPU cost for the query.

☐ d. Returns an estimated number of rows for the query.

☐ e. Returns a physical implementation for the query.

All the answers are correct.

Question 6

How does SQL Server handle statistics update by default? [Check all the correct answers]

☐ a. It doesn't.

☐ b. It updates statistics based on all the data in the table on a daily basis.

☐ c. It updates statistics based on a random sample of data performed periodically by the system administrator.

☐ d. It automatically updates statistics based on a random sample of data performed at intervals determined by the SQL Server.

☐ e. It automatically updates statistics based on all the table data, at intervals determined by the SQL Server.

The correct answer is d. SQL Server, by default, takes a random sample of data for updating statistics. This is done periodically, based on the table's size and growth rate. Answer a is incorrect; in older versions of SQL Server this was true, but SQL Server 7 handles statistics automatically. Answer b is incorrect; to do this on large tables could create severe locking contention on the updated table. It would be too costly, and SQL Server does not do this by default. Answer c is incorrect because by default, the statistics are automatic. Answer e is incorrect because the statistics are based on a sample of data.

Question 7

> What output does enabling SET SHOWPLAN_TEXT provide?
>
> ❏ a. Returns the results of the query.
>
> ❏ b. Returns an estimated I/O cost for the query.
>
> ❏ c. Returns an estimated CPU cost for the query.
>
> ❏ d. Returns an estimated number of rows for the query.
>
> ❏ e. Returns a physical implementation for the query.

The correct answer is e because this answer is one of the two outputs from SHOWPLAN_TEXT. The other output is a restatement of the query. Answer a is incorrect because SHOWPLAN_TEXT disables execution of the query. Answers b, c and d are incorrect because they are part of the output returned in SHOWPLAN_ALL.

Need To Know More?

 Amo, William C.: *Transact-SQL* (Foster City, CA, IDG Books Worldwide, 1998, ISBN 0-7645-8048-5). Chapter 17 describes how to use SQL Server Profiler.

 Coffman, Gayle: *SQL Server 7: The Complete Reference* (Berkley, CA, Osborne/McGraw-Hill, 1999, ISBN 0-07-882494-X). Chapter 17 describes SQL Server Profiler and SQL Server Performance Monitor. Chapter 21 provides a complete TSQL reference.

 McGehee, Brad and Shepker, Matthew: *Using Microsoft SQL Server 7.0* (Indianapolis, IN, QUE, 1998, ISBN 0-7897-1628-3). Chapter 10 describes monitoring log files, security, user activity, and performinance Chapter 18 covers setting up a baseline (so that you can monitor changes) and monitoring SQL Server.

 MS SQL Server Books Online.

 Search the TechNet CD-ROM (or its online version, through www.microsoft.com).

 www.microsoft.com/sql has current information on using SQL Server.

Automating Administrative Tasks

10

Terms you'll need to understand:

√ Job

√ Operator

√ Alert

√ SQL Server Agent

√ Database Maintenance Plan Wizard

Techniques you'll need to master:

√ Creating and scheduling tasks

√ Defining jobs, operators, and alerts

√ Creating tasks and alerts

√ Using SQL Server Agent Mail for notification and alerts

Overview Of Automated Administration

SQL Server is a database engine that requires periodic maintenance to ensure its continual, effective, correct operations. Rather than trying to remember to perform various maintenance duties on a periodic basis and to set aside resources on a periodic basis, you can (and should) automate and schedule these procedures.

Typical maintenance tasks that should be scheduled to run automatically include the following:

➤ Rebuilding indexes with a new **FILLFACTOR**.

➤ Compressing data files by removing empty database pages.

➤ Updating index statistics to ensure that the query optimizer has up-to-date information about the spread of data in the tables. (Although index statistics are automatically updated by SQL Server periodically, this feature can force the statistics to be updated immediately.)

➤ Performing internal consistency checks of the data and data pages within the database to ensure that a system or software problem has not damaged data.

➤ Backing up the database and transaction log files.

After you have scheduled these procedures and tasks to run automatically, you must make sure that they run correctly and to completion. When a problem arises, you need to act. Therefore, you need to be notified that the problem exists.

The tasks and procedures that system administrators need to perform are called *jobs*. The people who are brought in to solve problems are referred to as *operators*. The situations that require an operator's attention are known as *alerts*.

Components Of Automated Administration

The three main components of automated administration are jobs, operators, and alerts. The following sections describe these components.

Jobs

A *job* is an administrative task that is defined once so that it can be executed one or more times and can be monitored for success or failure each time it is executed. A job can be executed on one local server or on multiple remote servers, according to one or more schedules, by one or more alerts.

Job components can be executable programs, Windows NT commands, Transact-SQL statements, ActiveScript, or replication agents.

Operators

An *operator* is an individual responsible for the maintenance of the SQL Server(s). In some shops, operator responsibilities are assigned to one individual. In larger shops with multiple servers, many individuals share operator responsibilities.

Operators are notified of alerts in one or more ways: through email, via pager (through email), or through a netsend (that is, through the network, creating a dialog box or message box). If the operator's email alias is an alias assigned to a group of individuals, then all operators can be notified at once.

Alerts

An *alert* definition must match SQL Server events and list a task to perform if the event occurs. An administrator cannot usually control the occurrence of events, but can control the response to those events with alerts. Alerts can be defined to respond to SQL Server events by notifying one or more operators, raising an SNMP (Simple Network Management Protocol, an application protocol that offers network management services) trap, forwarding the event to another server, and/or executing a job.

Multiserver Administration

Multiserver administration is the process of automating administration across multiple servers in a network. This automation is a great idea if you are responsible for many servers. Scheduled information can flow between enterprise servers for data warehousing or any other purpose.

A multiserver administration configuration consists of at least one *master server* and at least one *target server*. The master server stores the central copy of job definitions to distribute jobs to and receive events from networked target servers. Target servers periodically connect to their master server to update their list of jobs. The target servers keep the master servers informed of job status.

Multiserver administration features are intended for members of the sa role. However, a member of the sa role on the target server cannot edit the operations performed on the target server by the master server. This security measure prevents accidental deletion of job steps and interruption of operations on the target server.

Steps For Automating Administration

Setting up automated administration involves five main steps, as follows:

1. First, you need to define yourself as an operator. You also should define an alternate, "fail-safe" operator, for times when you are unavailable.

2. Next, set up a nonproduction server as a master server and enlist the other company servers as targets in this master server. Doing so gives you the capability to centrally administer all the other servers' tasks.

3. After you know where you are going to back up *from*, create a backup job with Transact-SQL job steps, and schedule the jobs to occur according to your backup plan.

4. Define the job to notify yourself (by pager or email) and to write an event to the Microsoft Windows NT application event log if the job fails.

5. After you complete the previous steps, start the SQL Server Agent service, which must be running before administration tasks can be automated.

Defining Jobs, Operators, and Alerts

To define jobs, operators, and alerts, you can use SQL Server Enterprise Manager, Transact-SQL scripts, and/or SQL-DMO objects. Regardless of the method you use to define your administrative tasks, they do not run automatically until the SQL Server Agent service has been started.

Defining Jobs

To create a SQL Server Agent job, follow these steps:

1. Use SQL Server Enterprise Manager to create a Job object.

2. Set the name property; then, add the Job object to the jobs collection of a connected JobServer object to create the SQL Server Agent job.

After a SQL Server Agent job has at least one step and an execution target, you can use the start method of the Job object to execute the job. To schedule the job for execution by SQL Server Agent, use the JobSchedule object.

You can also create a job by using the Database Maintenance Plan Wizard.

Using The Database Maintenance Plan Wizard

The Database Maintenance Plan Wizard can be used to set up the core maintenance tasks that are necessary to ensure that your database performs well, is regularly backed up in case of system failure, and is checked for inconsistencies. The Database Maintenance Plan Wizard creates a Microsoft SQL Server job, scheduled for periodic execution, that automatically performs these maintenance tasks. (For a list of typical maintenance tasks that should be scheduled to run automatically, see "Overview Of Automated Administration," at the beginning of this chapter.)

Defining Operators

The primary attributes of an operator are name and contact information. Every operator must have a unique name, no longer than 128 characters. An operator's contact information defines how the operator is notified.

 Define operators before you define alerts so that you can point the alert to an action. Otherwise, you will have to come back to the alerts.

To notify an operator, you must set up one or more of the following:

➤ MAPI-1 compliant email client

➤ Third-party paging software and hardware with SQL Mail

➤ If you are installed on Microsoft Windows NT (or Windows 2000), netsend notifications

Operators can be notified by email, pager, or netsend (see the preceding list). Paging is implemented by using email. To set up pager notification, you must install software on the mail server to process inbound mail messages and convert them to pager messages. If all the operators share a pager provider, you can use SQL Server Enterprise Manager to specify any special email formatting required by the pager-to-email system. The netsend notification method specifies the recipient (computer or user) of a network message. This method is supported *only* on NT.

The fail-safe operator is notified about an alert after all pager notifications to the designated operators have failed. The fail-safe operator is notified when the operator(s) responsible for the alert could not be paged. Paging an operator can fail for several reasons. Pager addresses might be incorrect, operators might be off-duty, or the SQL Server Agent might be unable to access system tables in the MSDB database. The sysnotifications system table specifies operator responsibilities for alerts.

 Because the fail-safe operator is a safety feature, you cannot delete the operator assigned to fail-safe duty. Before you can delete the account of the operator assigned to fail-safe duty, you must reassign fail-safe duty to another operator or delete the fail-safe assignment.

Defining Alerts

Errors and messages, or *events*, are generated by SQL Server and entered into the NT application event log. The SQL Server Agent reads the application event log and compares events to alerts that you have defined. When the SQL Server Agent finds a match, it executes an alert.

By default, messages of severity 19 or higher are written to the Windows NT application event log. You can use **sp_altermessage** to designate specific sysmessages errors as "always logged" to log error messages with a severity lower than 19.

 The message severity setting gives you the capability to program your own events.

Alerts must be defined before notifications can be sent. The primary attributes of an alert are its name and its event specification:

➤ Every alert must have a name. Alert names must be unique and can be no longer than 128 characters.

➤ Alerts can occur in response to one or more events. You specify the set of events to trigger an alert according to error number or severity level.

Using SQL Enterprise Manager

You will probably use SQL Enterprise Manager to add and manage your jobs, operators, and alerts. Therefore, we are providing a complete walk-through in this section, which begins with Figure 10.1.

Below SQL Server Agent, you can see subheadings of Alerts, Operators, and Jobs. Note also that by right-clicking on the agent here, you have options to start and stop it. You can also see these options listed in the object window to the right.

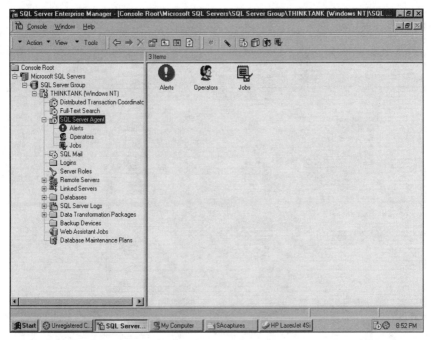

Figure 10.1   The SQL Server Enterprise Manager main window, with SQL Server Agent highlighted.

We'll look at these options one at a time. The next two figures (Figures 10.2 and 10.3) show the General and Response tabs in the alert Properties dialog box. An alert has a name, a type, and history associated with it.

This example shows one of the demonstration alerts that ships with SQL Server, which checks for a space-allocation error in tempdb. As you can see from the Response tab (see Figure 10.3), there are no actions currently assigned to the alert.

You would fill in the response tab at your convenience, to perform whatever tasks you think are necessary for a "full tempdb" error. (Tasks might include notifying the operator and automatically expanding tempdb.)

Next, look at the Operator Properties dialog box (see Figure 10.4). To define a new operator, you specify a logical name and contact information. The logical name is how you refer to the operator (for alert notification). You also specify the operator's email name, pager name, and/or netsend address. You can also specify a time window when the operator will be paged (so that operators can work in shifts).

The Notifications tab (see Figure 10.5) for the operator lets you visually scan the list of alerts and identify the ones for which this operator must be notified.

You also get a list of notifications so that if you are beeped, you can scan a list.

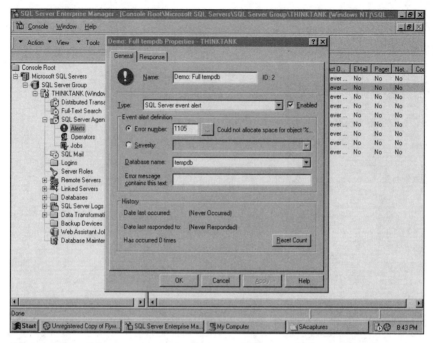

Figure 10.2 The General tab of the alert Properties dialog box.

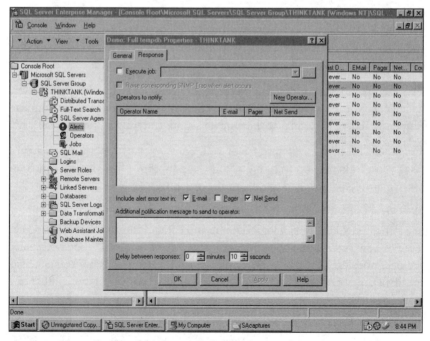

Figure 10.3 The Response tab of the alert Properties dialog box.

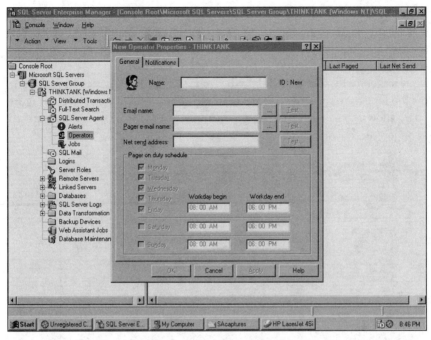

Figure 10.4   The General tab of the New Operator Properties dialog box.

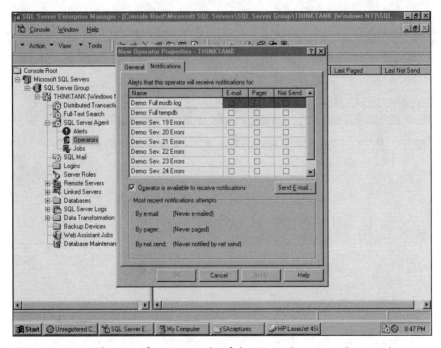

Figure 10.5   The Notifications tab of the New Operator Properties
dialog box.

Finally, you see a New Job Properties dialog box (see Figure 10.6). The General tab allows you to enter a name, category, and description. Also, you can specify on which server the job will run. The Steps tab allows you to list the steps in the job (see Figure 10.7). Further, you can rearrange the order of the steps rather easily. The Schedules tab (see Figure 10.8) allows you to schedule the job for execution according to your need. The Notifications tab (see Figure 10.9) allows you to have a specific operator or groups of operators notified upon job success or failure.

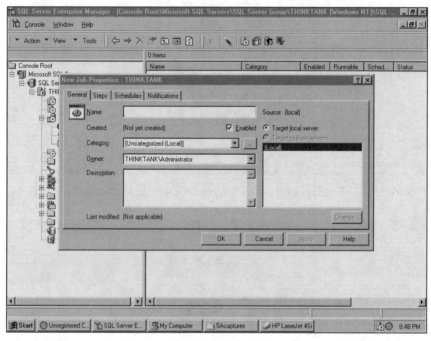

Figure 10.6   The General tab of the New Job Properties dialog box.

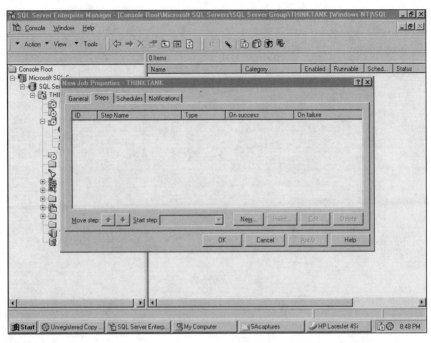

Figure 10.7   The Steps tab of the New Job Properties dialog box.

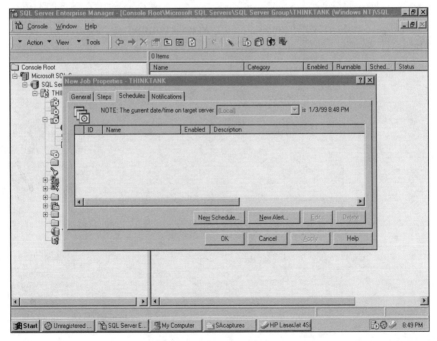

Figure 10.8   The Schedules tab of the New Job Properties dialog box.

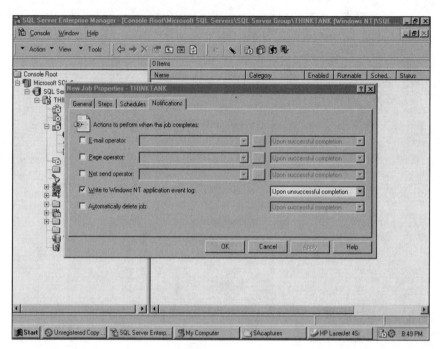

Figure 10.9 The Notifications tab of the Job Properties dialog box.

We recommend that you log anything important to the Windows NT application event log so that you know what ran, when it ran, and its current completion status.

Practice Questions

Question 1

Of jobs, operators, and events, which should be defined first?

- ○ a. Jobs.
- ○ b. Operators.
- ○ c. Alerts.
- ○ d. It doesn't matter.
- ○ e. It doesn't matter, but it makes sense to create operators before alerts.

The correct answer is e. Any of these three elements can be created first, but if you don't create the operators before you create the alerts, you cannot complete the alert definition.

Question 2

What has to be running in order for automated administration to work? [Check all the correct answers]

- ❏ a. SQL Server
- ❏ b. SQL Server Agent
- ❏ c. Replication Agent
- ❏ d. Backup Server
- ❏ e. All of the above

The correct answers are a and b. Answer a is correct because, if SQL Server is not running, you can't run any database queries. Answer b is also correct because SQL Server Agent monitors events. Answer c is incorrect; the Replication Agent isn't relevant. Answer d is incorrect because Backup Server doesn't exist. Answer e is incorrect because answers c and d are incorrect.

Question 3

> When do statistics need to be updated?
>
> ○ a. Never
>
> ○ b. Daily
>
> ○ c. Weekly
>
> ○ d. Quarterly
>
> ○ e. When you know more than the server about distribution skews of the data

The correct answer is e. Although the server updates statistics automatically, the statistics can become skewed in between the automatic update of the statistics and a long-running load or other task.

Question 4

> Which database maintenance tasks can be automated? [Check all the correct answers]
>
> ❑ a. Index rebuilds
>
> ❑ b. Updating of index statistics
>
> ❑ c. Database backups
>
> ❑ d. Transaction log backups
>
> ❑ e. None of the above

The correct answers are a, b, c, and d. Answer e is incorrect because the correct answers are provided.

Question 5

How can an operator be notified that a monitored event has occurred? [Check all the correct answers]

❑ a. Email

❑ b. Pager

❑ c. Telephone call

❑ d. By checking the Windows NT event log

❑ e. All of the above

The correct answers are a, b, and d. Answer c is incorrect because, although you might be able to find a product that enables telephone calls, this option isn't officially supported.

Need To Know More?

 Coffman, Gayle, *SQL Server 7: The Complete Reference* (Berkley, CA, Osborne/McGraw-Hill, 1999. ISBN 0-07-882494-X.) Chapter 4 describes how to use SQL Server Agent.

 McGehee, Brad and Shepker, Matthew, *Using Microsoft SQL Server 7.0* (Indianapolis, IN, QUE, 1998. ISBN 0-7897-1628-3). Chapter 10 covers SQL Server Maintenance Plan Wizard, and Chapter 9 covers how to use SQL Server Agent.

 MS SQL Server Books Online is a useful tool when you have an occasional question or when you need clarification of SQL terms.

 Search the TechNet CD-ROM (or its online version, which you can find at **www.microsoft.com**).

 www.microsoft.com/sql This Web site has up-to-date information about using SQL Server.

Replication

Terms you'll need to understand:

√ Replication

√ Publish and Subscribe model

√ Publisher

√ Distributor

√ Distribution database

√ Subscriber

√ Publication

Techniques you'll need to master:

√ Using Snapshot Replication

√ Understanding Transactional Replication

√ Performing Merge Replication

Overview

Replication is the mechanism provided by SQL Server that allows data and stored procedures to be distributed to other databases. These databases can reside on the same server as the source information, or they can reside on other servers. The other servers do not necessarily have to be running MS SQL Server. Replication also ensures that if the copied data is altered, the change will be reflected throughout the distributed data. In other words, the data will be synchronized so that one copy of the data will match all other copies.

This chapter describes the *Publish and Subscribe model* of replication, describes the three types of replication (Snapshot, Transactional, and Merge), and explains how to set up replication.

The Publish And Subscribe Model

Microsoft uses the Publish and Subscribe model for its implementation of replication. This model consists of the following three elements:

➤ Publisher

➤ Distributor

➤ Subscriber

The *Publisher* is the server that holds the data being distributed to other databases. The *Distributor* is the server that holds the distribution database. This database holds records of the published data and what acts as the medium to move the data between Publishers and Subscribers. The *Subscriber* is the server that holds copies of the published information. Subscribers can also receive changes to the published data.

For certain types of replication, subscribers can also implement changes to the data. These changes are then sent back to the Publisher (by way of the Distributor). Microsoft uses the Publish and Subscribe model to support three types of replication, as follows:

➤ Snapshot Replication

➤ Transactional Replication

➤ Merge Replication

Snapshot Replication

Snapshot Replication involves taking a *snapshot* of the published data. This snapshot is a copy of the schema of the published objects and the data stored in them. The snapshot is taken by a Snapshot Agent, which records schema and data. This snapshot is sent to the Distribution Agent, which sends the data on to the Subscribers. The Subscribers receive more than just changes to the data, but a whole new set of data to replace their old data. The old data is dropped and new data is re-created from the snapshot. You can think of this type of replication as removing an old photo from an album and replacing it with a new photo.

Transactional Replication

Transactional Replication, rather than transmitting whole tables (whole new sets of data), transmits just the modifications of published tables and executions of stored procedures (with their parameters). The process employs three key components: Snapshot Agent, Log Reader Agent, and Distribution Agent.

The Snapshot Agent provides the initial starting data for the subscribers. The Log Reader Agent searches the transaction log for instances of **INSERT, UPDATE,** or **DELETE** on the published objects and batch-copies them to the Distribution database. The Log Reader Agent can run continuously or on an administrator-defined schedule. The changes are stored in the Distribution database until the Distribution Agent, responsible for sending the data out to subscriber databases, "pushes" the data to the Subscribers. Data can also be "pulled" to the subscriber database (requested by the Distribution Agent). The Subscribers then make the appropriate changes or execute the forwarded procedure call in the subscriber database. The advantage of Transactional Replication is that only changes, rather than whole tables, are passed to the Subscribers.

Merge Replication

In Snapshot and Transactional Replication, the Publisher database is the source of all changes. With Merge Replication, modifications to a source database are tracked and are then synchronized with the Publisher and Subscriber databases. As with Snapshot and Transactional Replication, there is a Snapshot Agent, which records schema and data from a Publisher and sends them to the Distributor. As with Transactional Replication, this Snapshot Agent provides the initial starting data. In Merge Replication, however, this data is applied to the Subscribers by a Merge Agent. This Merge Agent applies the initial data from the Snapshot Agent and reconciles changes between the Publishers and Subscribers.

Setting Up Replication

For data in a replication environment to be accurately distributed to the appropriate database, the Publishers, Distributors, and Subscribers must be declared and configured properly in the system. Otherwise, data might not get to the appropriate Subscribers, or changes from the Subscribers might not be passed along to other databases.

SQL Server has two methods of configuring replication. The first method is to use the wizards provided in the Enterprise Manager. These wizards guide users step by step through the process of setting up Distributors, Publishers, and Subscribers. The second method, concentrated on in this book, is to use the stored procedures provided by SQL Server to configure the Distributors, Publishers, and Subscribers.

Configuring A Server As A Distributor

Before any Publishers can be declared, a Distributor server must be in existence. This server can be on the same server as the distribution database. After the server is configured, a distribution database must be created to store data and regulate replication.

To enable a server as a Distributor, you must add the server as a Distributor by using the **sp_adddistributor** stored procedure. Listing 11.1 shows the syntax of **sp_adddistributor**.

Listing 11.1   The syntax of sp_adddistributor.

```
sp_adddistributor [@distributor =] 'distributor'
[,[@heartbeat_interval =] heartbeat_interval]
[,[@password =] 'password']
```

The following list describes each parameter shown in Listing 11.1:

➤ *distributor* The name of the new Distributor server.

➤ *heartbeat_interval* The maximum length of time (in minutes) a replication agent can go on without logging a process message. The default interval is 10 minutes.

➤ *password* The password used by the distributor_admin login. The default *password* is NULL. The NULL or password is passed to the stored procedure. The password will be made a random value.

After a server has been enabled as a Distributor, it can hold distribution databases to store and process replication data. Distribution databases are created with the **sp_adddistributiondb** stored procedure (see Listing 11.2).

Listing 11.2   The syntax of sp_adddistributiondb.

```
sp_adddistributiondb [@database =] 'database'
[,[@data_folder =] 'data_folder'] [,[@data_file =] 'data_file']
[,[@data_file_size =] data_file_size] [,[@log_folder =] 'log_folder']
[,[@log_file =] 'log_file'] [,[@log_file_size =] log_file_size]
[,[@min_distretention =] min_distretention]
[,[@max_distretention =] max_distretention]
[,[@history_retention =] history_retention]
[,[@security_mode =] security_mode] [,[@login =] 'login']
[,[@password =] 'password']
[,[@createmode =] createmode]
```

The following list describes each parameter shown in Listing 11.2:

➤ *'database'* The name of the new distribution database.

➤ *'data_folder'* The name of the directory used to store the database files built by the procedure. By default, the data goes to \Mssql7\Data.

➤ *'data_file'* The name of the new database file.

➤ *'dat_file_size'* The size of the new database. The default size is 2MB.

➤ *'log_folder'* The directory for the database log file. By default, this is the same as the data directory.

➤ *'log_file'* The name of the log file for the database. If not provided, SQL Server will generate the name.

➤ *'log_file_size'* The size of the log files. The minimum size is 512K.

➤ *'min_distretention'* The minimum number of hours before stored transactions are deleted. The default is 0 hours.

➤ *'max_distretention'* The maximum number of hours before stored transactions are deleted. The default is 72 hours.

➤ *'history_retention'* The number of hours that the history will be retained. The default is to hold the history for 48 hours.

➤ *'security_mode'* The security mode used by the Distributor. The default mode is 0 for SQL Server Authentication. Windows NT Authentication is set by mode 1.

➤ *'login'* The name used when connecting to the Distributor. The default is sa (system administrator). A login is required when the security mode is 0.

➤ *'password'* The password used when connecting to the Distributor. A password is required when *security_mode* is set to 0. The default is NULL.

➤ *'createmode'* The creation mode for the procedure. Mode 0 creates a database for attaching. Mode 1 creates a database or uses an existing database but does not attach.

After a Distributor server is enabled and the distribution database is created, the Distributor server must be added to the list of distributors for each Publisher that will use this Distributor. The **sp_adddistpublisher** stored procedure allows remote Publishers to use the Distributor. Listing 11.3 shows the syntax for **sp_adddistpublisher**.

Listing 11.3   The syntax of sp_adddistpublisher.

```
sp_adddistpublisher [@publisher =] 'publisher',
[@distribution_db =] 'distribution_db'
[,[@security_mode =] security_mode]
[,[@login =] 'login']
[,[@password =] 'password']
{,[@working_directory =] 'working_directory'},
[,[@trusted =] 'trusted']
[,[@encrypted_password =] encrypted_password]
[,[@thirdparty_flag =] thirdparty_flag]
```

The following list describes each element shown in Listing 11.3:

➤ *'publisher'* The name of the Publisher server.

➤ *'distribution_db'* The name of the distribution database.

➤ *'security_mode'* The implemented security mode. Mode 0 uses SQL Server Authentication. Mode 1 uses Windows NT Authentication.

➤ *'login'* The login used by the replication agents to connect to the Publisher. The default is sa.

➤ *'password'* The password used by the replication agents to connect to the Publisher.

➤ *'working_directory'* The name of the working directory used to store data and schema files for the publication.

➤ *'trusted'* A **true** or **false** value that indicates whether the Publisher uses the same password as the Distributor.

➤ *encrypted_password* A Bit value set to 0 by default. Use 1 if the password is provided in encrypted form.

➤ *thirdparty_flag* A Bit value set to 0 by default. Use 1 if the data source is not Microsoft SQL Server.

Configuring A Server As A Publisher

Configuring a server as a Publisher enables it to send data to the distribution database. The configuration process includes enabling replication for the database and defining the articles that will be published. For Snapshot and Transaction Replication, the process for configuring a Publisher is the same. However, for Merge Replication, different stored procedures are used. These two processes will be looked at separately.

Configuring A Publisher For Snapshot Or Transactional Replication

To set up a Publisher for either Snapshot or Transactional Replication, take the following steps:

1. Execute **sp_replicationdboption**. This procedure enables publication for a database.

   Before replication can be configured for a database, replication must be enabled via the **sp_replicationdboption** stored procedure (see Listing 11.4).

Listing 11.4   The syntax of sp_replicationdboption.

```
sp_replicationdboption [@dbname =] 'db_name',
[@optname =] 'optname',
[@value =] 'value'
[,[@ignore_distributor =] ignore_distributor]
```

The following list describes each element shown in Listing 11.4:

➤ *'dbname'* Name of the database being altered for replication.

➤ *'optname'* The publishing mode for the database: *'merge publish'* is used for Merge Replication; *'publish'* is used for Transactional and Snapshot Replication.

➤ *'value'* A **true** or **false** value, used to enable (**true**) or disable (**false**) the replication option.

➤ *ignore_distributor* A value of 1 allows the stored procedure to run without connecting to the Distributor. The default is 0.

2. Execute **sp_addpublication** with *repl_freq* set to *Snapshot* for Snapshot Replication or to *Continuous* for Transactional Replication.

   After you configure the database to allow replication, you can configure the database to declare publications for Transactional Replication and

Snapshot Replication. This configuration is accomplished with the **sp_addpublication** stored procedure (see Listing 11.5).

Listing 11.5   The syntax of sp_addpublication.

```
sp_addpublication [@publication =] 'publication'
[,[@taskid =] taskid]
[,[@restricted =] 'restricted']
[,[@sync_method =] 'sync_method']
[,[@repl_freq =] 'repl_freq']
[,[@description =] 'description']
[,[@status =] 'status']
[,[@independent_agent =] 'independent_agent']
[,[@immediate_sync =] 'immediate_sync']
[,[@enabled_for_internet =] 'enabled_for_internet']
[,[@allow_push =] 'allow_push']
[,[@allow_pull =] 'allow_pull']
[,[@allow_anonymous =] 'allow_anonymous']
[,[@allow_sync_tran =] 'allow_sync_tran']
[,[@autogen_sync_procs =] 'autogen_sync_procs']
[,[@retention =] retention]
```

The following list describes each element shown in Listing 11.5:

➤ *'publication'* The name of the publication.

➤ *taskid* A unique scheduler task ID. This parameter is provided only for backward compatibility with previous versions of Microsoft SQL Server.

➤ *'restricted'* A parameter provided for backward compatibility only. Use *default_access* instead.

➤ *'sync_method'* The nature of the bulk-copy output used to copy the table rows. The choices are Native mode and Character mode.

➤ *'repl_freq'* The type of replication being performed. The Continuous option is used for Transactional Replication. The Snapshot option is used for Snapshot Replication.

➤ *'description'* A description of the publication.

➤ *'status'* A parameter that indicates whether the publication data will be made available immediately (Active) or later (Inactive).

➤ *'independent_agent'* A parameter that indicates—with an entry of **true** or **false**—whether there is a standalone Distribution Agent for the publication.

➤ *'immediate_sync'* A **true** or **false** option that indicates whether the synchronization files for the publication are created each time the Snapshot Agent runs.

➤ *'enabled_for_internet'* A **true** or **false** option that indicates whether the publication will be enabled for Internet use.

➤ *'allow_push'* A **true** or **false** option that indicates whether the publication will allow push Subscribers.

➤ *'allow_pull'* A **true** or **false** option that indicates whether the publication will allow pull Subscribers.

➤ *'allow_anonymous'* A **true** or **false** option that indicates whether the publication will allow anonymous Subscribers.

➤ *'allow_sync_tran'* If set to **true**, immediate-updating subscriptions will be permitted by the publication. This option is set to **false** by default.

➤ *'autogen_sync_procs'* This option is set to **true** by default so that the stored procedure used to synchronize immediate-updating subscriptions will be created automatically by the Publisher.

➤ *'retention'* The number of hours a subscription may be inactive before it expires and is removed from the distribution database.

3. Execute **sp_addpublication_snapshot** to create a Snapshot Agent and to place the schema and data into the replication working directory (see Listing 11.6).

After the database has been configured for the appropriate replication types, the publications can be defined. This step defines the behavior of the Snapshot Agent required for all types of replication.

Listing 11.6 The syntax of sp_addpublication_ snapshot.

```
sp_addpublication_snapshot [@publication =] 'publication'
[,[@frequency_type =] frequency_type]
[,[@frequency_interval =] frequency_interval]
[,[@frequency_subday =] frequency_subday]
[,[@frequency_subday_interval =] frequency_subday_interval]
[,[@frequency_relative_interval =] frequency_relative_interval]
[,[@frequency_recurrence_factor =] frequency_recurrence_factor]
[,[@active_start_date =] active_start_date]
[,[@active_end_date =] active_end_date]
[,[@active_start_time_of_day =] active_start_time_of_day]
[,[@active_end_time_of_day =] active_end_time_of_day]
```

The following list describes each element shown in Listing 11.6:

➤ *'publication'* The name of the publication.

➤ *frequency_type* An option that describes the frequency in which the Snapshot Agent is applied, as follows:

Value	Description
1	Once
4	Daily
8	Weekly
10	Monthly
20	Monthly, relative to the frequency interval
40	When SQL Server Agent starts

➤ *frequency_interval* The value to apply to the frequency set by *frequency_type*.

➤ *frequency_subday* The units for *freq_subday_interval*, as follows:

Value	Description
1	Once
2	Second
4	Minute
8	Hour

➤ *frequency_subday_interval* The interval for *frequency_subday*.

➤ *frequency_relative_interval* The date the Snapshot Agent runs.

➤ *frequency_recurrence_factor* The recurrence factor used by *frequency_type*.

➤ *active_start_date* The date when the Snapshot Agent is first scheduled. The format is YYYYMMDD.

➤ *active_end_date* The date when the Snapshot Agent stops being scheduled, formatted as YYYYMMDD.

➤ *active_start_time_of_day* The time when the Snapshot Agent is first scheduled, formatted as HHMMSS.

➤ *active_end_time_of_day* The time when the Snapshot Agent stops being scheduled, formatted as HHMMSS using a 24-hour clock.

4. Execute **sp_addarticle** for each article defined in the publication.

After the snapshot behavior has been defined, a publication can have articles added to it. The articles can be stored procedures or tables. They are added with the **sp_addarticle** stored procedure. See Listing 11.7 for the syntax of the **sp_addarticle** stored procedure.

Listing 11.7   The syntax of the sp_addarticle stored procedure.

```
sp_addarticle [@publication =] 'publication',
[@article =] 'article', [@source_table =] 'source_table'
[,[@destination_table =] 'destination_table']
[,[@vertical_partition =] 'vertical_partition']
[,[@type =] 'type'] [,[@filter =] 'filter']
[,[@sync_object =] 'sync_object']
[,[@ins_cmd =] 'ins_cmd'] [,[@del_cmd =] 'del_cmd']
[,[@upd_cmd =] 'upd_cmd']
[,[@creation_script =] 'creation_script']
[,[@description =] 'description']
[,[@pre_creation_cmd =] 'pre_creation_cmd']
[,[@filter_clause =] 'filter_clause']
[,[@schema_option =] schema_option]
[,[@destination_owner =] 'destination_owner']
[,[@status =] status]
[,[@source_owner =] 'source_owner']
[,[@sync_object_owner =] 'sync_object_owner']
[,[@filter_owner =] 'filter_owner']
[,[@source_object =] 'source_object']
```

The following list describes each element shown in Listing 11.7:

➤ *'publication'* The name of the publication that contains the article.

➤ *'article'* The name of the article.

➤ *'source_table'* The name of the original source table.

➤ *'destination_table'* The name of the destination table in the subscriber database.

➤ *'vertical_partition'* An option that specifies whether all columns are being replicated, or only columns specified using the **sp_articlecolumn** stored procedure are being replicated.

➤ *'type'* The type of article. The different values available are as follows:

Value	Description
logbased	Log-based article
logbased manualfilter	Log-based article with manual filter
logbased manualview	Log-based article with manual view
logbased manualboth	Log-based article with manual filter and manual view
proc exec	Replicates the execution of the stored procedure to all Subscribers of the article
serializable proc exec	Replicates the execution of the stored procedure only if it is executed within the context of a serializable transaction

➤ *'filter'* The name of the newly created stored procedure (created with **FOR REPLICATION**) used to horizontally filter the table.

➤ *'sync_object'* The name of the table or view used for producing a synchronization output file.

➤ *'ins_cmd'* The replication mechanism used when replicating inserts. The different options are as follows:

Value	Description
NONE	No action is taken.
CALL sp_MSins_*article*	Calls a stored procedure to be executed at the Subscriber, or creates the specified stored procedure in the destination database of each Subscriber of the article.
SQL	Performs replication by using **INSERT** statements.

➤ *'del_cmd'* The replication mechanism used when replicating deletes. The options are as follows:

Value	Description
NONE	No action is taken.
CALL sp_MSdel_*article*	Calls a stored procedure to be executed at the Subscriber.

| XCALL sp_MSdel_*article* | Calls a stored procedure taking **XCALL** style parameters. |
| SQL | Replicates using **DELETE** statements. |

➤ *'upd_cmd'* The replication mechanism used to resolve updates. The options are as follows:

Value	Description
NONE	No action is taken.
CALL sp_MSupd_*article*	Calls a stored procedure to be executed at the Subscriber.
MCALL sp_MSupd_*article*	Calls a stored procedure taking **MCALL** style parameters.
XCALL sp_MSupd_*article*	Calls a stored procedure taking **XCALL** style parameters.
SQL	Replicates using **UPDATE** statements.

➤ *'creation_script'* The path and name of a schema script used to create target tables.

➤ *'description'* A description of the article.

➤ *'pre_creation_cmd'* A parameter that indicates the type of statement to be issued before the replicated table is created. The choices are as follows:

Value	Description
none	Does not execute a command
delete	Deletes the destination table
drop	Drops the destination table
truncate	Truncates the destination table

➤ *'filter_clause'* A **WHERE** clause used to exclude rows from replication.

➤ *schema_option* A bitmap of the schema generation options stored in a binary (8) variable.

➤ *'destination_owner'* The name of the owner of the replicated object in the destination database.

➤ *status* A bitmap of the article options stored in a tinyint.

➤ *'source_owner'* The owner of the object in the publishing database.

➤ *'sync_object_owner'* The owner of the synchronization object.

➤ *'filter_owner'* The owner of the filter.

➤ *'source_object'* The source object being replicated. Microsoft recommends using this parameter instead of *source_table*, which is provided for backward compatibility with SQL Server 6.5.

Configuring A Publisher For Merge Replication

Merge Replication is configured by using some different stored procedures when defining the publication and the articles to be published. To set up a Publisher for a Merge Replication, follow these steps:

1. Execute **sp_replicationdboption** to enable publication of the current database.

2. Execute **sp_addmergepublication** to define the publication.

   For Merge Replication, use the **sp_addmergepublication** stored procedure (see Listing 11.8) instead of **sp_addpublication**.

Listing 11.8   The syntax of sp_addmergepublication.

```
sp_addmergepublication [@publication =] 'publication'
[,[@description =] 'description' [,[@retention =] retention]
[,[@sync_mode =] 'sync_mode', [@allow_push =] 'allow_push']
[,[@allow_pull =] 'allow_pull']
[,@allow_anonymous =] 'allow_anonymous']
[,[@enabled_for_internet =] 'enabled_for_internet']
[,[@centralized_conflicts =] 'centralized_conflicts']
[,[@dynamic_filters =] 'dynamic_filters']
```

The following list describes each element shown in Listing 11.8:

➤ *'publication'* The name of the new merge publication.

➤ *'description'* A description of the new publication.

➤ *retention* A parameter that sets the number of days the publication will be saved before it expires. Expired publications will be removed.

➤ *'sync_mode'* A parameter that describes the nature of the bulk-copy output used to copy the table rows. The choices are Native mode and Character mode.

➤ *'allow_push'* A **true** or **false** option that indicates whether the publication will allow push subscribers.

➤ *'allow_pull'* A **true** or **false** option that indicates whether the publication will allow pull subscribers.

➤ *'allow_anonymous'* A **true** or **false** option that indicates whether the publication will allow anonymous subscribers.

➤ *'enabled_for_internet'* A **true** or **false** option that indicates whether the publication will be enabled for Internet use.

➤ *'centralized_conflicts'* If set to **true**, replication conflicts are stored on the Publisher. If set to **false**, replication conflicts are stored with the Subscriber.

➤ *'dynamic_filters'* A **true** or **false** setting that determines whether the publication is filtered on a dynamic clause.

3. Execute **sp_addpublication_snapshot** to define the Snapshot Agent.

4. Execute **sp_addmergearticle** for each article in the publication.

The **sp_addmergearticle** stored procedure (see Listing 11.9) defines a new article for Merge Replication only.

Listing 11.9   The syntax of sp_addmergearticle.

```
sp_addmergearticle [@publication =] 'publication',
[@article =] 'article',
[@source_object =] 'source_object' [,[@type =] 'type']
[,[@description =] 'description']
[,[@column_tracking =] 'column_tracking']
[,[@status =] 'status']
[,[@pre_creation_cmd =] 'pre_creation_cmd']
[,[@creation_script =] 'creation_script']
[,[@schema_option =] schema_option]
[,[@subset_filterclause =] 'subset_filterclause']
[,[@article_resolver =] 'article_resolver']
[,[@resolver_info =] 'resolver_info']
[,[@source_owner =] 'source_owner']
```

The following list describes each element shown in Listing 11.9:

➤ *'publication'* The name of the publication that contains the article.

➤ *'article'* The name of the article.

➤ *'source_object'* The name of the source table from which the article will be added. *source_object* is sysname, with no default.

➤ *'type'* The type of article. The default is Table.

➤ *'description'* A description of the article.

➤ *'column_tracking'* The setting for column-level tracking.

➤ *'status'* The status of the article. If Active, the initial processing script to publish the table is run. If Unsynced, the initial processing script to publish the table is run the next time the Snapshot Agent runs.

➤ *'pre_creation_cmd'* A method that indicates the type of statement to be issued before the replicated table is created. The choices are as follows:

Value	Description
none	Does not execute a command
delete	Deletes the destination table
drop	Drops the destination table
truncate	Truncates the destination table

➤ *'creation_script'* An optional pre-creation script for the article. *creation_script* is nvarchar(255), with a default of NULL.

➤ *schema_option* A bitmap of the schema generation options stored in a binary (8) variable.

➤ *'subset_filterclause'* A **WHERE** clause used to exclude rows from replication.

➤ *'article_resolver'* A parameter set to either Custom Resolver or NULL. If Custom Resolver, SQL Server uses a custom resolver rather than the system-supplied resolver.

➤ *'resolver_info'* The name of the stored procedure used as a custom article resolver.

➤ *'source_owner'* The owner of the *source_object*.

Configuring Subscribers

There are two types of subscriptions—push subscriptions and pull subscriptions. Push subscriptions are managed centrally and are *pushed* (sent out) from the publisher to the subscribers. Pull subscriptions are managed at the Subscribers. The Subscribers *pull* (request) the subscribed data from the Publishers.

Push Subscriptions Using Snapshot Or Transaction Replication

To add a push subscription for publications by using Snapshot or Transactional Replication, take the following steps:

1. Execute **sp_addsubscriber** (see Listing 11.10) to register the Subscriber at the Publisher.

Listing 11.10   The syntax of sp_addsubscriber.

```
sp_addsubscriber [@subscriber =] 'subscriber' [,[@type =] type]
[,[@login =] 'login'] [,[@password =] 'password']
[,[@commit_batch_size =] commit_batch_size]
[,[@status_batch_size =] status_batch_size]
[,[@flush_frequency =] flush_frequency]
[,[@frequency_type =] frequency_type]
[,[@frequency_interval =] frequency_interval]
[,[@frequency_relative_interval =] frequency_relative_interval]
[,[@frequency_recurrence_factor =] frequency_recurrence_factor]
[,[@frequency_subday =] frequency_subday]
[,[@frequency_subday_interval =] frequency_subday_interval]
[,[@active_start_time_of_day =] active_start_time_of_day]
[,[@active_end_time_of_day =] active_end_time_of_day]
[,[@active_start_date =] active_start_date]
[,[@active_end_date =] active_end_date]
[,[@description =] 'description']
[,[@security_mode =] security_mode]
[,[@encrypted_password =] encrypted_password]
```

The following list describes each element shown in Listing 11.10:

➤ *'subscriber'* The name of the server to be added as a valid Subscriber to the server's publications.

➤ *type* The type of Subscriber. *Type* can be one of these values:

Value	Description
0 (default)	Microsoft SQL Server Subscriber
1	ODBC data source server
2	Microsoft Jet database
3	OLE DB provider

➤ *'login'* The login ID for SQL Server Authentication. The default *login* is sa.

➤ *'password'* The password for SQL Server Authentication.

➤ *commit_batch_size* This parameter is not used in SQL Server 7. Supported for backward compatibility only.

➤ *status_batch_size* This parameter is not used in SQL Server 7. Supported for backward compatibility only.

➤ *flush_frequency* This parameter is not used in SQL Server 7. Supported for backward compatibility only.

➤ *frequency_type* The frequency with which to schedule the Distribution Agent. *frequency_type* can be one of the following values:

Value	Description
1	One time
2	On demand
4	Daily
8	Weekly
16	Monthly
32	Monthly relative
64 (default)	Autostart
124	Recurring

➤ *frequency_interval* The value to apply to the frequency set by *frequency_type*. The default *frequency_interval* is 1.

➤ *frequency_relative_interval* The date of the Distribution Agent. This parameter is used when *frequency_type* is set to 32 (monthly relative). *frequency_relative_interval* can be one of these values:

Value	Description
1 (default)	First
2	Second
4	Third
8	Fourth
16	Last

➤ *frequency_recurrence_factor* The recurrence factor used by *frequency_type*. The default *frequency_recurrence_factor* is 0.

➤ *frequency_subday* This parameter that specifies how often to re-schedule during the defined period. *frequency_subday* can be one of the following values:

Value	Description
1	Once
2	Second
4 (default)	Minute
8	Hour

➤ *frequency_subday_interval* The interval for *frequency_subday*. The default *frequency_subday_interval* is 5.

➤ *active_start_time_of_day* The time of day when the Distribution Agent is first scheduled, formatted as HHMMSS. The default *active_start_ time_of_day* is 0.

➤ *active_end_time_of_day* The time of day when the Distribution Agent stops being scheduled, formatted as HHMMSS. *active_ end_time_of_day* is int, with a default of 235959, which means 11:59:59 P.M. as measured on a 24-hour clock.

➤ *active_start_date* The date when the Distribution Agent is first scheduled, formatted as YYYYMMDD. The default *active_start_ date* is 0.

➤ *active_end_date* The date when the Distribution Agent stops being scheduled, formatted as YYYYMMDD. The default *active_end_date* is 99991231, which means December 31, 9999.

➤ *'description'* A text description of the Subscriber. When upgrading, existing MSsubscriber_info tables are modified to include a description column, which is initialized to SQL Server 7.

➤ *security_mode* The implemented security mode. The default *security_ mode* is 1. Mode 0 specifies SQL Server Authentication. Mode 1 specifies Windows NT Authentication.

➤ *encrypted_password* A parameter used for internal use only.

2. Execute **sp_addpublication** with *allow_push* set to **true** to enable push subscriptions.

3. Execute **sp_addsubscription** (see Listing 11.11) to create the subscription.

Listing 11.11   The syntax of sp_addsubscription.

```
sp_addsubscription [@publication =] 'publication'
[,[@article =] 'article'] [,[@subscriber =] 'subscriber']
[,[@destination_db =] 'destination_db',
[@sync_type =] 'sync_type']
[,[@status =] 'status',
[@subscription_type =] 'subscription_type']
[,[@update_mode =] 'update_mode']
[,[@loopback_detection =] 'loopback_detection']
[,[@frequency_type =] frequency_type]
[,[@frequency_interval =] frequency_interval]
[,[@frequency_relative_interval =] frequency_relative_interval]
[,[@frequency_recurrence_factor =] frequency_recurrence_factor]
[,[@frequency_subday =] frequency_subday]
[,[@frequency_subday_interval =] frequency_subday_interval]
[,[@active_start_time_of_day =] active_start_time_of_day]
[,[@active_end_time_of_day =] active_end_time_of_day]
[,[@active_start_date =] active_start_date]
[,[@active_end_date =] active_end_date]
[,[@optional_command_line =] 'optional_command_line']
[,[@reserved =] 'reserved']
[,[@enabled_for_syncmgr =] 'enabled_for_syncmgr']
```

The following list describes each element shown in Listing 11.11:

➤ *'publication'* The name of the publication.

➤ *'article'* The article that is subscribed to. The default *article* is All. The article name must be unique within the publication. If All is not supplied, a subscription is added to all articles in that publication.

➤ *'subscriber'* The name of the Subscriber.

➤ *'destination_db'* The name of the destination database in which to place replicated data. The *destination_db* is NULL and uses the same name as the publication database.

➤ *'sync_type'* The subscription synchronization type. *sync_type* can be one of the following values:

Value	Description
automatic (default)	Synchronization is applied to the Subscriber through the distribution process.
manual	A synchronization file is automatically produced, but it must be manually applied to the Subscriber.
none	No initial synchronization.

➤ *'status'* The subscription status. *status* is **sysname** and can be one of these values:

Value	Description
active	If *sync_type* is none, the default for *status* is active. To enable a Subscriber to see articles in a restricted publication article, a placeholder subscription must be created with inactive status. If *sync_type* is automatic, *status* cannot be set to active.
subscribed	If *sync_type* is other than none, the default for *status* is subscribed.

➤ *'subscription_type'* The type of subscription. The default *subscription_type* is push. Can be push or pull.

Note: Anonymous subscriptions do not need to use this stored procedure. The Distribution Agents of push subscriptions reside at the Distributor, and the Distribution Agents of pull subscriptions reside at the Subscriber.

➤ *'update_mode'* The type of update. *update_mode* can be one of these values:

Value	Description
read-only (default)	Disables support for immediate-updating Subscribers
synctran	Enables support for immediate-updating Subscribers

➤ *'loopback_detection'* A parameter that determines whether the Distribution Agent sends transactions originated at the Subscriber back to the Subscriber. *loopback_detection* can be one of these values:

Value	Description
true	Distribution Agent doesn't send transactions originated at the Subscriber back to the Subscriber. The value can be set to **true** if and only if the subscription *update_mode* is synctran and the article table has a published timestamp column.
false	Distribution Agent sends transactions originated at the Subscriber back to the Subscriber.
NULL (default)	

➤ *frequency_type* The frequency with which to schedule the Distribution Agent. If no value is specified, **sp_addsubscription** uses the value specified in **sp_addsubscriber**.

➤ *frequency_interval* The value to apply to the frequency set by *frequency_type*.

➤ *frequency_relative_interval* The date of the Distribution Agent. This parameter is used when *frequency_type* is set to 32 (monthly relative). The *frequency_relative_interval* can be one of these values:

Value	Description
1	First
2	Second
4	Third
8	Fourth
16	Last

NULL (default)

➤ *frequency_recurrence_factor* The recurrence factor used by *frequency_type*.

➤ *frequency_subday* The parameter that defines how often, in minutes, to reschedule during the defined period. *frequency_subday* can be one of these values:

Value	Description
1	Once
2	Second
4	Minute
8	Hour

NULL (default)

➤ *frequency_subday_interval* The interval for *frequency_subday*.

➤ *active_start_time_of_day* The time of day when the Distribution Agent is first scheduled, formatted as HHMMSS.

➤ *active_end_time_of_day* The time of day when the Distribution Agent stops being scheduled, formatted as HHMMSS.

➤ *active_start_date* The date when the Distribution Agent is first scheduled, formatted as YYYYMMDD.

➤ *active_end_date* The date when the Distribution Agent stops being scheduled, formatted as YYYYMMDD.

➤ *'optional_command_line'* The optional command prompt to execute.

➤ *'reserved'* Reserved.

➤ *'enabled_for_syncmgr'* Determines whether the subscription can be synchronized through the Microsoft Synchronization Manager. The default for *enabled_for_syncmgr* is **false.** If **false,** the subscription is not registered with Synchronization Manager. If **true,** the subscription is registered with Synchronization Manager and can be synchronized without launching SQL Server Enterprise Manager.

Push Subscriptions Using Merge Replication

To add a push subscription for Merge Replication, take these steps:

1. Execute **sp_addsubscriber** to register the Subscriber at the Publisher.

2. Execute **sp_addmergepublication** with *allow_push* set to **true** to enable push subscriptions.

3. Execute **sp_addmergesubscription** (see Listing 11.12) to create the subscription.

Listing 11.12   The syntax of sp_addmergesubscription.

```
sp_addmergesubscription [@publication =] 'publication'
[,[@subscriber =] 'subscriber']
[,[@subscriber_db =] 'subscriber_db']
[,[@subscription_type =] 'subscription_type']
[,[@subscriber_type =] 'subscriber_type']
[,[@subscription_priority =] subscription_priority]
[,[@sync_type =] 'sync_type']
[,[@frequency_type =] frequency_type]
[,[@frequency_interval =] frequency_interval]
[,[@frequency_relative_interval =] frequency_relative_interval]
[,[@frequency_recurrence_factor =] frequency_recurrence_factor]
[,[@frequency_subday =] frequency_subday]
[,[@frequency_subday_interval =] frequency_subday_interval]
[,[@active_start_time_of_day =] active_start_time_of_day]
[,[@active_end_time_of_day =] active_end_time_of_day]
[,[@active_start_date =] active_start_date]
[,[@active_end_date =] active_end_date]
[,[@optional_command_line =] 'optional_command_line']
[,[@description =] 'description']
[,[@enabled_for_syncmgr =] 'enabled_for_syncmgr']
```

The following list describes each element shown in Listing 11.12:

➤ *'publication'* The name of the publication. The publication must already exist.

➤ *'subscriber'* The name of the Subscriber.

➤ *'subscriber_db'* The name of the subscription database.

➤ *'subscription_type'* If set to push, a push subscription is added and the Merge Agent is added at the Distributor. The default is push. If set to pull, a pull subscription is added without adding a Merge Agent at the Distributor.

➤ *'subscriber_type'* The type of Subscriber. Can be one of these values:

Value	Description
local (default)	Subscriber known only to the Publisher
global	Subscriber known to all servers
anonymous	Subscriber known only to itself

➤ *subscription_priority* A number indicating the priority for the subscription. *subscription_priority* is a real number, with a default of NULL. For local and anonymous subscriptions, the priority is 0.0. For global subscriptions, the priority must be less than 100.0.

➤ *'sync_type'* The subscription sync type has a default of automatic. *sync_type* can be automatic or nosync. If automatic, the schema and initial data are transferred to the Subscriber first. If nosync, it is assumed that the Subscriber already has the schema and initial data.

➤ *frequency_type* A value indicating when the Merge Agent will run. *frequency_type* can be one of these values:

Value	Description
1	Once
4	Daily
8	Weekly
10	Monthly
20	Monthly, relative to the frequency interval
40	When SQL Server Agent starts
NULL (default)	

➤ *frequency_interval* The days that the Merge Agent runs. *frequency_interval* can be one of these values:

Value	Description
1	Sunday
2	Monday
3	Tuesday
4	Wednesday
5	Thursday
6	Friday
7	Saturday
8	Day
9	Weekdays
10	Weekend days

NULL (default)

➤ *frequency_relative_interval* The scheduled merge occurrence of the frequency interval in each month. *frequency_relative_interval* can be one of these values:

Value	Description
1	First
2	Second
4	Third
8	Fourth
16	Last

NULL (default)

➤ *frequency_recurrence_factor* The recurrence factor used by *frequency_type*. *frequency_recurrence_factor* has a default of NULL.

➤ *frequency_subday* Describes the units for *freq_subday_interval* and can be one of these values:

Value	Description
1	Once
2	Second
4 (default)	Minute
8	Hour

➤ *frequency_subday_interval* The frequency for *frequency_subday* to occur between each merge.

➤ *active_start_time_of_day* The time of day when the Merge Agent is first scheduled, formatted as HHMMSS.

➤ *active_end_time_of_day* The time of day when the Merge Agent stops being scheduled, formatted as HHMMSS.

➤ *active_start_date* The date when the Merge Agent is first scheduled, formatted as YYYYMMDD.

➤ *active_end_date* The date when the Merge Agent stops being scheduled, formatted as YYYYMMDD.

➤ *'optional_command_line'* The optional command prompt to execute. This parameter is used either to add a command that captures the output and saves it to a file, or to specify a configuration file or attribute.

➤ *'description'* A brief description of the merge subscription.

➤ *'enabled_for_syncmgr'* The parameter that determines whether the subscription can be synchronized through the Microsoft Synchronization Manager. The default value is **false**. If **false**, the subscription is not registered with Synchronization Manager. If **true**, the subscription is registered with Synchronization Manager and can be synchronized without launching SQL Server Enterprise Manager.

Pull Subscriptions Using Snapshot Or Transactional Replication

With pull subsciptions, the movement of replicated data is initiated at the Subscriber. It's no longer adequate to register subscriptions solely with the Publishers. You need to take additional steps to also register the subscription at the Subscriber end.

To add pull subscriptions for publications by using Snapshot or Transactional Replication, take these steps:

1. Execute **sp_addpublication** with *allow_pull* set to **true** to enable pull subscriptions at the Publisher.

2. Execute **sp_addsubscriber** to register the Subscriber at the Publisher.

3. Execute **sp_addsubscription** to create the subscription at the Publisher.

4. Execute **sp_addpullsubscription** (see Listing 11.13) to create the pull subscription at the Subscriber.

Listing 11.13   The syntax of sp_addpullsubscription.

```
sp_addpullsubscription [@publisher =] 'publisher',
[@publisher_db =] 'publisher_db',
[@publication =] 'publication'
[,[@independent_agent =] 'independent_agent']
[,[@subscription_type =] 'subscription_type']
[,[@description =] 'description']
[,
[@update_mode =] 'update_mode']
[,[@immediate_sync =] immediate_sync]
```

The following list describes each element shown in Listing 11.13:

➤ *'publisher'* The name of the Publisher.

➤ *'publisher_db'* The name of the publisher database.

➤ *'publication'* The name of the publication.

➤ *'independent_agent'* The parameter that determines whether there is a standalone Distribution Agent for this publication. *independent_agent* has a default of **true**. If **true**, there is a standalone Distribution Agent for this publication. If **false**, there is one Distribution Agent for each publisher database/subscriber database pair. *independent_agent* is a property of the publication and must have the same value here as it has at the Publisher.

➤ *'subscription_type'* The subscription type of the publication. Can be one of these values:

Value	Description
Pull	Pull subscription
Anonymous (default)	Anonymous subscription

➤ *'description'* The description of the publication.

➤ *'update_mode'* The type of update. *update_mode* can be one of these values:

Value	Description
read-only (default)	Disables support for immediate-updating Subscribers.
Synctran	Enables support for immediate-updating Subscribers.

➤ *immediate_sync* The parameter that determines whether the synchronization files are created or re-created each time the Snapshot Agent runs. *immediate_sync* is a bit with a default of 1, and must be set to the same value as *immediate_sync* in **sp_addpublication**. *immediate_sync* is a property of the publication and must have the same value here as it has at the Publisher.

5. Execute **sp_addpullsubscription_agent** (see Listing 11.14) to create a scheduled job for the Distribution Agent at the Subscriber.

Listing 11.14   The syntax of sp_addpullsubscription_agent.

```
sp_addpullsubscription_agent [@publisher =] 'publisher',
[@publisher_db =] 'publisher_db',
[@publication =] 'publication'
[,[@subscriber =] 'subscriber']
[,[@subscriber_db =] 'subscriber_db']
[,[@subscriber_security_mode =] subscriber_security_mode]
[,[@subscriber_login =] 'subscriber_login']
[,[@subscriber_password =] 'subscriber_password']
[,[@distributor =] 'distributor',
[,[@distribution_db =] 'distribution_db']
[,[@distributor_security_mode =] distributor_security_mode]
[,[@distributor_login =] 'distributor_login']
[,[@distributor_password =] 'distributor_password']
[,[@optional_command_line =] 'optional_command_line']
[,[@frequency_type =] frequency_type]
[,[@frequency_interval =] frequency_interval]
[,[@frequency_relative_interval =] frequency_relative_interval]
[,[@frequency_recurrence_factor =] frequency_recurrence_factor]
[,[@frequency_subday =] frequency_subday]
[,[@frequency_subday_interval =] frequency_subday_interval]
[,[@active_start_time_of_day =] active_start_time_of_day]
[,[@active_end_time_of_day =] active_end_time_of_day]
[,[@active_start_date =] active_start_date]
```

```
[,[@active_end_date =] active_end_date]
[,[@distribution_jobid =] distribution_jobid OUTPUT]
[,[@encrypted_distributor_password =]
     encrypted_distributor_password]
[,[@enabled_for_syncmgr =] 'enabled_for_syncmgr']
[,[@ftp_address =] 'ftp_address']
[,[@ftp_port =] ftp_port]
[,[@ftp_login =] 'ftp_login']
[,[@ftp_password =] 'ftp_password']
```

The following list describes each element shown in Listing 11.14:

➤ *'publisher'* The name of the Publisher.

➤ *'publisher_db'* The name of the publisher database.

➤ *'publication'* The name of the publication.

➤ *'subscriber'* The name of the Subscriber.

➤ *'subscriber_db'* The name of the subscription database.

➤ *subscriber_security_mode* Valid modes are mode 0, which specifies Microsoft SQL Server Authentication, and mode 1, which specifies Microsoft SQL Server Authentication.

➤ *'subscriber_login'* The login used by the subscriber to receive data from the Publishers.

➤ *'subscriber_password'* The password used by the subscriber to receive data from the Publishers.

➤ *'distributor'* The name of the Distributor.

➤ *'distribution_db'* The name of the Distributor's distribution database.

➤ *distributor_security_mode* The security mode implemented. Mode 0 specifies Microsoft SQL Server Authentication. Mode 1 specifies Microsoft SQL Server Authentication. The default mode is 0.

➤ *'distributor_login'* The Distributor login. *distributor_login* is required if *distributor_security_mode* is set to 0.

➤ *'distributor_password'* The Distributor password. *distributor_password* is required if *distributor_security_mode* is set to 0.

➤ *'optional_command_line'* An optional command prompt statement supplied to the Distribution Agent. This can be an NT command or the name of an NT program to be executed.

➤ *frequency_type* The frequency with which to schedule the Distribution Agent. *frequency_type* can be one of the following values:

Value	Description
1	One time
2 (default)	On demand
4	Daily
8	Weekly
16	Monthly
32	Monthly relative
64	Autostart
124	Recurring

➤ *frequency_interval* The value to apply to the frequency set by *frequency_type*. *frequency_interval* has a default of 1.

➤ *frequency_relative_interval* The date of the Distribution Agent. This parameter is used when *frequency_type* is set to 32 (monthly relative). *frequency_relative_interval* can be one of these values:

Value	Description
1 (default)	First
2	Second
4	Third
8	Fourth
16	Last

➤ *frequency_recurrence_factor* The recurrence factor used by *frequency_type*. *frequency_recurrence_factor* has a default of 1.

➤ *frequency_subday* The parameter that determines how often to reschedule during the defined period. *frequency_subday* can be one of these values:

Value	Description
1 (default)	Once
2	Second

4	Minute
8	Hour

➤ *frequency_subday_interval* The interval for *frequency_subday*. *frequency_subday_interval* has a default of 1.

➤ *active_start_time_of_day* The time of day when the Distribution Agent is first scheduled, formatted as HHMMSS.

➤ *active_end_time_of_day* The time of day when the Distribution Agent stops being scheduled, formatted as HHMMSS.

➤ *active_start_date* The date when the Distribution Agent is first scheduled, formatted as YYYYMMDD.

➤ *active_end_date* The date when the Distribution Agent stops being scheduled, formatted as YYYYMMDD.

➤ *distribution_jobid* OUTPUT The ID of the Distribution Agent for this job.

➤ *encrypted_distributor_password* A parameter used for internal use only.

➤ *'enabled_for_syncmgr'* The parameter that determines whether the subscription can be synchronized through the Microsoft Synchronization Manager. *enabled_for_syncmgr* has a default of **false**. If **false**, the subscription is not registered with Synchronization Manager. If **true**, the subscription is registered with Synchronization Manager and can be synchronized without launching SQL Server Enterprise Manager.

➤ *'ftp_address'* The network address of the FTP service for the Distributor.

➤ *ftp_port* The port number of the FTP service for the Distributor.

➤ *'ftp_login'* The username used to connect to the FTP service.

➤ *'ftp_password'* The user password used to connect to the FTP service.

Pull Subscription Using Merge Replication

For Merge Replication, different stored procedures are used for the configuration of subscriptions and publications. To add a pull subscription for Merge Replication, take these steps:

1. Execute **sp_addmergepublication** with *allow_pull* set to **true** to enable pull subscriptions at the Publisher.

2. Execute **sp_addsubscriber** to register the Subscriber at the Publisher.

3. Execute **sp_addmergesubscription** (refer to Listing 11.12) to create the subscription at the Publisher.

4. Execute **sp_addmergepullsubscription** (see Listing 11.15) to create the subscription at the Subscriber.

Listing 11.15 The syntax of sp_addmergepullsubscription.

```
sp_addmergepullsubscription [@publication =] 'publication'
[,[@publisher =] 'publisher']
[,[@publisher_db =] 'publisher_db']
[,[@subscriber_type =] 'subscriber_type']
[,[@subscription_priority =] subscription_priority]
[,[@sync_type =] 'sync_type']
[,[@description =] 'description']
```

The following list describes each element shown in Listing 11.15:

➤ *'publication'* The name of the publication.

➤ *'publisher'* The name of the Publisher. *publisher* defaults to the local server name. The Publisher must be a valid server.

➤ *'publisher_db'* The name of the publisher database.

➤ *'subscriber_type'* The type of Subscriber. *subscriber_type* can be type 1, 2, or 3. Type 1 is a global subscriber. Type 2 is a local subscriber. Type 3 is an anonymous subscriber. The default is 2.

➤ *subscription_priority* The subscription priority. For local and anonymous subscriptions, the priority is 0.0. The priority is used by the default resolver to pick a winner when conflicts are detected.

➤ *'sync_type'* The subscription synchronization type. Valid values for *sync_type* are automatic or nosync. The default is automatic. If automatic, the schema and initial data are transferred to the Subscriber first. If nosync, it is assumed that the Subscriber already has the schema and initial data.

➤ *'description'* A brief description of this pull subscription.

5. Execute **sp_addmergepullsubscription_agent** (see Listing 11.16) to create a scheduled job for the Distribution Agent at the Subscriber.

Listing 11.16   The syntax of sp_addmergepullsubscription_agent.

```
sp_addmergepullsubscription_agent [[@name =] 'name']
{,[@publisher =] 'publisher',
[@publisher_db =] 'publisher_db',
[@publication =] 'publication'}
[,[@publisher_security_mode =] publisher_security_mode]
[,[@publisher_login =] 'publisher_login']
[,[@publisher_password =] 'publisher_password']
[,[@publisher_encrypted_password =] publisher_encrypted_password]
[,[@subscriber =] 'subscriber']
[,[@subscriber_db =] 'subscriber_db']
[,[@subscriber_security_mode =] subscriber_security_mode]
[,[@subscriber_login =] 'subscriber_login']
[,[@subscriber_password =] 'subscriber_password']
[,[@distributor =] 'distributor']
[,[@distributor_security_mode =] distributor_security_mode]
[,[@distributor_login =] 'distributor_login']
[,[@distributor_password =] 'distributor_password']
[,[@encrypted_password =] encrypted_password]
[,[@frequency_type =] frequency_type]
[,[@frequency_interval =] frequency_interval]
[,[@frequency_relative_interval =] frequency_relative_interval]
[,[@frequency_recurrence_factor =] frequency_recurrence_factor]
[,[@frequency_subday =] frequency_subday]
[,[@frequency_subday_interval =] frequency_subday_interva]
[,[@active_start_time_of_day =] active_start_time_of_day]
[,[@active_end_time_of_day =] active_end_time_of_day]
[,[@active_start_date =] active_start_date]
[,[@active_end_date =] active_end_date]
[,[@optional_command_line =] 'optional_command_line']
[,[@merge_jobid =] merge_jobid]
[,[@enabled_for_syncmgr =] 'enabled_for_syncmgr']
[,[@ftp_address =] 'ftp_address']
[,[@ftp_port =] ftp_port]
[,[@ftp_login =] 'ftp_login']
[,[@ftp_password =] 'ftp_password']
```

The following list describes each element shown in Listing 11.16:

➤ *'name'* The name of the agent.

➤ *'publisher'* The name of the Publisher server.

➤ *'publisher_db'* The name of the Publisher database.

➤ *'publication'* The name of the publication.

➤ *publisher_security_mode* The security mode at the Publisher. The default is 1.

➤ *'publisher_login'* The login used at the Publisher.

➤ *'publisher_password'* The password used at the Publisher.

➤ *publisher_encrypted_password* The parameter that spesifies whether the password is stored in encrypted format.

➤ *'subscriber'* The name of the Subscriber.

➤ *'subscriber_db'* The name of the subscription database.

➤ *subscriber_security_mode* The security mode of the Subscriber. *subscriber_security_mode* has a default of 1. Mode 1 specifies Windows NT Authentication. Mode 0 specifies SQL Server Authentication.

➤ *'subscriber_login'* The Subscriber login. *subscriber_login* is required if *subscriber_security_mode* is set to 0.

➤ *'subscriber_password'* The Subscriber password. *subscriber_password* is required if *subscriber_security_mode* is set to 0.

➤ *'distributor'* The name of the Distributor. *distributor* has a default of *publisher*. This means the Publisher is also the Distributor.

➤ *distributor_security_mode* The security mode of the Distributor. *distributor_security_mode* has a default of 0. Mode 0 specifies SQL Server Authentication. Mode 1 specifies Windows NT Authentication.

➤ *'distributor_login'* The Distributor login. *distributor_login* is required if *distributor_security_mode* is set to 0.

➤ *'distributor_password'* The Distributor password. *distributor_password* is required if *distributor_security_mode* is set to 0.

➤ *encrypted_password* The parameter that determines whether the password is encrypted. *encrypted_password* is bit, with a default of 0. When *encrypted_password* is set to 1, the password is encrypted. This is used in generating replication scripts.

➤ *frequency_type* The frequency with which to schedule the Distribution Agent. *frequency_type* can be one of these values:

Value	Description
1	One time
2	On demand

4	Daily
8	Weekly
16	Monthly
32	Monthly relative
64	Autostart
124	Recurring

NULL (default)

➤ *frequency_interval* The days that the Distribution Agent runs. *frequency_interval* can be one of these values:

Value	Description
1	Sunday
2	Monday
3	Tuesday
4	Wednesday
5	Thursday
6	Friday
7	Saturday
8	Day
9	Weekdays
10	Weekend days

NULL (default)

➤ *frequency_relative_interval* The date of the Distribution Agent. This parameter is used when *frequency_type* is set to 32 (monthly relative) and can be one of these values:

Value	Description
1	First
2	Second
4	Third
8	Fourth

16   Last

NULL (default)

➤ *frequency_recurrence_factor* The recurrence factor used by *frequency_type*.

➤ *frequency_subday* Determines how often to reschedule during the defined period and can be one of these values:

Value	Description
1	Once
2	Second
4	Minute
8	Hour

NULL (default)

➤ *frequency_subday_interval* The interval for *frequency_subday*.

➤ *active_start_time_of_day* The time of day when the Distribution Agent is first scheduled, formatted as HHMMSS.

➤ *active_end_time_of_day* The time of day when the Distribution Agent stops being scheduled, formatted as HHMMSS.

➤ *active_start_date* The date when the Distribution Agent is first scheduled, formatted as YYYYMMDD.

➤ *active_end_date* The date when the Distribution Agent stops being scheduled, formatted as YYYYMMDD.

➤ *'optional_command_line'* An optional command prompt that is supplied to the Distribution Agent.

➤ *merge_jobid* The output parameter for the job ID.

➤ *'enabled_for_syncmgr'* The option that determines whether the subscription can be synchronized through the Microsoft Synchronization Manager. *enabled_for_syncmgr* has a default of **false**. If **false**, the subscription is not registered with Synchronization Manager. If **true**, the subscription is registered with Synchronization Manager and can be synchronized without launching SQL Server Enterprise Manager.

➤ *'ftp_address'* The network address of the FTP service for the

Distributor.

➤ *ftp_port* The port number of the FTP service for the Distributor.

➤ *'ftp_login'* The username used to connect to the FTP service.

➤ *'ftp_password'* The user password used to connect to the FTP service.

Practice Questions

Question 1

Which type(s) of replication require a Snapshot Agent?

○ a. Transaction Replication

○ b. Snapshot Replication

○ c. Merge Replication

○ d. Transaction and Snapshot Replication only

○ e. Transaction, Snapshot, and Merge Replication

The only correct answer is e. Answers a, b, c, and d are incorrect because Transaction, Merge, and Snapshot replication all require a Snapshot Agent.

Question 2

Sp_replicationdboption performs which function?

○ a. Enables replication for a server

○ b. Enables replication for a database

○ c. Enables replication for a remote database

○ d. Enables replication for transactions

○ e. Enables replication for snapshots

The correct answer is b. Replication is enabled at the database level. Answer a is incorrect because replication is enabled at the database level. Answer c is incorrect because a stored procedure must be run in the affected database—it is not run remotely. Answer d is incorrect because transactions are replicated by creating a Publisher for Transaction Replication. Answer e is incorrect because snapshots are replicated by creating a Publisher.

Question 3

> What is being accomplished by the following stored procedure?
> [Check all the correct answers]
>
> ```
> exec sp_addpublication @publication = 'newpub',
> @restricted = 'false', @sync_method = 'native',
> @repl_freq = 'snapshot',
> @description = 'Snapshot publication from
>         tenchi perftune',
> @status = 'active', @allow_push = 'true',
> @allow_pull = 'true', @allow_anonymous = 'false',
> @enabled_for_internet = 'false',
> @independent_agent = 'false',
> @immediate_sync = 'false',
> @allow_sync_tran = 'false',
> @autogen_sync_procs = 'false', @retention = 72
> ```
>
> ❑ a. A publication called newpub is created.
>
> ❑ b. A new publication is enabled for push subscriptions.
>
> ❑ c. A new publication id disabled for pull subscriptions.
>
> ❑ d. A new publication is created for Transaction Replication.
>
> ❑ e. A new publication is created for Snapshot Replication.

The correct answers are a, b, and e. Answer a is correct because the **@publication** parameter receives newpub as input. Answer b is correct because **@allow_pus** is set to **true**. Answer c is incorrect because **@allow_pull** is set to false. Answer d is incorrect because **@repl_freq** is set to **snapshot**. Answer e is correct because **@repl_freq** is set to **snapshot**.

Question 4

> Which of the following are true when adding a pull subscription for Merge Replication? [Check all the correct answers]
>
> ❑ a. The sp_addmergepublication must be run at the publisher with 'allow_pull' set to true.
>
> ❑ b. The sp_addsubscriber must be run to register at the subscriber.
>
> ❑ c. The sp_addmergepullsubscription must be run at the Publisher.
>
> ❑ d. The sp_addmergepullsubscription must be run at the Subscriber.
>
> ❑ e. The sp_addmergepullsubscription_agent must be run on the Subscriber.

The correct answers are a, c, and e. Answer a is correct because, for pull subscription to work, **allow_pull** must be set to **true**. Answer b incorrect because the **sp_addsubscriber** must be run at the publisher for pull Merge Replication. Answer c is correct; for pull Merge Replication, the **sp_addmergesubscription** must be run at the Publisher. This also makes answer d incorrect.

Need To Know More?

 Coffman, Gayle, *SQL Server 7: The Complete Reference*, (Berkley, CA, Osborne/McGraw-Hill, 1999. ISBN 0-07-882494-X). Chapter 9 covers SQL Server 7 replication enhancements.

 McGehee, Brad and Matthew Shepker, *Using Microsoft SQL Server 7.0*, (Indianapolis, IN, QUE, 1998. ISBN 0-7897-1628-3). Chapter 17 provides an overview of replication and how to use replication.

 MS SQL Server Books Online is always a solid resource.

 Search the TechNet CD-ROM (or its online version, through **www.microsoft.com**).

 www.microsoft.com/sql This Web site has up-to-date information about using SQL Server.

Remote Data Access

· ·

Terms you'll need to understand:

√ Distributed query

√ Distributed transaction

√ Distributed transaction Service

√ Friendly name

√ Fully qualified object name

√ Linked server

√ Remote procedure call (RPC)

√ Resource manager

√ Rowset

√ Transaction manager

√ Two-phase commit

Techniques you'll need to master:

√ Configuring SQL Server for RPCs

√ Executing remote procedure calls (RPCs)

√ Removing servers that have been configured for remote data access

√ Being able to decided whether to use an RPC or a distributed query

√ Configuring SQL Server for distributed queries

√ Accessing remote data through linked servers

√ Accessing remote data through ad hoc queries

√ Using distributed queries when the remote server has a different character set

Overview

Most of the time, all the data an application needs to access resides in one SQL Server. There are exceptions, however. Sometimes the data is stored in multiple SQL Servers, and sometimes the data is not stored in any SQL Server. Microsoft SQL Server provides two ways to access data that does not reside in a SQL Server: remote procedure calls and distributed queries.

 Although both remote procedure calls and distributed queries can access data in a remote SQL Server (a SQL Server besides the one that the SQL is issued against), Microsoft recommends that you use distributed queries when accessing remote data.

Remote Procedure Calls

A remote procedure call, or RPC, is used to access data that resides on another SQL Server. RPCs, which are a legacy feature of SQL Server, cannot access data that isn't stored in a SQL Server.

 SQL Server 7 can *receive* remote procedure calls from SQL Server 4.2a or higher. However, SQL Server 7 can *make* remote procedure calls to only SQL Server 6.0 or higher.

Adding And Removing Servers

Before you can use an RPC to access a remote SQL Server, the local SQL Server must know its own name and the name of the remote SQL Server. You make a remote SQL Server known to the local SQL Server with the **sp_addserver** stored procedure. The syntax of **sp_addserver** is as follows:

```
sp_addserver [@server =] 'server'
   [,[@local =] 'local']
   [,[@duplicate_ok =] 'duplicate_OK']
```

The parameters of **sp_addserver** are as follows:

➤ **@server** Specifies the name of the Microsoft SQL Server.

➤ **@local** Specifies whether the server is a local or remote server. You can have only one local server defined. If you are setting a local server name, it will not take effect until after you restart SQL Server. For a local SQL Server, **@local** must be set to 'local'. For a remote SQL Server, **@local** is NULL.

When you're installing SQL Server, the setup program will set the local server name to the name you pick for the server. You should not have to change the local server name unless you are renaming the SQL Server. To verify a SQL Server name, you use the **@@servername** function, as illustrated in the following code snippet:

```
SELECT @@SERVERNAME
```

➤ **@duplicate_ok** Specifies the behavior when you add a duplicate server name. If **@duplicate_ok** is set to **duplicate_OK,** no error is generated when you add a duplicate server name. If **@duplicate_ok** is set to **NULL,** an error is generated when you add a duplicate server name.

When you no longer want to be able to access a remote server, you use the **sp_drop-server** stored procedure to remove the remote server. You can use the **sp_dropserver** stored procedure to remove servers that were added with the **sp_addserver** stored procedure and to remove linked servers that were added with the **sp_addlinkedserver** stored procedure. The syntax of **sp_dropserver** is as follows:

```
sp_dropserver [@server =] 'server'
    [, [@droplogins =]{'droplogins' | NULL}]
```

The **@server** parameter specifies the name of the server to remove. If the **@droplogins** parameter is set to **'droplogins'** any logins that were added for the remote data server with either the **sp_addremotelogin** stored procedure or the **sp_addlinkedsrvlogin** stored procedure will be dropped from the local SQL Server.

Configuring SQL Server For RPCs

To make a remote procedure call, the system administrator has to configure both the SQL Server making the RPC and the SQL Server receiving the RPC. SQL Server default configuration allows it to make and receive RPCs. To reconfigure SQL Server's RPC capability, use the **sp_configure** stored procedure with the **remote access** option. The syntax is as follows:

```
sp_configure 'remote access',[1|0]
reconfigure
```

Setting the **remote access** option to 1 enables other SQL Server instances to access the local server. Setting the **remote access** option to 0 disables other SQL Server instances from being able to access the local server. You must have the sysadmin role to execute the **sp_configure** stored procedure.

The **sp_serveroption** stored procedure can be used to specify what servers can take part in an RPC. The syntax of **sp_serveroption** is as follows:

```
sp_serveroption [[@server =] 'server']
   [,[@optname =] 'option_name']
   [,[@optvalue =] 'option_value'
```

The **@server** parameter is the server that you want to configure. The options that you can configure that affect RPCs are **'rpc'** and **'rpc out'**. If you set **'rpc'** to **On** or **True**, the local SQL Server can receive an RPC from the server specified with the **@server** parameter. If **'rpc out'** is set to **On** or **True**, the local SQL Server can send an RPC to the server specified with the **@server** option.

Mapping Remote Logins To Local Logins

The **sp_addremotelogin** stored procedure is used to map remote logins to logins on the local SQL Server. The syntax of **sp_addremotelogin** is as follows:

```
sp_addremotelogin [@remoteserver =] 'remoteserver'
   [,[@loginame =] 'login']
   [,[@remotename =] 'remote_name']
```

The **@remoteserver** parameter is used to specify the remote server from which you want to add logins. The remote server must first have been added with the **sp_addserver** command. If this is the only parameter passed to **sp_addremotelogin,** then all remote logins will map to a login on the local SQL Server with the same login name.

The **@loginame** parameter is used to specify the login name of an existing local SQL Server to which you want to map remote logins. The **@remotename** parameter is used to specify which logins on the remote SQL Server will map to the login specified in the **@loginame** parameter.

Dropping Remote Logins

The **sp_dropremotelogin** stored procedure is used to unmap remote logins from local logins. The syntax of **sp_dropremotelogin** is as follows:

```
sp_dropremotelogin [@remoteserver =] 'remoteserver'
   [,[@loginame =] 'login']
   [,[@remotename =] 'remote_name']
```

The parameters for **sp_dropremotelogin** are the same as the parameters for **sp_addremotelogin**.

Configuring A Remote Login

To configure the behavior of a remote login, you use the **sp_remoteoption** stored procedure. The syntax of **sp_remoteoption** is as follows:

```
sp_remoteoption [[@remoteserver =] 'remoteserver']
    [,[@loginame =] 'loginame']
    [,[@remotename =] 'remotename']
    [,[@optname =] 'optname']
    [,[@optvalue =] 'optvalue']
```

The parameters for **sp_remoteoption** are as follows:

➤ **@remoteserver** The name of the remote SQL Server.

➤ **@loginame** The local login that you are configuring.

➤ **@remotename** The remote server login that you are configuring.

➤ **@optname** The option that you are setting. The only configurable option is '**trusted**'. If the **trusted** option is turned on, the local login's password does not have to match the remote server's password. If **trusted** is turned off, the local passwords must match the remote password.

➤ **@optvalue** The option that turns the remote option on or off. If **@optvalue** is set to FALSE, the option is turned off. If **@optvalue** is set to TRUE, the option is turned on.

Executing An RPC

After both servers have been configured, you execute a remote stored procedure by using its fully qualified name, as follows:

```
[exec[ute]] server_name.[database_name].[owner].stored_procedure
    [parameters[, parameter . . . ]]
```

A remote stored procedure can be used anywhere in SQL that a local stored procedure can be used. That is, a remote stored procedure can be in a batch by itself, mixed with other queries in a batch, or called from inside a stored procedure as a **EXECUTE** statement in an **INSERT** statement. The following example illustrates how to call remote stored procedures:

```
exec MyOtherServer...sp_who
```

The preceding example illustrates the simplest way to call a remote stored procedure. In the following example, the system stored procedure, **sp_who**, is executed on the server MyOtherServer with no parameters:

```
insert Names execute MyOtherServer.pubs.joe.RetrieveAuthorNames
       @parm1 = 'A'
```

This example uses an RPC to retrieve data to insert into a table called Names. The procedure **RetrieveAuthorNames**, owned by Joe, in the database Pubs on MyOtherServer is executed with the parameter **@parm1** being set to 'A'.

Anything that you can do in a local stored procedure, you can do in a remote stored procedure. Any procedure that you can execute if you log onto the remote server, you can execute through an RPC. An RPC can return data in a result set, return output parameters, and return a return status to the calling SQL Server. Listing 12.1 shows a stored procedure that returns data with a result set, output parameters, a return status, and the SQL to execute it.

Listing 12.1   An example of a remote procedure.

```
-- execute on the remote server in tempdb
CREATE PROC SysObjName
    @NumObj INT OUTPUT
as
SELECT name FROM sysobjects
    WHERE type = 'S'
SELECT @NumObj = @@ROWCOUNT
RETURN -30000
Go
--execute on the local server
declare @RetCnt int,
    @result int
exec @result = MyRemoteServer.tempdb..myp1 @RetCnt output
select ReturnStatus=@result, OutputParm=@RetCount
go
--   The following is the result set
name
----------
sysobjects
sysindexes
syscolumns
systypes
syscomments
sysfiles1
syspermissions
sysusers
```

```
sysdepends
sysreferences
sysfulltextcatalogs
sysindexkeys
sysforeignkeys
sysmembers
sysprotects
sysfiles
sysfilegroups
sysallocations

ReturnStatus OutputParm
----------   ----------
-30000       18
```

Distributed Queries

SQL Server provides a method to access data in any data source that uses an OLE DB provider. You can access data from any OLE DB data source. A distributed query allows you to access data in one or more remote data sources as if the data is a local table. The following list describes some of the capabilities of distributed queries:

➤ Unlike an RPC, a distributed query can access data from multiple data sources in the same query.

➤ A distributed query executes SQL on the local server that affects the data on the remote server.

Before you can use distributed queries, the connection must have the **ANSI_NULLS** and **ANSI_WARNINGS** options turned on, as in the following code snippet.

```
SET ANSI_NULLS ON
SET ANSI_WARNINGS ON
```

Although data sources queried through distributed queries are usually databases, OLE DB providers exist for a wide variety of files and file formats, including text files and spreadsheet data. If an OLE DB provider has not been created for your specific data source, you can probably use the OLE DB provider for ODBC to access your data source.

Linked Servers

A *linked server* is a preconfigured OLE DB data source. SQL statements can refer to a linked server by using the fully qualified object name. Before using a linked server, you must first configure the local SQL Server to access the remote OLE DB data source. The fully qualified object name is *ServerName.DatabaseName.ObjectOwner.ObjectName*. The following example illustrates a linked server being used in a **SELECT** statement as part of a fully qualified object name:

```
SELECT * FROM OtherServer.SalesDB.dbo.Sale
```

Besides using the remote server name as part of a fully qualified object name, the linked server name can also be specified in an **OPENQUERY** function, which is covered later in this chapter. The **OPENQUERY** function returns a rowset that can be used in place of a table or view in SQL statements.

 A rowset is a set of rows that contains columns of data. Rowsets are central objects that OLE DB data providers use to return result set data in tabular form.

The main benefits of a linked server are the following:

➤ A linked server provides remote data access.

➤ A linked server allows you to use distributed queries and transactions on heterogeneous data sources.

➤ A linked server allows you to access multiple heterogeneous data sources the same way.

Adding Linked Servers

Before you can access a linked server, you must first add the linked server with the **sp_addlinkedserver** stored procedure. The syntax of **sp_addlinkedserver** is as follows:

```
sp_addlinkedserver [@server =] 'server'
    [, [@srvproduct =] 'product_name']
    [, [@provider =] 'provider_name']
    [, [@datasrc =] 'data_source']
    [, [@location =] 'location']
    [, [@provstr =] 'provider_string']
    [, [@catalog =] 'catalog']
```

The parameters for **sp_addlinkedserver** are as follows:

➤ **@server** The name used in SQL on the local SQL Server to refer to the linked server.

➤ **@srvproduct** The product name of the OLE DB data source.

Note: If @srvproduct is SQL Server, then provider_name, data_source, location, provider_string, and catalog do not need to be specified.

➤ **@provider** The unique programmatic identifier (PROGID) of the OLE DB provider for the data source. The OLE DB provider is expected to be registered with the given PROGID in the Registry.

➤ **@datasrc** The name of the data source as understood by the OLE DB provider.

➤ **@location** The location of the database as understood by the OLE DB provider.

➤ **@provstr** The OLE DB provider-specific connection string that identifies a unique data source.

➤ **@catalog** The catalog to be used when making a connection to the OLE DB provider.

The information for the parameters for **sp_addlinkedserver** are all provided by the OLE DB provider.

To connect to a linked server, the local SQL Server must be configured to allow distributed queries to access the remote server with the **sp_serveroption** stored procedure as follows:

```
sp_serveroption 'servername','data access','true'
```

Removing Linked Servers

When you no longer want to be able to access a linked server, use the **sp_dropserver** stored procedure to remove access to the linked server. The **sp_dropserver** stored procedure can be used to remove servers that were added with the **sp_addserver** stored procedure and to remove linked servers that were added with the **sp_addlinkedserver** stored procedure. The syntax of **sp_dropserver** is as follows:

```
sp_dropserver [@server =] 'server'
    [, [@droplogins =]{'droplogins' | NULL}]
```

The **@server** parameter specifies the name of the server to remove. If the **@droplogins** parameter is set to '**droplogins**', any logins that were added for the remote data server with either the **sp_addremotelogin** stored procedure or the **sp_addlinkedsrvlogin** stored procedure will be dropped from the local SQL Server. Drop logins must execute exactly what the add login did to succeed.

Adding Linked Server Logins

With RPC, you map the logins for the remote server to the logins on the local server. When mapping logins for a linked server, you map the local logins to the logins that will be used when accessing data on the remote server. When you add a remote server with **sp_addlinkedserver**, a default mapping between all logins on the local server and logins with the same credentials on the remote server will be established. The command to map local logins to remote logins is **sp_addlinkedsrvlogin**. The syntax of **sp_addlinkedsrvlogin** is as follows:

```
sp_addlinkedsrvlogin [@rmtsrvname =] 'rmtsrvname'
   [,[@useself =] TRUE|FALSE]
   [,[@locallogin =] 'locallogin']
   [,[@rmtuser =] 'rmtuser']
   [,[@rmtpassword =] 'rmtpassword']
```

The parameters for **sp_addlinkedsrvlogin** are:

➤ **@rmtsrvname** The name of a linked server.

➤ **@useself** The name of the login to use when connecting to the linked server. If **@useself** is **TRUE**, the connections to the linked server are made with the login name and password of the connection executing the SQL statement requesting data from the remote server. If **@useself** is **FALSE**, the **@rmtuser** and **@rmtpassword** parameters are used when accessing data on the remote server. You cannot set **@useself** to **TRUE** in a Windows NT authenticated login unless the Microsoft Windows NT environment supports security account delegation, which allows the connections Windows NT security credentials to be passed on to another server, and the provider supports Windows NT Authentication.

➤ **@locallogin** A login on the local server. If **@locallogin** is **NULL**, this call to **sp_addlinkedsrvlogin** applies to all local logins that connect to **@rmtsrvname**.

➤ **@rmtuser** The username used to connect to **@rmtsrvname** when **@useself** is **FALSE**.

➤ **@rmtpassword** The password associated with **@rmtuser**.

If **@useself** is **FALSE** and both **@rmtuser** and **@rmtpassword** are **NULL**, no login or password is used to connect to the remote server.

Removing Linked Server Logins

When you want to remove the mapping of a local login to a remote login, use the **sp_droplinkedsrvlogin** stored procedure. The syntax of **sp_dropedlinkedsrvlogin** is as follows:

```
sp_droplinkedsrvlogin [@rmtsrvname =] 'rmtsrvname',
   [@locallogin =] 'locallogin'
```

If **@locallogin** is not null, the local login must already be mapped to a login on the remote server with **sp_addlinkedsrvlogin**. If **@locallogin** is null, the default mapping that was created with **sp_addlinkedserver** will be dropped.

The OPENQUERY Function

The **OPENQUERY** function is used to execute a *pass-through query* (the query is passed on to the other data source without SQL Server parsing or compiling the query) at an OLE DB data source. The syntax of the **OPENQUERY** function is as follows:

```
OPENQUERY(linked_server, 'query')
```

The parameters of the **OPENSERVER** function are the linked server's name and the query to be executed. Before the **OPENSERVER** function can be used, the local SQL Server must first be configured to access the linked server. The following example illustrates the use of the **OPENQUERY** function.

```
SELECT *
FROM OPENQUERY(OtherSvr,
        'SELECT au_lname, au_fname FROM pubs..authors')
```

Ad Hoc Distributed Queries

If you haven't defined your remote data source, you can still access the remote data with an ad hoc distributed query by using the **OPENROWSET** function. When using the **OPENROWSET** function, you specify the information needed to connect to the linked server. The rowset can then be referred to the same way a table is referred to. The syntax of **OPENROWSET** is as follows:

```
OPENROWSET('provider_name'
   {'datasource';'user_id';'password' | 'provider_string' },
   {[catalog.][schema.]object | 'query'})
```

The **OPENROWSET** function is passed all the information necessary to connect to a remote data source as follows:

➤ *'provider_name'* A character string that represents the registered name of the OLE DB provider as specified in the Registry. This is also called a friendly name.

➤ *'datasource'* A string that corresponds to a particular OLE DB data source. This string's format is specific to the OLE DB data source.

➤ *'user_id'* The username that is passed to the specified OLE DB provider.

➤ *'password'* The password that is associated with the *'user_id'*.

➤ *'provider_string'* Provider-specific connection information needed to initialize the OLE DB datasource.

➤ *catalog* The name of the catalog or database that the ad hoc query will be accessing.

➤ *schema* The name of the schema or object owner.

➤ *object* The object name.

➤ *'query'* The query that is sent to and executed by the provider.

*Note: If the query returns multiple result sets, the **OPENROWSET** function will return only the first result set.*

Data Conversion

When remote data is accessed, the data will be converted to and from the local SQL Server's data type and code page. When data is retrieved with a **SELECT, UPDATE, INSERT,** or **DELETE** statement, the remote data will be converted to the local SQL Server's data types and code page. When data is modified with an **INSERT** or **UPDATE** statement, the local SQL Server's data will be converted to the remote data source's data type and code page.

If the code page of the remote data is different from the local server's code page, the query results may be meaningless. For this discussion, look at the following query:

```
SELECT FirstName, LastName
   FROM OtherDataSource.DBName.ObjectOwner.PersonNames
   WHERE PersonKey = 'ABC'
   ORDER BY LastName, FirstName
```

If the remote data source has a code page different from the local SQL Server's code page, the comparison in the **WHERE** clause may not have the results you expect. If you run the query on the remote server, it will return any row in which **PersonKey** is equal to 'ABC'. If you run the query on the local SQL

Server, **PersonKey** will be converted to the local code page before the comparison takes place.

Limitations Of Distributed Queries

By not supporting the functionality, the OLE DB provider can further limit the SQL that can be used. The following list contains SQL Server's rules and limitations in using distributed queries:

➤ **SELECT** statements that contain only **SELECT, FROM,** and **WHERE** clauses are allowed in a distributed query.

➤ The **INTO** clause is allowed if the table being created is on the local SQL Server.

➤ If the select_list contains a BLOB column from a remote table, the **SELECT** statement cannot contain an **ORDER BY** clause.

➤ The local SQL statement cannot refer to remote BLOB columns with **IS NULL** and **IS NOT NULL.**

➤ All **INSERT, UPDATE,** and **DELETE** statements that modify data on the remote data server must meet the OLE DB data-modification requirements.

➤ When accessing the remote table with a cursor, the **WHERE CURRENT OF UPDATE** and **DELETE** clause can be used only if the OLE DB provides the functionality.

➤ **READTEXT, WRITETEXT,** and **UPDATETEXT** are not supported against remote tables.

➤ **CREATE, ALTER,** and **DROP** statements cannot be used against remote servers.

➤ **STATIC** or **INSENSITIVE** cursors can refer to remote tables.

➤ **KEYSET** cursors can refer to remote tables only if the OLE DB provider meets the requirements documented in **KEYSET** cursor functionality.

➤ You cannot use **FORWARD-ONLY** cursor to refer to a remote table.

Distributed Transactions

When a transaction accesses data on two or more servers, the transaction is known as a *distributed transaction*. There are two main components in a distributed transaction: the resource manager and the transaction manager. A SQL

Server (6.5 or greater) can participate in a distributed transaction with another SQL Server (6.5 or greater), or with any data source that complies with the X/Open XA specification for Distributed Transaction Processing.

 A transaction within a single SQL Server that spans two or more databases is actually a distributed transaction. In this case, SQL Server manages the distributed transaction.

Resource Managers

The *resource managers* are the servers that contain the data. A resource manager provides the resources to resolve part of a distributed transaction. SQL Server can operate as a resource manager in a distributed transaction that complies with the X/Open XA specification for Distributed Transaction Processing.

Transaction Managers

The *transaction manager* coordinates the transaction among the resource managers, Microsoft Distributed Transaction Coordinator (MS DTC), or any transaction managers that support the X/Open XA specification for Distributed Transaction Processing, can be a transaction manager in a distributed transaction. The transaction manager will coordinate the transaction with the resource managers to ensure that the complete transaction is committed or rolled backed together.

Note: If the transaction manager is not running, you cannot start a distributed transaction.

The Two-Phase Commit

A distributed transaction is treated much like a local transaction. When the transaction is complete, the application must issue a commit or a rollback transaction statement. The transaction manager then coordinates the commit or rollback transaction statement by using a two-part process (two-phase commit). The two-phase commit consists of the Prepare phase and the Commit phase.

The Prepare Phase

In the Prepare phase, the transaction manager sends a Prepare command to all the resource managers that are taking part in the distributed transaction. The resource managers then prepare the transaction so that it can be committed or rolled back. The resource managers then notify the transaction manager that they have completed the Prepare phase. If any resource manager cannot complete the Prepare request, the transaction is rolled back.

The Commit Phase

After all the resource managers have notified the transaction manager that the Prepare phase has been completed, the transaction manager notifies the resource managers to either commit or roll back the transaction. If any resource manager cannot complete the transaction, the transaction is rolled back.

SQL Server In Distributed Transactions

SQL Server can be included in a distributed transaction in several of the following ways:

➤ If a local transaction is active and a distributed query is issued, the local transaction will be converted to a distributed transaction. The following code snippet illustrates a local transaction escalating to a distributed transaction:

```
BEGIN TRANSACTION
GO
UPDATE authors SET contract = 1
GO -- at this point it is a local transaction
UPDATE MyServer.Pubs.dbo.authos SET contract = 1
GO -- this transaction is now escalated
   -- to a distributed transaction
COMMIT TRANSACTION
GO
```

➤ A distributed transaction can be explicitly started with the **BEGIN DISTRIBUTED TRANSACTION** statement.

➤ Remote procedure calls can escalate a local transaction to a distributed transaction.

➤ ODBC or OLE DB methods can be used to start a distributed transaction.

The SQL Server in which the distributed transaction is initiated is the transaction originator and therefore controls the completion of the transaction. After the distributed transaction is initiated, when a **COMMIT TRANSACTION** or **ROLLBACK TRANSACTION** statement is issued for the connection, the controlling server requests that the transaction manager complete the distributed transaction across all resource managers involved.

The BEGIN DISTRIBIBUTED TRANSACTION Statement

The **BEGIN DISTRIBUTED TRANSACTION** statement is used to explicitly start a distributed transaction. The syntax of the **BEGIN DISTRIBUTED TRANSACTION** statement is as follows:

```
BEGIN DISTRIBUTED TRAN[SACTION]
        [transaction_name | @tran_name_variable]
```

RPCs Escalating Transaction

When executing an RPC inside a local transaction, SQL Server can be configured so that the local transaction will be escalated to a distributed transaction. The **sp_configure** stored procedure is used to configure SQL Server. The syntax of **sp_configure** to configure SQL Server's remote procedure escalation is as follows:

```
sp_configure "remote proc trans", [1 | 0]
```

If the **remote proc trans** option of **sp_configure** is set to 0, then a remote procedure call inside a local transaction doesn't escalate to a distributed transaction. If the **remote proc trans** option of **sp_configure** is set to 1, then a remote procedure call inside a local transaction escalates to a distributed transaction.

Remember to issue the **reconfigure** command after configuring SQL Server. If you do not, the configuration changes will not take effect.

Practice Questions

Question 1

> In the following SELECT statement, what are the names of the
> tables being accessed? [Check all the correct answers]
>
> ```
> select * from sales..thisyear cross join
>     old.othersales.joe.lastweek
> ```
>
> ❑ a. thisyear
> ❑ b. lastweek
> ❑ c. sales
> ❑ d. old
> ❑ e. joe

The correct answers are a and b. Answer c is incorrect because *sales* is the name of a database. Answer d is incorrect because *old* is the name of the remote server. Answer e is incorrect because *joe* is the owner of the table *lastweek*.

Question 2

Which of the following SQL batches will run a distributed transaction? [Check all the correct answers]

❑ a.
```
begin transaction
go
delete table1
go
update MyServer.dbo.Mytable set Column1 = 1234
go
commit transaction
go
```

❑ b.
```
sp_configure 'remote proc tran',1
reconfigure
go
exec Server2.mydb.myproc
go
```

❑ c.
```
begin distributed transaction
go
update server2.pubs..authors set contract = 1
go
commit transaction
go
```

❑ d.
```
begin transaction
go
delete mydb..table1
delete m2.mydb..table2
go
rollback transaction
go
```

The correct answers are d and c. Answer a is incorrect in the update statement because MyServer is a database name, not a remote server name, so there is no distributed transaction. Answer b is incorrect because although the server is configured to automatically escalate local transactions to a distributed transaction when an RPC is issued, a local transaction was not in effect when the RPC was issued.

Question 3

The OPENQUERY function is used to do which of the following?

○ a. The OPENQUERY function is used to modify data on a remote server.

○ b. The OPENQUERY function is used to execute an RPC.

○ c. The OPENQUERY function can make an ad hoc connection to an OLE DB data source.

○ d. The OPENQUERY function is used to access predefined remote data sources.

○ e. All of the above.

The correct answer is c; the **OPENQUERY** function is used for ad hoc queries against remote data sources. Answer a is incorrect because the **OPENQUERY** function doesn't directly modify data. Answer b is incorrect because the **OPENQUERY** function doesn't execute RPCs. Answer d is incorrect because the **OPENQUERY** function isn't used with predefined data sources.

Question 4

> Which of the following steps must be completed to access data on a remote server with an RPC? [Check all the correct answers]
>
> ❑ a. The remote proc tran ser ver option must be turned on.
>
> ❑ b. The local server must be configured for remote access.
>
> ❑ c. The remote ser ver must be configured for remote access.
>
> ❑ d. The passwords must match on the remote ser ver and the local server.
>
> ❑ e. The logins must match on the remote ser ver and the local server.

The correct answer is c. Answer a is incorrect because the remote **proc tran server** option controls transactions in RPCs. Answer b is incorrect because the local server doesn't have to be configured for remote access to execute an RPC to another server. Answers d and e are incorrect because logins and passwords can be configured so that they have to match between the local and remote servers. Logins and passwords, however, do not have to match unless the servers are configured so they must match.

Question 5

> Which of the following SQL statements are valid in distributed queries? [Check all the correct answers]
>
> ❑ a. `select * into MyServer.tempdb..t1 from pubs..authors`
>
> ❑ b. `insert S2.pubs..jobs (job_desc,min_lvl,mxm_lvl)`
>
> ❑ c. `values ( 'My Job',1,2)`
>
> ❑ d. `select * from s3.pubs..authors`
>
> ❑ e. `drop table S2.tempdb..t3`

The correct answers are b and c. Answer a is incorrect; you cannot use a remote table as the table being created with a **SELECT INTO** statement. Answer d is incorrect; you cannot drop a table in a distributed query.

Need To Know More?

 Amo, William C, *Transact-SQL* (Foster City, CA, IDG Books Worldwide. 1998, ISBN 0-7645-8048-5). Chapter 16 covers distributed transactions.

 Coffman, Gayle, *SQL Server 7: The Complete Reference* (Berkley, CA, Osborne/McGraw-Hill, 1999. ISBN 0-07-882494-X). Chapter 16 covers both linked servers and remote servers.

 MS SQL Server Books Online.

 Search the TechNet CD-ROM (or its online version, through **www.microsoft.com**).

 www.microsoft.com/sql has current information about using SQL Server.

SQL Server 7 Troubleshooting

Techniques you'll need to master:

- √ Diagnosing and resolving problems with upgrading from SQL Server 6.x

- √ Diagnosing and resolving problems with backup and restore operations

- √ Diagnosing and resolving replication problems

- √ Diagnosing and resolving distributed query problems

- √ Diagnosing and resolving problems with access to SQL Server, databases, and database objects

Handling Problems With Upgrading From SQL Server 6.x

The following sections cover techniques that you can use to successfully diagnose and resolve problems encountered during and after upgrading from SQL Server 6.x to SQL Server 7. These techniques are using SQL's Upgrade Wizard and the Upgrade Log files.

Using The SQL Server Upgrade Wizard

SQL Server 7 comes with an Upgrade Wizard that converts databases from SQL Server 6.x servers to the new version. When the wizard performs an upgrade, the earlier server and its data remains intact throughout the upgrade process.

During the upgrade process, stored procedures are checked against the contents of the syscomments table for inconsistencies. All logins, users, and permissions are validated. If any inconsistencies or problems are detected, the wizard prompts the user that warnings have been logged. The specific errors are noted in error files placed in a subdirectory under the Upgrade directory. The directory name is based on the servername and on the date and time when the Upgrade Wizard was run (see Listing 13.1). Error files have the .ERR suffix.

The wizard also displays a dialog box named Summary Of Warnings. This dialog box displays inconsistencies found in the user objects. Users shouldn't work with the database until these inconsistencies are resolved. This data is also available in an output file located in the server's upgrade directory. The file name is based on the database name and ID (see Listing 13.1).

Listing 13.1　Structure of error file names.

```
"Check65-<servername><dbid><dbname>_err.out"
```

If stored procedures were renamed with **sp_rename**, the source stored in the **syscomments** table will not match the procedure. The stored procedures need to be dropped and re-created.

Using The Upgrade Log Files

The Upgrade directory contains a series of log files describing each of the upgrade steps. Each upgraded database receives a subdirectory under this parent directory. Each database directory contains log files that detail the success and failure of object creation for the database. Files that have a suffix of .ok indicate that all instances of that type of object were created successfully. Files that have an extension suffix of .err indicate that at least one object of a specific type was not created successfully. The error files list each failed object creation statement and the reason the object wasn't created successfully. You can inspect these log files to determine what failures occurred and why.

Handling Problems With BACKUP And RESTORE Operations

A variety of problems can interfere with **BACKUP** and **RESTORE** operations. These problems can include syntax errors and situations when the **BACKUP** and **RESTORE** commands refuse to execute. The following sections deal with how to diagnose and resolve these problems.

Syntax Errors

A syntax error can occur when you use the **BACKUP** or **RESTORE** statement. If the syntax is in fact correct for SQL Server 7, but the operation does not work correctly, then the database is in SQL Server 6.5 Compatibility Mode. The **BACKUP** and **RESTORE** keywords are valid only with SQL Server 7 databases.

Set the SQL Server compatibility level to 70 before using **BACKUP** and **RE-STORE** statements. To set the compatibility level, use the **sp_dbcmptlevel** stored procedure (see Listing 13.2).

Listing 13.2   Syntax for the **sp_dbcmptlevel** stored procedure.

```
sp_dbcmptlevel dbname, versionum
```

The *dbname* is the name of the database. The *versionum* is a version number. Valid values are 70 for SQL Server 7, 65 for SQL Server 6.5, and 60 for SQL Server 6.

BACKUP Refuses To Execute

When certain commands are in progress, the **BACKUP** statement cannot be performed. The backup program returns an Error 3023 Severity Level 16 when it's executed while the following commands or tasks are being performed:

➤ DBCC CHECKALLOC

➤ DBCC SHRINKDATABASE

➤ bcp

➤ SELECT INTO

➤ File manipulation

The solution to this problem is to allow the conflicting processes to end and run the backup at a later time.

Truncate Log On Checkpoint

Another reason why a backup program may refuse to execute is because the **trunc. log on chkpt** option has been enabled for the database. This database option is used as a method of keeping a log from growing too fast or from filling an entire log device when autogrow is not permitted. This database option truncates the log whenever periodic checkpoints occur. If this option is enabled, then only full database and differential database backups are allowed, because the log no longer contains all the changes that have occurred in the database and is therefore considered unusable. This will cause any attempts to execute a **BACKUP LOG** to fail.

The solution is to make one of two choices: accept only full or differential backups for the Backup and Recovery scheme, or disable the **trunc. log on chkpt** option and allow for regularly scheduled transaction log backups to trim the log.

Database Refuses To Be Restored

When a database is restored from backups, the process must begin with a full database backup followed by any differential backups or transaction log backups performed in order. If the order is not correct, the restoration will fail.

A database restoration also will fail if the sort order, collation sequence, Unicode locale ID, and Unicode of the backup does not match the server. If these settings do not match, the **BACKUP** and **RESTORE** operations produce either an Error 3120 for sort order problems or an Error 3149 for a Unicode locale mismatch.

The solution to this problem is to change the settings of the server. However, changing these settings requires the rebuilding of the master database. The process of building a new master database can produce the loss of all data in all databases. It is recommended that before you rebuild the master database, you back up the creation scripts of all objects so the objects can be re-created later. All data from user tables should be copied out of the databases by using BCP or Data Transformation Services. After the objects, scripts, and data have been safely produced, you can rebuild the master database from the command prompt by using the **rebuildm** program and changing the settings to match the backup of the database that caused the problem.

After the master database has been re-created, the database backup can be restored. The other databases also have to be re-created.

Handling Replication Problems

SQL Server is designed to detect and correct most replication problems automatically, but users may still encounter problems. Most replication problems can be resolved by following a general troubleshooting approach. The following sections deal with diagnosing and resolving replication problems.

General Approach To Troubleshooting Replication Problems

You can begin troubleshooting replication problems by using the Enterprise Manager to view task history to determine which tasks failed and the reasons for their failure. The message details may not always identify the actual problems, but they might list symptoms that result from the problems. You can also use the Replication Monitor in the Enterprise Manager to view the status of replication agents. If you suspect that the data is not being transferred correctly, you can use the **sp_table_validation** stored procedure to test for row count or checksum differences. Listing 13.3 provides the syntax for sp_table_validation.

Listing 13.3   Syntax for the sp_table_validation stored procedure

```
sp_table_validation 'tablename', expected_rowcount
expected_checksum, rowcount_only , 'owner',
full_or_fast, shutdown_agent, 'output_table'
```

The following list describes the parameters for the **sp_table_validation** stored procedure:

➤ *'tablename'* The name of the table.

➤ *expected_rowcount* The number of rows expected in the table. The default is **NULL**. If **NULL**, the actual rowcount is returned as an output parameter.

➤ *expected_checksum* The parameter that determines whether to return the expected checksum for the table. *expected_checksum* is numeric with a default of **NULL**. If **NULL**, the actual checksum is returned as an output parameter. If a value is provided, that value is checked against the actual checksum to identify any differences.

➤ *rowcount_only* The default for *rowcount_only* is 1. When set to 1, the stored procedure returns only the rowcount for the table. The other valid value for *rowcount_only* is 0.

➤ *'owner'* The name of the owner of the table.

➤ *full_or_fast* The parameter that determines which of two methods is used to calculate the rowcount. The first method, when *full_or_fast* is set to 0, uses **count(*)**. When *full_or_fast* is set to 1, SQL Server uses the sysindexes table to count rows. This is faster than rowcount, but may not be accurate because the sysindexes table is not necessarily up-to-date. When *full_or_fast* is set to 2, the fast method is tried first and then **count(*)** is used if differences are found. If an *expected_rowcount* is not provided for this option, only **count(*)** is used for the rowcount.

➤ *shutdown_agent* A bit field with possible values of 1 or 0. The default is 0. If 0, the replication agent does not shut down when the command is executed. If 1, an Error 20578 is raised, and the replication agent is signaled to shut down.

➤ *'output_table'* The table name of the view used for output messages.

Specific Problems

Specific problems that can arise with replication include not being able to start replication agents and jobs and not being able to resolve data conflicts when working with Merge Replication.

Cannot Start A Replication Agent

A replication agent may not start because of inadequate security settings. Before the replication agent is started, SQL Server Agent calls the **xp_logininfo** stored procedure to validate that you still belong to your Windows NT user groups and to verify your login permissions to the server. If the security check does not pass, the agent does not start, and an error is returned. This error shows only in the Jobs folder. The solution to this problem is to either rework security at the NT level or use standard SQL Server security.

Cannot Start Another Replication Job

Some replication agents allow only one instance of certain jobs to run at a time. For example, one log reader can run per publication database or one Distributor or Merge Agent per Publication/Subscriber pair. If a failure occurs with one of these jobs due to a connection failure, it's possible that other jobs will not start until the network connection timeout is reached or the system process ID (SPID) of the failed job is killed.

Cannot Find Conflicts

In Merge Replication, the Merge Agent synchronizes the data changes between the Publisher and its Subscribers. In this process, three kinds of conflicts can occur:

➤ **Insert/Update conflicts** The same data is changed at more than one location.

➤ **Delete conflicts** The same row of data is deleted at one location but updated at another.

➤ **Constraint conflicts** Data is modified at one location, but the change violates constraints at another location.

These conflicts are resolved by a conflict resolver. The resolver determines which changes are kept (the winner) and which changes are discarded (the loser), and stores the outcome in a conflict table. Conflict tables are named **conflict_tablename.** SQL Server also provides a Replication Conflict Viewer to review the outcomes of the conflicts and to change these outcomes. If replication has been configured for centralized logging of conflicts, the tables will be stored with the Publisher. If replication was configured for decentralized logging of conflicts, then the conflict tables can appear at either the Publisher or the Subscriber, depending on who lost the conflicts.

Access Denied When Reading Or Writing Snapshot Files

If the Snapshot Agent fails to start and an "Access Denied" message is received, there is an NT-based security problem. The first trouble spot to look at is the security on the SQL Server Agent. Run the Dcomcnfg.exe program, and check the Default Security. The NT account running the SQL Server Agent should have default access and launch permissions.

Also, verify that the snapshot folder on the Distributor is shared properly. On an NT computer, the snapshot folder is shared by default. On a Windows 95/98 computer, the folder is not shared by default and must be manually configured for sharing.

Replicating From SQL Server 7 To SQL Server 6.5

SQL Server 7 supports replication with SQL Server 6.x servers, but with a limited capacity. The following combinations are supported:

➤ Replication is permitted from a SQL Server 7 Publisher/Distributor (Publisher/Distributor means the both Publication and Distribution functions are performed on the same server) to a SQL Server 6.5

Subscriber. However, any new features that are unique to SQL Server 7, and are not supported in SQL Server 6.5, cannot be used.

➤ Replication from a SQL Server 7 Publisher/Distributor to a SQL Server 6 Subscriber. The SQL Server 6 Subscriber must be configured as an ODBC Subscriber and not as a native SQL Server Subscriber.

➤ Replication from a SQL Server 6.5 Publisher/Distributor to a SQL Server 7 Subscriber.

➤ Replication from a SQL Server 6.5 Publisher to a SQL Server 7 Distributor.

When you attempt to replicate from a SQL Server 7 to SQL Server 6.5 Subscriber, certain additional objects are required on the SQL Server 6.5 server. If these objects do not yet exist, an Invalid Object error is returned. These objects are created by running the Replp70.sql script at the SQL Server 6.5 Subscriber. After this script is run, the Publisher can be registered with the Subscriber; this is done with the **sp_addpublisher70** stored procedure. The syntax is provided in Listing 13.4.

Listing 13.4 Syntax for the sp_addpublisher70 stored procedure.

```
sp_addpublisher70 publisher_name, NT_account
```

After the Publisher is registered, the SQL Server 6.5 Subscriber should be registered with the SQL Server 7 Enterprise Manager. The publication can also be made on the SQL Server 7 Publisher.

Data Validation Appears To Fail

Data validation uses rowcounts and checksums to determine if data at the Subscriber has diverged from data at the Publisher. However, there are several conditions other than actual data divergence that could cause data validation to fail.

Checksum computes a 32-bit cyclic redundancy check (CRC) on the entire row image on the page. It cannot operate on a view unless the view includes all columns of only a single table or vertical partition of the table. The checksum also skips the contents of text and image columns.

Checksum also requires the structure of the table to be identical between the Publishers and Subscribers. If the Publisher has a table generated by a **CRE-ATE TABLE** statement, and the Subscribers receive the table from a **CREATE TABLE** statement followed by an **ALTER TABLE** statement to add specific columns to complete the table, then the tables are not considered identical. This difference in the tables can be verified by checking the syscolumns tables. The replication process must be redeveloped to ensure that the tables are created the same way.

Real or floating-point values may produce checksum differences if character-mode **bcp** was used to move the data. This often occurs when the publication is distributed to non-SQL Server Subscribers. These problems are the results of unavoidable differences in precision when converting data to and from character mode. The problem is considered minor (by Microsoft), and there is no real solution.

Another source of data validation errors can be a custom resolver for Merge Replication. If a custom resolver is written that doesn't provide a resolution to all possible combinations of data changes, data validation will fail. For example, a custom resolver may be designed to resolve data movement only from the Publisher to the Subscriber but not the reverse. In this situation, the conflict tables and error tables should be checked for any possible explanations. It may also be helpful to do a distributed query between the two computers that could pinpoint where the differences lie. If the resolver is the problem, it may have to be rewritten.

Handling Distributed Query Problems

SQL Server 7 allows you to create distributed queries by creating links to OLE DB data sources. This section deals with diagnosing and resolving distributed query problems.

When errors occur, two sets of error messages are returned. One set comes from the OLE DB provider. The second set comes from SQL Server. When these errors occur, the SQL Server should be checked to see if the parameters for the link with the **sp_addlinkedserver** stored procedure are set up correctly. If the parameters are correct, the parameters used to login to the linked server should also be checked. These parameters are passed from the **sp_addlinkedserverlogin** stored procedure. Any problems with these settings will produce an Error 7303.

Other errors reflect inconsistencies in the data or metadata between the servers. In these cases, the structures and permissions set on the tables at the OLE DB source should be checked. In some cases, the objects may not even exist. A trace on OLE DB using the SQL Server Profiler is recommended. Common error messages for these problems include the following:

➤ **Error 7306** Could not open table '%ls' from OLE DB provider '%ls'. %ls.

➤ **Error 7314** OLE DB provider '%ls' does not contain table '%ls'.

➤ **Error 7321** An error occurred while preparing a query for execution against OLE DB provider '%ls'. %ls.

➤ **Error 7356** OLE DB provider '%ls' supplied inconsistent metadata for a column. Metadata information was changed at execution time.

➤ **Error 7357** Could not process object '%ls'. The OLE DB provider '%ls' indicates that the object has no columns.

Other problems that can occur with distributed queries deal with the control of transactions. SQL Server supports the use of distributed and nested transactions, but many systems do not. It is important that the OLE DB source be configured to work properly. When the OLE DB source doesn't support distributed transactions, the queries must be rewritten to not use transaction control statements, or the **SET XACT_ABORT** option can be set to **On** for the SQL Server session. This aborts transactions when errors occur in processing the data. The following error messages relate to transaction control problems with distributed queries:

➤ **Error 7391** Couldn't perform the operation because the OLE DB provider '%ls' doesn't support distributed transactions.

➤ **Error 7392** Couldn't start a transaction for OLE DB provider '%ls'.

If the OLE DB source is misconfigured or if Windows NT is not configured properly to work with the OLE DB source, the following error messages may be returned:

➤ **Error 7399** OLE DB provider '%ls' reported an error. %ls.

➤ **Error 7403** Could not locate the Registry entry for an OLE DB provider '%ls'.

➤ **Error 7413** Could not perform a Windows NT authenticated login because delegation is not available.

➤ **Error 8114** Error converting data type %ls to %ls.

➤ **Error 8501** MS DTC on server '%.*ls' is unavailable.

Handling Problems With Access To SQL Server, Databases, And Database Objects

The following sections cover diagnosing and resolving problems when accessing SQL Server, database, and database objects.

SQL Server

When users have trouble connecting to the SQL Server, first verify that the server is still running. You can verify this by checking the services from the Control Panel of Windows NT or by running the Enterprise Manager. If the server is running, clients should verify connectivity to the server on the network. This can be done with the **ping** *servername* command on TCP/IP networks or with the **net view** command for Named Pipes connections. It is also important to never forget the simple solutions, such as verifying that the correct logins and passwords are being used to connect to the server. These kinds of problems of tracing failed logins when using the SQL Server Profiler.

Suspect Database

During recovery, SQL Server may mark a database as suspect and return an error code of 1105. This usually happens when the disk has run out of free space during the recovery process. A database is marked suspect by setting the eighth bit of the status column in the sysdatabases table. This problem can be remedied by executing the **sp_resetstatus** stored procedure. This procedure resets the eighth bit of the status column so the database is no longer considered corrupt. However, using this stored procedure will make changes to system tables that are not considered "usual." The process to follow for using the **sp_resetstatus** procedure and providing more space to the database so recovery can be completed, is as follows:

1. Execute the **sp_configure 'allow updates',1** stored procedure. This enables the ability to make changes directly on the system tables, including sysdatabases. This is required for the **sp_resetstatus** procedure.

2. Execute the **reconfigure with override** command. This command allows the 'allow updates' configuration option to take effect immediately.

3. Execute **sp_resetstatus** *'databasename'*. This modifies the status column of the sysdatabases table and removes the suspect marking.

4. Use **ALTER DATABASE** to add a data file or log file to the database. This provides more space for the data.

5. Execute the **sp_configure 'allow updates',0** stored procedure. This disables the ability to update the system tables directly.

6. Stop and restart SQL Server. With the extra space provided by the new data file or log file, SQL Server should be able to complete recovery of the database.

There are other reasons that a database may be marked as corrupt. For example, the space allocations for the database may become corrupt. In these situtations, you can still use **sp_resetstatus** to unmark the suspect bit; however, the repairs to the database may require either using DBCC commands to repair the database or dropping and re-creating the database.

Database Access

When users have trouble accessing the database, the most common problem is usually associated with the login. It's possible for users to have many logins and to use the wrong login to access the wrong database. To verify which logins the users have and which databases they should have access to, look at the syslogins table in the master database and the sysusers table in the user databases.

Database Objects

When users have trouble accessing specific objects, this is usually a problem with permissions. Verify that the user is a valid user for the database. Then, verify that the user has permissions to access the objects in the database. This can be done with the **sp_helprotect** stored procedure. Again, never forget the simple solutions. It's possible that the user may be misspelling the name of the object being accessed.

Practice Questions

Question 1

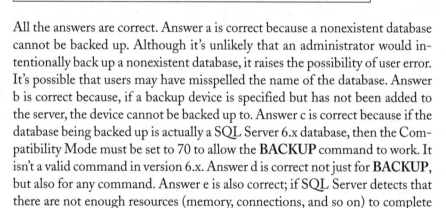

Which potential problems can prevent a BACKUP command from executing? [Check all the correct answers]

- ❏ a. The database does not exist.
- ❏ b. The backup device does not exist.
- ❏ c. The database is not configured for SQL Server 7 compatibility mode.
- ❏ d. Syntax errors.
- ❏ e. There are not enough resources to run the BACKUP command.

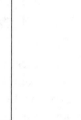

All the answers are correct. Answer a is correct because a nonexistent database cannot be backed up. Although it's unlikely that an administrator would intentionally back up a nonexistent database, it raises the possibility of user error. It's possible that users may have misspelled the name of the database. Answer b is correct because, if a backup device is specified but has not been added to the server, the device cannot be backed up to. Answer c is correct because if the database being backed up is actually a SQL Server 6.x database, then the Compatibility Mode must be set to 70 to allow the **BACKUP** command to work. It isn't a valid command in version 6.x. Answer d is correct not just for **BACKUP**, but also for any command. Answer e is also correct; if SQL Server detects that there are not enough resources (memory, connections, and so on) to complete the **BACKUP** operation, it refuses to run it. This can happen if a backup is scheduled during the peak operating times for the database (not a good time to run backup). The alternative is to wait for a nonpeak period to run **BACKUP**.

Question 2

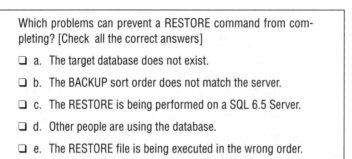

Which problems can prevent a RESTORE command from completing? [Check all the correct answers]

❏ a. The target database does not exist.

❏ b. The BACKUP sort order does not match the server.

❏ c. The RESTORE is being performed on a SQL 6.5 Server.

❏ d. Other people are using the database.

❏ e. The RESTORE file is being executed in the wrong order.

The correct answers are b, c, d, and e. Answer b is correct; if the sort order of the backup doesn't match the server's, the master database must be rebuilt to complete the restore. Answer c is correct; backups created in SQL Server 7 are not backward compatible with earlier versions. Answer d is correct; if other users are in the database when a restoration is performed, they may alter data before the entire process completes. This solution is to restart the restoration process. Answer e is correct; if several **RESTORE** commands are used to return a database to a prior state, the backup files must be loaded in order, or an error is returned. Answer a is incorrect; in earlier versions of SQL Server, the database had to exist. In SQL Server 7, the database is created with the **RESTORE** command.

Question 3

Which process best describes how a suspect marking can be removed from a database?

○ a. Configure the database to allow updates, and alter the sixth bit in the sysdatabases table for the suspect database.

○ b. Execute the sp_resetstatus stored procedure for the database.

○ c. Configure the server to allow updates, and execute the sp_resetstatus stored procedure for the database.

○ d. Reset the sixth status bit in the sysdatabases table for the suspect database.

○ e. There is no way to remove the suspect flag from a database without dropping the database.

The correct answer is c. Answers a and d are incorrect because the correct status bit is the eighth status bit. Answer b is technically correct, but answer c is better because it includes the fact that the Allow Updates must be configured for the server. Answer e is incorrect because there is a way to drop the suspect flag.

Question 4

> Which of the following situations can cause replication between SQL Server 7 and SQL Server 6.x to fail? [Check all the correct answers]
>
> ❑ a. Failure to execute a replp70.sql script
>
> ❑ b. SQL Server does not support all forms of replication from SQL Server 6.5
>
> ❑ c. Use of table names longer than 30 characters
>
> ❑ d. Use of the uniqueidentifier column
>
> ❑ e. SQL Server does not support replication to SQL Server 6

Answers a, b, c, d, and e are correct. Answer a is correct because the replp70.sql script creates objects that are required for replication compatibility between SQL Server 7 and SQL server 6.5. Answer b is correct; replication is supported for older versions of SQL Server in a limited capacity. Certain features of replication in SQL Server 7 will not work with SQL Server 6.x. Answers c and d are correct because these are features that exist solely in SQL Server 7 and are incompatible with SQL Server 6.5, so they cannot be used in replication. Answer e is correct. SQL Server supports replication with SQL Server 6 databases, but the databases must be configured as ODBC data sources.

Need To Know More?

 Coffman, Gayle, *SQL Server 7: The Complete Reference* (Berkley, CA, Osborne/McGraw-Hill, 1999, ISBN 0-07-882494-X). Chapter 21 provides a complete TSQL syntax, including the DBCC commands used to detect and fix problems with SQL Server.

 McGehee, Brad and Shepker, Matthew, *Using Microsoft SQL Server 7.0* (Indianapolis, IN, QUE, 1998, ISBN 0-7897-1628-3). Chapter 19 covers troubleshooting and fixing problems with SQL Server.

 MS SQL Server Books Online

 Search the TechNet CD-ROM (or its online version, through www.microsoft.com).

 www.microsoft.com/test_info

 www.microsoft.com/sql has up-to-date information about using SQL Server.

Sample Test

In this chapter, we provide pointers to help you develop a successful test-taking strategy, including how to choose proper answers, how to decode ambiguity, how to work within the Microsoft testing framework, how to decide what you need to memorize, and how to prepare for the test. At the end of the chapter, we include 40 questions on subject matter pertinent to Microsoft Exam 70-028: "Administering Microsoft SQL Server 7.0."

Questions, Questions, Questions

There should be no doubt in your mind that you face a test full of specific and pointed questions. If the version of the Administering Microsoft SQL Server 7 exam is fixed-length, it will include 52 questions; and you will be allotted 90 minutes to complete the exam and need to get 68 percent of the questions correct. If it is an adaptive test (and the software should tell you this as you begin the exam), it will consist of somewhere from 25 through 50 questions (on average) and take from 30 through 60 minutes. At the time of writing this book, the test is fixed-length.

Whichever type of test you take, for this exam, questions belong to one of five basic types:

➤ Multiple-choice with a single answer

➤ Multiple-choice with multiple answers

➤ Multipart with a single answer

➤ Multipart with multiple answers

➤ Simulations (that is, operating on a GUI screen capture to simulate using the SQL Server interface with your mouse and/or your keyboard)

Always read a question at least twice before answering, and always look for an Exhibit button as you examine each question. Exhibits include graphical information related to a question. An exhibit is usually a screen capture of program output or GUI information that you must examine to analyze the question's contents and formulate an answer. The Exhibit button brings up graphics and charts that help explain a question, provide additional data, or illustrate page layout or program behavior.

Not every question has only one answer; many questions require multiple answers. Therefore, read each question carefully to determine how many answers are necessary or possible and to look for additional hints or instructions when selecting answers. Such instructions often occur in brackets, immediately following the question (as they do for all multiple-choice, multiple-answer questions).

Picking Proper Answers

Obviously, the only way to pass any exam is to select enough of the right answers to obtain a passing score. However, Microsoft's exams are not standardized like the SAT and GRE exams; Microsoft's exams are far more diabolical and convoluted. In some cases, questions are strangely worded, and deciphering them can be a real challenge. In those cases, you may need to rely on answer-elimination skills. Almost always, at least one answer out of the possible choices for a question can be eliminated immediately because it matches one of these conditions:

➤ The answer does not apply to the situation.

➤ The answer describes a nonexistent issue, an invalid option, or an imaginary state.

➤ The answer may be eliminated because of the question itself.

After you eliminate all answers that are obviously wrong, you can apply your retained knowledge to eliminate further answers. Look for items that sound correct but refer to actions, commands, or features that are not present or not available in the situation that the question describes.

If you're still faced with a blind guess among two or more potentially correct answers, reread the question. Try to picture how each of the possible remaining answers would alter the situation. Be especially sensitive to terminology; sometimes the choice of words ("remove" instead of "disable") can make the difference between a right answer and a wrong one.

Only when you've exhausted your ability to eliminate answers, but remain unclear about which of the remaining possibilities is correct, should you guess at an answer. An unanswered question offers you no points, but guessing gives you at least some chance of getting a question right; just don't be too hasty when making a blind guess.

If you're taking a fixed-length test, you can wait until the last round of reviewing marked questions (just as you're about to run out of time or out of unanswered questions) before you start making guesses. If you're taking an adaptive test, you'll have to guess to move on to the next question if you can't figure out an answer some other way. Either way, guessing should be your technique of last resort!

Decoding Ambiguity

Microsoft exams have a reputation for including questions that can be difficult to interpret, confusing, or ambiguous. In our experience with numerous exams, we consider this reputation to be completely justified. The Microsoft exams are tough and deliberately made that way.

The only way to beat Microsoft at its own game is to be prepared. You'll discover that many exam questions test your knowledge of things that are not directly related to the issue raised by a question. This means that the answers you must choose from, even incorrect ones, are just as much a part of the skill assessment as the question itself. If you don't know something about most aspects of SQL Server 7, you may not be able to eliminate obviously wrong answers because they relate to a different area of SQL Server than the one that's addressed by the question at hand. In other words, the more you know about the software, the easier it will be for you to tell right from wrong.

Questions often give away their answers, but you have to be Sherlock Holmes to see the clues. Often, subtle hints appear in the question text in such a way that they seem almost irrelevant to the situation. You must realize that each question is a test unto itself and that you need to inspect and successfully navigate each question to pass the exam. Look for small clues, such as the mention of times, group permissions and names, and configuration settings. Little things like these can point at the right answer if properly understood; if missed, they can leave you facing a blind guess.

Another common difficulty with certification exams is vocabulary. Microsoft has an uncanny knack for naming some utilities and features entirely obviously in some cases, and completely inanely in other instances. Be sure to brush up on the key terms presented at the beginning of each chapter. You may also want to read through the Glossary at the end of this book the day before you take the test.

Working Within The Framework

The test questions appear in random order, and many elements or issues that receive mention in one question may also crop up in other questions. It's not uncommon to find that an incorrect answer to one question is the correct answer to another question, and vice versa. Take the time to read every answer to each question, even if you recognize the correct answer to a question immediately. That extra reading may spark a memory or remind you about a SQL Server 7 feature or function that helps you on another question elsewhere in the exam.

If you're taking a fixed-length test, you can revisit any question as many times as you like. If you're uncertain of the answer to a question, check the box that's provided to mark it for easy return later on. You should also mark questions you think may offer information that you can use to answer other questions. On fixed-length tests, we usually mark somewhere between 25 and 50 percent of the questions on exams we've taken. The testing software is designed to let you mark every question if you choose; use this framework to your advantage. Everything you will want to see again should be marked; the testing software can then help you return to marked questions quickly and easily.

For fixed-length tests, we strongly recommend that you first read through the entire test quickly, before getting caught up in answering individual questions. This will help to jog your memory as you review the potential answers and can help identify questions that you want to mark for easy access to their contents. It will also let you identify and mark the really tricky questions for easy return as well. The key is to make a quick pass over the territory to begin with, so that you know what you're up against; and then to survey that territory more thoroughly on a second pass, when you can begin to answer all questions systematically and consistently.

If you're taking an adaptive test, and you see something in a question or one of the answers that jogs your memory on a topic or that you feel you should record if the topic appears in another question, write it down on your piece of paper. Just because you can't go back to a question in an adaptive test doesn't mean you can't take notes on what you see early in the test, in hopes that it might help you later.

 For adaptive tests, don't be afraid to take notes on what you see in various questions. Sometimes, what you record from one question, especially if it's not as familiar as it should be or reminds you of the name or use of some utility or interface details, can help you on other questions later on.

Deciding What To Memorize

The amount of memorization you must undertake for an exam depends on how well you remember what you've read and how well you know the software by heart. If you are a visual thinker, and you can see the drop-down menus and dialog boxes in your head, you won't need to memorize as much as someone who's less visually oriented. The tests will stretch your recollection of commands and functions of SQL Server 7.

At a minimum, you'll want to memorize the following kinds of information:

➤ The components used in replication

➤ How to monitor SQL Server

➤ How to create databases

➤ The functionality of security components

If you work your way through this book while sitting at a machine with SQL Server 7 installed, and try to manipulate this environment's features and functions as they're discussed, you should have little or no difficulty mastering this material. Also, don't forget that The Cram Sheet at the front of the book is designed to capture the material that is most important to memorize; use this to guide your studies as well.

Preparing For The Test

The best way to prepare for the test—after you've studied—is to take at least one practice exam. We've included one here in this chapter for that reason. The test questions are located in the pages that follow (and unlike the preceding chapters in this book, the answers don't follow the questions immediately; you'll have to flip to Chapter 15 to review the answers separately).

Give yourself 70 minutes to take this exam, keep yourself on the honor system, and don't look at earlier text in the book or jump ahead to the answer key. When your time is up or you've finished the questions, you can use Chapter 15 to check your work. Pay special attention to the explanations for the incorrect answers; these can also help to reinforce your knowledge of the material. Knowing how to recognize correct answers is good, but understanding why incorrect answers are wrong can be equally valuable.

Taking The Test

Relax. Once you're sitting in front of the testing computer, there's nothing more you can do to increase your knowledge or preparation. Take a deep breath, stretch, and start reading that first question.

There's no need to rush; you have plenty of time to complete each question and to return to those questions that you skip or mark for return (if you are taking a fixed-length test). If you read a question twice and remain clueless, you can mark it if you're taking a fixed-length test; if you're taking an adaptive test, you'll have to guess and move on. Both easy and difficult questions are intermixed throughout the test in random order. If you're taking a fixed-length test, don't cheat yourself by spending too much time on a hard question early on in the test, thereby depriving yourself of the time you need to answer the questions at the end of the test. If you're taking an adaptive test, don't spend more than five minutes on any single question—if it takes you that long to get nowhere, it's time to guess and move on.

On a fixed-length test, you can read through the entire test, and, before returning to marked questions for a second visit, figure out how much time you've got per question. As you answer each question, remove its mark. Continue to review the remaining marked questions until you run out of time or complete the test.

On an adaptive test, set a maximum time limit for questions and watch your time on long or complex questions. If you hit your limit, it's time to guess and move on. Don't deprive yourself of the opportunity to see more questions by taking too long to puzzle over questions, unless you think you can figure out the answer. Otherwise, you're limiting your opportunities to pass.

That's it for pointers. Here are some questions for you to practice on.

Question 1

How can deadlocking be reduced? [Check all the correct answers]

- ❏ a. Minimize the use of Holdlock
- ❏ b. SET DEADLOCK_PRIORITY for a connection to high
- ❏ c. Avoid user interaction in transactions
- ❏ d. Access objects in the same order
- ❏ e. None of the above

Question 2

Joe's user account is currently a member of the db_owner fixed database role for the Sales database. If you want Joe to be able to maintain user and permissions for the databases and have no other permissions in the database, what of the following must be done?

- ○ a. Remove Joe from the db_owner role

  Add Joe to the sysadmin role
- ○ b. Add Joe to the db_accessadmin role

  Add Joe to the db_securityadmin role
- ○ c. Remove Joe from the db_owner role

  Add Joe to the db_security role
- ○ d. Remove Joe from the db_owner role

  Add Joe to the db_accessadmin role

  Add Joe to the db_securityadmin role

Question 3

You are about to bring a decision support system live. The data is updated during a nightly update via replication from several sites. How often should you back up the database? [Choose the best answer]

○ a. Daily.

○ b. Weekly.

○ c. Monthly.

○ d. Databases do not need to be backed up.

○ e. Any of the above.

Question 4

Which of the following conditions may cause BACKUP (Database/Differential or Log) to fail? [Check all the correct answers]

❑ a. Select Into/Bulkcopy has been enabled for the database.

❑ b. The tables in the database are being modified.

❑ c. The database is being shrunk.

❑ d. A database file is being shrunk.

Question 5

If the only network protocol SQL Server is configured to use is TCP/IP on port 5023, which of the following must be performed on the client so the client can connect to SQL Server? [Check all the correct answers]

❑ a. The client must be configured to use TCP/IP and port 5023.

❑ b. ODBC must be configured to connect to the SQL Server.

❑ c. The client must be configured to use multiprotocol connection.

❑ d. The default network library must be set to TCP/IP.

❑ e. The client tools must be installed on the client.

Question 6

You are about to bring a decision support system live. The data is updated during a nightly update via replication from several sites How often should you run the basic dbcc commands to verify data integrity?

○ a. Daily.

○ b. Weekly.

○ c. Monthly.

○ d. It isn't necessary to run dbcc commands on a periodic basis.

○ e. Insufficient information is provided to make an intelligent decision.

Question 7

What stored procedure can reset the suspect status of a data-base? [Check all the correct answers]

❏ a. sp_dbstatus

❏ b. sp_configure

❏ c. sp_resetstatus

❏ d. sp_dboption

❏ e. All of the above

Question 8

If you need to access data from a remote SQL Server as part of a SELECT statement, which of the following is the best approach?

○ a. Add the remote server as a remote server.

○ b. Add the remote server as a Publisher.

○ c. Copy the data from the remote server to the local server.

○ d. Add the remote server as a linked server.

Question 9

You are about to bring an OLTP (online transaction processing) system live. You have 200 users, averaging about 15 transactions per second (total, not each). What needs to be part of your preventive maintenance regimen? [Check all the correct answers]

❑ a. A backup of the database.

❑ b. Frequent backup of the transaction log.

❑ c. Periodic execution of dbcc checkalloc.

❑ d. Frequent backups of the physical drives on which the databases reside.

❑ e. SQL Server 7 doesn't require any periodic maintenance.

Question 10

Where can messages passed back from the SQL Server be found for monitoring? [Check all the correct answers]

❑ a. In the NT Event Viewer

❑ b. In the SQL Server Errorlog

❑ c. In the SQL Server Agent Errorlog

❑ d. None of the above

Question 11

Which of the following is the best way to allow a Unix user to access a SQL Server?

○ a. Grant the Windows NT Guest account access to the SQL Server.

○ b. Configure SQL Server to use Mixed Mode Security, and then create a SQL Server login for the Unix user.

○ c. Configure SQL Server to user Standard Security Mode, and then create a SQL Server login for the Unix user.

○ d. Set the server option "no_security" to true.

Question 12

What system database contains information about the interaction between the server and all resources, physical and logical, outside the server?

○ a. master

○ b. MASTER

○ c. system

○ d. SYSTEM

○ e. tempdb

○ f. msdb

Question 13

What are possible causes of a login failure to SQL Server? [Check all the correct answers]

❑ a. The SQL Server login has been mistyped.

❑ b. The network is unavailable.

❑ c. The password for the SQL Server login has expired.

❑ d. The login is not a valid user for its default database.

❑ e. All of the above.

Question 14

If you need to install SQL Server on Windows 98 and want SQL Server to use Named Pipes as one of its network protocols, which of the following installation types should you use? [Check all the correct answers]

❑ a. Typical installation

❑ b. Compact installation

❑ c. Custom installation

❑ d. None of the above

Question 15

What stored procedure will give you information pertaining to SQL Server locking?

- ○ a. sp_lock
- ○ b. sp_locking
- ○ c. sp_helplock
- ○ d. sp_processes
- ○ e. This information is available only graphically.

Question 16

A full-text query is failing to execute. What tasks can be performed to verify that full text is running and configured properly? [Check all the correct answers]

- ❑ a. Run the SELECT fulltextserviceproperty ('IsFulltextInstalled') query
- ❑ b. Run the sp_fulltext_database stored procedure
- ❑ c. SELECT the PopulateStatus property of fulltextcatalogproperty for the full-text index
- ❑ d. All of the above

Question 17

Bailey is currently a member of the Critic role. This role has select, insert, delete, and update permissions on the Movie table; the Critic role has no other permissions. If you want Bailey to be able to retrieve data through any tool, but have the ability to read, insert, and update the table through your application, which of the following is the best way to do this?

○ a. Remove Bailey from the Critic role.

Add Bailey to an application role that has select, insert, and update permissions on the Movie table.

○ b. Create an application role that has insert and update permissions on the Movie table, and change your application to use this new role.

Grant select permissions to Bailey on the Movie table.

○ c. Add Bailey to the db_denydatareader and db_denydatawriter roles.

Create an application role that has select, insert, and update permissions on the Movie table, and change your application to use this new role.

Grant select permissions to Bailey on the Movie table.

○ d. Remove Bailey from the Critic role.

Create an application role that has select, insert, and update permissions on the Movie table and change your application to use this new role.

Grant select permissions to Bailey on the Movie table.

Question 18

The following SQL has been executed by user jsmith, who has create table and create procedure permissions:

```
Create table a (b int, c int)
Create procedure insertit as
     Insert a values (1,2)
```

Another user, bjones, executes the procedure. What happens?

○ a. A row is inserted into the table.

○ b. The procedure runs, but the table insert fails.

○ c. The procedure runs, then terminates abruptly.

○ d. The procedure will not run.

Question 19

Given the following query and SHOWPLAN_TEXT output, what is true about the query? [Choose the best answer]

```
select * from titles
where title_id = 'BU1111'

StmtText
_____

  |--Clustered Index Seek
            (pubs..titles.UPKCL_titleidind,
             SEEK:(titles.title_id=@1) ORDERED)
```

○ a. The query would be executed using the clustered index.

○ b. The query would be executed using the non-clustered index.

○ c. The clustered index, UPKCL_titleidind, would be used to execute the query.

○ d. A table scan would be performed.

○ e. The non-clustered index, UPKCL_titleidind, would be used to execute the query.

Question 20

If you want to find out all of the current processes on a SQL Server, you must run which of the following stored procedures?

○ a. sp_users

○ b. sp_who

○ c. sp_processes

○ d. sp_active

○ e. sp_lock

Question 21

The following SQL has been executed by user jsmith, who has create table and create procedure permissions:

```
Create table a (b int, c int)
Create procedure insertit as
     Insert a values (1,2)
Grant execute on  insertit to bjones
```

Another user, bjones, executes the procedure. What happens?

○ a. A row is inserted into the table.

○ b. The procedure runs, but the table insert fails.

○ c. The procedure runs, then terminates abruptly.

○ d. The procedure will not run.

Question 22

You want to set up servers that will replicate information that will be changed at the source server as well as on the remote servers. What kind of replication will best accomplish this task? [Choose the best answer]

○ a. Snapshot Replication

○ b. Transaction Replication

○ c. Merge Replication

○ d. Answers a and b only

○ e. Answers a and c only

Question 23

If a restore operation is aborted during the middle of the restore, what is the best way to complete the restore?

○ a. Run the complete restore.

○ b. Run the restore with the recovery clause.

○ c. Run the restore with the restart clause.

○ d. Drop and re-create the database, and then restart the restore.

Question 24

The following SQL has been executed by user jsmith, who has create table and create procedure permissions:

```
Create table a (b int, c int)
Create procedure insertit as
     Insert a values (1,2)
Grant insert on a to bjones
```

Another user, bjones, executes the procedure. What happens?

○ a. A row is inserted into the table.

○ b. The procedure runs, but the table insert fails.

○ c. The procedure runs, then terminates abruptly.

○ d. The procedure will not run.

Question 25

What sequence of commands will properly implement a Subscriber for transactional pull replication [Choose the best answer]

○ a. Execute sp_addpublication with allow_pull set to true to enable pull subscriptions at the Publisher.

Execute sp_addsubscriber to register the Subscriber at the Publisher.

Execute sp_addsubscription to create the subscription at the Publisher.

Execute sp_addsubscription with pull to create the pull subscription at the Subscriber.

○ b. Execute sp_addpublication with allow_pull set to true to enable pull subscriptions at the Publisher.

Execute sp_addsubscriber to register the Subscriber at the Publisher.

Execute sp_addsubscription to create the subscription at the Publisher.

Execute sp_addpullsubscription to create the pull subscription at the Subscriber.

○ c. Execute sp_addpublication with allow_pull set to true to enable pull subscriptions at the Publisher.

Execute sp_addsubscriber to register the Subscriber at the Publisher.

Execute sp_addsubscription to create the subscription at the Publisher.

Execute sp_addpullsubscription to create the pull subscription at the Subscriber.

Execute sp_addsubscription_agent with allow_pull to create a scheduled job for the Distribution Agent at the Subscriber.

○ d. Execute sp_addpublication with allow_pull set to true to enable pull subscriptions from the Publisher.

Execute sp_addsubscriber to register the Subscriber at the Publisher.

Execute sp_addsubscription to create the subscription at the Publisher.

Execute sp_addpullsubscription to create the pull subscription at the Subscriber.

Execute sp_addpullsubscription_agent to create a scheduled job for the Distribution Agent at the Subscriber.

Question 26

After you issue a full database backup, the backup command abnormally terminates. Which of the following could be causing the problem? [Check all the correct answers]

❑ a. A user could be creating a large database file in the database backup.

❑ b. SQL Server Recovery interval could be set too high.

❑ c. A user could be creating an index in the database being backed up.

❑ d. An unlogged operation could have been performed since the last backup.

Question 27

Which of the following rules pertain to logins, users, roles, and passwords? [Check all the correct answers]

❑ a. There is a maximum character width of 32.

❑ b. There is a maximum character width of 128.

❑ c. They can contain letters, symbols, and digits.

❑ d. Passwords cannot contain a space, $, or @.

❑ e. Passwords can contain a space, $, or @ only if the character is delimited with quotes.

Question 28

Which of the following processes correctly describers the creation of a Distributor? [Check all the correct answers]

❑ a. Execute sp_adddistributor on the Publisher server.

Execute sp_adddistributiondb on the server to generate a new distribution database.

Execute sp_adddistpublisher at each Publisher server that will use this Distributor.

❑ b. Execute sp_adddistributor on the Publisher server.

Execute sp_adddistributiondb on the server to generate a new distribution database.

Execute sp_adddistpublisher on the server for each Publisher server that will use this Distributor.

❑ c. Execute sp_adddistributor on the new Distributor server.

Execute sp_adddistributiondb on the Publisher server to generate a new distribution database.

Execute sp_adddistpublisher at each Publisher server that will use this Distributor.

❑ d. Execute sp_adddistributor on the new Distributor server.

Execute sp_adddistributiondb on the Distributor server to generate a new distribution database.

Execute sp_adddistpublisher at each Publisher server that will use this Distributor.

❑ e. None of the above.

Question 29

On which of the following machines can you perform a full install of SQL Server enterprise? [Check all the correct answers]

❑ a. Dec Alpha, running Windows NT 4 Enterprise SP4, 64MB of memory, and 175MB of free space on the hard drives

❑ b. Pentium 133, NT 4 Enterprise SP4, 128MB of memory, and 2GB free space on the hard drives

❑ c. Pentium II 300, NT 4 Enterprise SP4, 128MB of memory, and 2GB free space on the hard drives

❑ d. Pentium II 300, NT 4 SP4, 32MB of memory, and 2GB free space on the hard drives

❑ e. Pentium Pro 200, NT 4 Enterprise SP4, 128MB of memory, and 2GB free space on the hard drives

Question 30

What stored procedure adds a security account in the current database for a Microsoft SQL Server login or Microsoft Windows NT user or group, and enables it to be granted permissions to perform activities in the database?

○ a. sp_addlogin.

○ b. sp_adduser.

○ c. sp_grantaccess.

○ d. sp_grantdbaccess.

○ e. There is no way to do this.

Question 31

Which stored procedure can add a Publisher to a distribution database? [Choose the best answer]

○ a. sp_addpublisher

○ b. sp_addpublisher70

○ c. sp_adddistpublisher

○ d. sp_addpublication

Question 32

If Conner creates a table SalesData in the Sales database and you then execute the sp_dropuser command for Conner, what happens to the table SalesData?

○ a. dbo becomes the owner

○ b. SalesData is removed from the database

○ c. The ddl_admin group becomes the owner of the table

○ d. Nothing

Question 33

What stored procedure allows you to register a local or remote server before you can administer and manage it by using SQL Server Enterprise Manager?

○ a. sp_addserver.

○ b. sp_addipaddress.

○ c. sp_addsqlserver.

○ d. It isn't necessary to register remote servers.

○ e. None of the above.

Question 34

What types of replication are supported by SQL Server 7? [Check all the correct answers]

❏ a. Transaction Replication

❏ b. Merge Replication

❏ c. Snapshot Replication

❏ d. Snapshot Replication with pull subscriptions

❏ e. Merge Replication with pull subscriptions

Question 35

If you are running SQL Server 4.2 on Windows NT 3.5.1, which of the following must be done to upgrade to SQL Server 7? [Check all the correct answers]

❑ a. You must upgrade NT to 4 SP4.

❑ b. SQL server must have all of its data bcp out.

❑ c. SQL Server must be upgraded to 6.5 first.

❑ d. You must configure the existing SQL Server to use TCP/IP network protocol.

Question 36

You can start the SQL Server manually with which of the following methods? [Check all the correct answers]

❑ a. SQL Server Enterprise Manager.

❑ b. SQL Server Service Manager.

❑ c. The Services application in Control Panel.

❑ d. At the command prompt, in a variety of ways.

❑ e. SQL Server can only be started automatically at system startup.

Question 37

What tasks are required to drop a distribution database?

○ a. Disable all Subscribers that use the distribution database

○ b. Drop all publication databases

○ c. Disable all Publishers that use the Distributor

○ d. Execute the sp_dropdistributiondb stored procedure

○ e. c and d only

Question 38

Suppose that you perform a full backup every Friday at 10:00 P.M., differential backups Saturday through Thursday at 10:00 P.M., and transaction backups every day at 8:00 A.M. and 1:00 P.M.. Suppose further that you have a database failure on Wednesday at 1:15 P.M. and you do not need to recover any database changes that occurred between 1:00 P.M. and 1:15 P.M. on Wednesday. Which of the following series of steps is the best one to use to recover the database?

○ a. Restore the full backups

Restore Saturday's, Sunday's, Monday's, and Tuesday's differential backup

Restore Wednesday's transaction backup

○ b. Restore the full backup

Restore every Saturday through Wednesday transaction backups that were performed since the last full backup

○ c. Restore the full backup

Restore Tuesday's differential backup

Restore Wednesday's transaction backup

○ d. Restore the full backup

Restore Tuesday's differential backup

Restore Wednesday's 1:00 P.M. transaction backup

Question 39

What happens if you add a guest user to the model database? [Check all the correct answers]

❑ a. Any valid login can access any database.

❑ b. Any valid login can access any subsequently created database.

❑ c. Any valid login can access the model database.

❑ d. No database permissions are affected.

❑ e. Nothing, unless you first add a guest login.

Question 40

Which of the following statements best describes what will happen when the following bcp statement is executed?

```
bcp tempdb..#t1 in myfile -Usa -Ppassword
```

○ a. If the temporary table #t1 exists, it will be loaded with data from myfile. Otherwise, the bcp will abort.

○ b. If the temporary table #t1 exists, it will be loaded with data from myfile. Otherwise, the bcp will first create the temporary table.

○ c. bcp will fail because you did not specify a server name.

○ d. bcp will fail because you cannot bcp data into a temporary table.

Answer Key To Sample Test

1. a, c, d
2. d
3. a
4. a, c, d
5. a, e
6. e
7. b, c
8. d
9. a, b, c
10. a, b, c
11. b
12. a
13. a, b
14. d

15. a
16. a, c
17. d
18. d
19. c
20. b
21. a
22. c
23. c
24. d
25. d
26. a, c
27. b, c, e
28. a, d

29. c, e
30. d
31. c
32. d
33. a
34. a, b, c, e
35. a, c
36. a, b, c, d
37. e
38. c
39. b, c
40. d

Question 1

The correct answers are a, c, and d. Answer b is incorrect because setting **DEADLOCK_PRIORITY** helps determine the behavior of the SQL Server when a deadlock occurs. Answer e is, therefore, incorrect.

Question 2

The correct answer is d. Answer a is incorrect because, when you give Joe the sysadmin role, he will have the db_admin role in every database. Answer b is incorrect because, although you grant Joe the appropriate roles to maintain users and grant permissions, he was not removed from his current db_owner role. Answer c is incorrect because you remove Joe from the db_owner role but there isn't a db_security role.

Question 3

The correct answer is a. If data is only updated on a daily basis, a once-a-day backup is sufficient. Therefore, answers b, c and e are incorrect. Answer d is incorrect because it is included for comic relief.

Question 4

The correct answers are a, c, and d. Answer b is incorrect because the Backup program is capable of being executed while the database is in use; this includes the modification of tables.

Question 5

The correct answers are a and e. Answer b is incorrect because ODBC can be configured, but doesn't have to be configured for a client to connect to SQL Server. Answer c is incorrect because you do not have to configure multiprotocol. Answer d is incorrect because the default network library doesn't have to be set to use TCP/IP.

Question 6

The correct answer is e. The dbcc commands should be run prior to aging out backups. This is the information needed prior to making these decisions. Answer a is a likely possibility, but not a fixed requirement.

Question 7

The correct answers are b and c. Only sp_configure and sp_resetstatus can perform this task. Answer a is incorrect because sp_dbstatus doesn't exist. Answer d is incorrect because the sp_dboption cannot alter the suspect status bits for a database.

Question 8

The correct answer is d. Answer a is incorrect because it allows you to access the data with a remote procedure call. Answer b allows you to replicate data from the remote server to the local server, but doesn't allow you to directly access the remote server's data. Answer c is incorrect because it allows you to access a copy of the remote data, but it doesn't allow you to access the current data.

Question 9

The correct answers are a, b, and c. Answer d is incorrect because database backups are a better solution. Answer e is wrong because the correct answer is provided.

Question 10

The correct answers are a, b, and c. You can see the messages that SQL Server generated by the NT Event Viewer in the SQL Server Errorlog and the SQL Server Agent Errorlog.

Question 11

The correct answer is b. Answer a is incorrect; the Unix user doesn't log on to any NT domain, so the user will not have an NT account to map to the Guest account. Answer c is incorrect because you cannot configure SQL Server to run in Standard Security Mode. Answer d is incorrect because there is no "no_security" server option.

Question 12

The correct answer is a. Answer b is incorrect because database names are case-sensitive. Answers c and d are incorrect because those databases do not exist. Answers e and f are incorrect because they handle temporary tables and replication information, respectively.

Question 13

The correct answers are a and b. Answer c is incorrect because passwords for SQL Server logins do not expire. Answer d is incorrect because if this situation occurs, the user will be sent to the master database. Answer e is incorrect because only answers a and b are correct.

Question 14

The correct answer is d. Windows 95/98 cannot run a SQL Server that uses Named Pipes protocol.

Question 15

The correct answer is a. Answers b, c, and d are incorrect because these stored procedures do not exist. Answer e is incorrect because you can use a stored procedure to obtain SQL Server locking information.

Question 16

The correct answers are a and c. Answer b is incorrect because it isn't a good method for verifying whether the full-text feature is enabled for a database. This command enables or disables full-text indexing for a database. A better choice is to select the IsFullTextEnabled property for the DATABASE-PROPERTY() function to verify if full-text indexing is enabled.

Question 17

The correct answer is d. Answer a is incorrect because application roles do not have members. Answer b is incorrect because Bailey still has her permissions from being a member of the Critic role. Answer c is incorrect because, if you want to remove all the permissions that Bailey has from being a member of a role, you should remove Bailey from the role.

Question 18

The correct answer is d. Permission has not been granted to the user to execute the procedure. Answers a, b, and c are incorrect because the procedure cannot be run.

Question 19

The correct answer is c. Answer a is technically correct, but answer c is a better answer. Answers b and e are incorrect because the output indicates that the selected index is a clustered index. Answer d is incorrect because the table scan will not be performed if an index is chosen.

Question 20

The correct answer is b. Answers a, c, and d are incorrect because they are not valid procedures. Answer e is incorrect because sp_lock shows the current locks on the server.

Question 21

The correct answer is a. After permission has been granted on the procedure, the additional permissions do not need to be granted on the table because both have the same owner. Answers b, c, and d are incorrect because the procedures run and complete their tasks.

Question 22

The correct answer is c. Merge Replication allows for changes to be made at the Publisher and Subscribers. The Snapshot and Transaction Replication allows changes to be made at the publisher and distributed to subscribers.

Question 23

The correct answer is c. The restart clause will restart a restore from the point where it left off. Answer a is incorrect because, although it will complete the task, it isn't as good as answer c. Answer b is incorrect; the recovery clause instructs SQL Server to perform the recovery process. Answer d is incorrect because, although it will produce the correct results, it isn't as good as answer c.

Question 24

The correct answer is d. Execute permission has not been granted to the user to execute the procedure. Answers a, b, and c are incorrect because the procedure cannot be run.

Question 25

The correct answer is d. The last step is included in answer d. Answer a refers to an option for sp_addpullsubscription agent, which doesn't exist. Answer c is incorrect because the sp_addsubscription_agent stored procedure doesn't exist. Answer b is incomplete.

Question 26

The correct answers are a and c. When a database file is being created or an index is being created on a table in the database, you cannot perform a database backup. Answer b is incorrect because the recovery interval governs the amount of time between system-generated checkpoints. Answer d is incorrect because, if an unlogged operation was performed, you can still do a full database backup. You cannot do the backup while the unlogged operation is being performed.

Question 27

The correct answers are b, c, and e. Answer a is incorrect because the maximum character width is 128. Answer d is incorrect because passwords can contain spaces, $, and @ characters.

Question 28

The correct answers are a and d. Answers a and d correctly describe the implementation of a distribution server. Answer b is incorrect because the sp_adddistpublisher should be run on each publisher that will use the distributor. Answer c is incorrect because sp_adddistributiondb should be run on the new distribution server. Answer e is incorrect because the correct answer is provided.

Question 29

The correct answers are c and e. Answer a is incorrect because you need at least 180MB of free space to perform a full installation. Answer b is incorrect because you cannot install SQL Server on a Pentium 133. Answer d is incorrect because SQL Server Enterprise must be installed on NT Enterprise, and it requires at least 64MB of memory.

Question 30

The correct answer is d. There is no way to do this. Answers a and b are an alternate method of granting access to a specific user. Answer c is incorrect because this procedure doesn't exist. Answer e is incorrect because the correct answer is provided.

Question 31

The correct answer is c. Answer a is incorrect because it is an old SQL Server 6.5 stored procedure. Answer b is incorrect because the procedure is used to add a SQL Server 7 publisher to a SQL Server 6.5 database. Answer d is incorrect because it is used to create a new publication.

Question 32

The correct answer is d. Nothing will happen because the sp_dropuser command will not drop a user if the user owns a table. Therefore, answers a, b, and c are incorrect.

Question 33

The correct answer is a. Answers b and c are incorrect because these don't exist. Answers d and e are incorrect because the correct answer is provided.

Question 34

The correct answers are a, b, c, and e. All the answers except answer d are valid forms of replication. Snapshot Replication doesn't allow pull subscriptions.

Question 35

The correct answers are a and c. Answer b is incorrect because you do not need to bcp data out of the database to upgrade. Answer d is incorrect because you must use the Named Pipes protocol when upgrading a database.

Question 36

The correct answers are a, b, c, and d. Answer e is incorrect because the correct answer (for manually starting SQL Server) is provided.

Question 37

The correct answer is e—answers c and d are correct. Answer a is incorrect because the subscribers do not need to be disabled for you to drop the distribution database. Answer b is incorrect because the publications need only to be disabled, not dropped.

Question 38

The correct answer is c. Answer a will recover the database, but you are performing extra restores of the differential backup. Answer b will recover the database, but you are loading more backups than needed. Answer d is incorrect; you did not recover the 8:00 A.M. transaction backup, so you cannot install the 1:00 P.M. transaction backup.

Question 39

The correct answers are b and c. Answer a is incorrect because valid logins can only access subsequently created databases. Answer d is incorrect because the model database is immediately affected. Answer e is incorrect because guest is a special case of user.

Question 40

The correct answer is d. bcp doesn't allow you to load data into a temporary table.

Appendix
Pubs Database

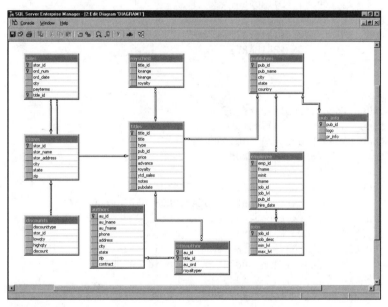

Figure A.1 The Pubs Database diagram

Pubs SQL

```
EXEC sp_addtype N'empid', N'char (9)', N'NOT NULL'
GO

EXEC sp_addtype N'id', N'varchar (11)', N'not null'
GO

EXEC sp_addtype N'tid', N'varchar (6)', N'not null'
GO
CREATE TABLE [dbo].[stores] (
       [stor_id] [char] (4) NOT NULL ,
       [stor_name] [varchar] (40) NULL ,
       [stor_address] [varchar] (40) NULL ,
       [city] [varchar] (20) NULL ,
       [state] [char] (2) NULL ,
       [zip] [char] (5) NULL ,
       CONSTRAINT [UPK_storeid] PRIMARY KEY  CLUSTERED
       ([stor_id])  ON [PRIMARY]
)
GO

CREATE TABLE [dbo].[publishers] (
       [pub_id] [char] (4) NOT NULL ,
       [pub_name] [varchar] (40) NULL ,
       [city] [varchar] (20) NULL ,
       [state] [char] (2) NULL ,
       [country] [varchar] (30) NULL CONSTRAINT
         [DF__publishers__country__0EA330E9] DEFAULT ('USA'),
       CONSTRAINT [UPKCL_pubind] PRIMARY KEY  CLUSTERED
       ([pub_id])  ON [PRIMARY] ,
        CHECK ([pub_id] = '1756' or [pub_id] = '1622'
               or [pub_id] = '0877' or [pub_id] = '0736'
               or [pub_id] = '1389'
               or ([pub_id] like '99[0-9][0-9]'))
)
GO

CREATE TABLE [dbo].[authors] (
       [au_id] [id] NOT NULL ,
       [au_lname] [varchar] (40) NOT NULL ,
       [au_fname] [varchar] (20) NOT NULL ,
       [phone] [char] (12) NOT NULL
               CONSTRAINT [DF__authors__phone__09DE7BCC]
                   DEFAULT ('UNKNOWN'),
       [address] [varchar] (40) NULL ,
```

```
        [city] [varchar] (20) NULL ,
        [state] [char] (2) NULL ,
        [zip] [char] (5) NULL ,
        [contract] [bit] NOT NULL ,
        CONSTRAINT [UPKCL_auidind] PRIMARY KEY  CLUSTERED
        ([au_id])  ON [PRIMARY] ,
         CHECK (([au_id] like
                '[0-9][0-9][0-9]-[0-9][0-9]-[0-9][0-9][0-9][0-9]')),
         CHECK (([zip] like '[0-9][0-9][0-9][0-9][0-9]'))
)
GO


CREATE  INDEX [aunmind] ON [dbo].[authors]([au_lname], [au_fname])
        ON [PRIMARY]
GO


CREATE TABLE [dbo].[titles] (
        [title_id] [tid] NOT NULL ,
        [title] [varchar] (80) NOT NULL ,
        [type] [char] (12) NOT NULL
                CONSTRAINT [DF__titles__type__117F9D94]
                DEFAULT ('UNDECIDED'),
        [pub_id] [char] (4) NULL ,
        [price] [money] NULL ,
        [advance] [money] NULL ,
        [royalty] [int] NULL ,
        [ytd_sales] [int] NULL ,
        [notes] [varchar] (200) NULL ,
        [pubdate] [datetime] NOT NULL
                CONSTRAINT [DF__titles__pubdate__1367E606]
                DEFAULT (getdate()),
        CONSTRAINT [UPKCL_titleidind] PRIMARY KEY  CLUSTERED
        ([title_id]       ) ON [PRIMARY] ,
         FOREIGN KEY
        ([pub_id]) REFERENCES [dbo].[publishers] ([pub_id])
)
GO


 CREATE  INDEX [titleind] ON [dbo].[titles]([title]) ON [PRIMARY]
GO


CREATE TABLE [dbo].[discounts] (
        [discounttype] [varchar] (40) NOT NULL ,
        [stor_id] [char] (4) NULL ,
        [lowqty] [smallint] NULL ,
        [highqty] [smallint] NULL ,
        [discount] [decimal](4, 2) NOT NULL ,
         FOREIGN KEY
```

```
        ([stor_id]) REFERENCES [dbo].[stores] ([stor_id])
) ON [PRIMARY]
GO
CREATE TABLE [dbo].[jobs] (
        [job_id] [smallint] IDENTITY (1, 1) NOT NULL ,
        [job_desc] [varchar] (50) NOT NULL
                CONSTRAINT [DF__jobs__job_desc__239E4DCF]
                DEFAULT ('New Position - title not formalized yet'),
        [min_lvl] [tinyint] NOT NULL ,
        [max_lvl] [tinyint] NOT NULL ,
         PRIMARY KEY  CLUSTERED
        ([job_id])  ON [PRIMARY] ,
         CHECK ([max_lvl] <= 250),
         CHECK ([min_lvl] >= 10)
)
GO


CREATE TABLE [dbo].[employee] (
        [emp_id] [empid] NOT NULL ,
        [fname] [varchar] (20) NOT NULL ,
        [minit] [char] (1) NULL ,
        [lname] [varchar] (30) NOT NULL ,
        [job_id] [smallint] NOT NULL
                CONSTRAINT [DF__employee__job_id__2C3393D0]
                DEFAULT (1),
        [job_lvl] [tinyint] NOT NULL
                CONSTRAINT [DF__employee__job_lvl__2E1BDC42]
                DEFAULT (10),
        [pub_id] [char] (4) NOT NULL
                CONSTRAINT [DF__employee__pub_id__2F10007B]
                DEFAULT ('9952'),
        [hire_date] [datetime] NOT NULL
                CONSTRAINT [DF__employee__hire_date__30F848ED]
                DEFAULT (getdate()),
        CONSTRAINT [PK_emp_id] PRIMARY KEY  NONCLUSTERED
        ([emp_id])  ON [PRIMARY] ,
        FOREIGN KEY ([job_id]) REFERENCES [dbo].[jobs] ([job_id]),
         FOREIGN KEY ([pub_id]) REFERENCES
                [dbo].[publishers] ([pub_id]),
        CONSTRAINT [CK_emp_id] CHECK (([emp_id] like
                '[A-Z][A-Z][A-Z][1-9][0-9][0-9][0-9][0-9][FM]') or
                ([emp_id] like
                '[A-Z]-[A-Z][1-9][0-9][0-9][0-9][0-9][FM]'))
)
GO
```

```
CREATE  CLUSTERED  INDEX [employee_ind] ON
      [dbo].[employee]([lname], [fname], [minit]) ON [PRIMARY]
GO

CREATE TABLE [dbo].[pub_info] (
      [pub_id] [char] (4) NOT NULL ,
      [logo] [image] NULL ,
      [pr_info] [text] NULL ,
      CONSTRAINT [UPKCL_pubinfo] PRIMARY KEY  CLUSTERED
      ([pub_id])  ON [PRIMARY] ,
       FOREIGN KEY ([pub_id]) REFERENCES
            [dbo].[publishers] ([pub_id])
)
GO

CREATE TABLE [dbo].[roysched] (
      [title_id] [tid] NOT NULL ,
      [lorange] [int] NULL ,
      [hirange] [int] NULL ,
      [royalty] [int] NULL ,
       FOREIGN KEY
      ([title_id]) REFERENCES [dbo].[titles] ([title_id])
) ON [PRIMARY]
GO

CREATE  INDEX [titleidind] ON [dbo].[roysched]([title_id])
      ON [PRIMARY]
GO

CREATE TABLE [dbo].[sales] (
      [stor_id] [char] (4) NOT NULL ,
      [ord_num] [varchar] (20) NOT NULL ,
      [ord_date] [datetime] NOT NULL ,
      [qty] [smallint] NOT NULL ,
      [payterms] [varchar] (12) NOT NULL ,
      [title_id] [tid] NOT NULL ,
      CONSTRAINT [UPKCL_sales] PRIMARY KEY  CLUSTERED
      ([stor_id],[ord_num],[title_id])  ON [PRIMARY] ,
       FOREIGN KEY
      ([stor_id]) REFERENCES [dbo].[stores] ([stor_id]),
       FOREIGN KEY
      ([title_id]) REFERENCES [dbo].[titles] ([title_id])
)
GO

 CREATE  INDEX [titleidind] ON [dbo].[sales]([title_id])
      ON [PRIMARY]
GO
```

```
CREATE TABLE [dbo].[titleauthor] (
      [au_id] [id] NOT NULL ,
      [title_id] [tid] NOT NULL ,
      [au_ord] [tinyint] NULL ,
      [royaltyper] [int] NULL ,
      CONSTRAINT [UPKCL_taind] PRIMARY KEY  CLUSTERED
      ([au_id],[title_id])  ON [PRIMARY] ,
       FOREIGN KEY
      ([au_id]) REFERENCES [dbo].[authors] ([au_id]),
       FOREIGN KEY
      ([title_id]) REFERENCES [dbo].[titles] ([title_id])
)
GO


CREATE  INDEX [auidind] ON [dbo].[titleauthor]([au_id])
      ON [PRIMARY]
GO


CREATE  INDEX [titleidind] ON [dbo].[titleauthor]([title_id])
      ON [PRIMARY]
GO


CREATE VIEW titleview
AS
select title, au_ord, au_lname, price, ytd_sales, pub_id
from authors, titles, titleauthor
where authors.au_id - titleauthor.au_id
   AND titles.title_id - titleauthor.title_id


GO
CREATE  PROCEDURE acur
  @auth_cur cursor varying output,
  @state char(2)  - "CA",
  @ctype int - 1
AS
if (@ctype - 1)
      set @auth_cur - cursor SCROLL for
            select au_lname
            from authors where state - @state
else
      set @auth_cur - cursor SCROLL for
            select au_lname, au_fname from authors

open @auth_cur
return 1

GO
```

```
CREATE PROCEDURE byroyalty @percentage int
AS
select au_id from titleauthor
where titleauthor.royaltyper = @percentage


GO


CREATE PROCEDURE reptq1 AS
select pub_id, title_id, price, pubdate
from titles
where price is NOT NULL
order by pub_id
COMPUTE avg(price) BY pub_id
COMPUTE avg(price)


GO


CREATE PROCEDURE reptq2 AS
select type, pub_id, titles.title_id, au_ord,
   Name = substring (au_lname, 1,15), ytd_sales
from titles, authors, titleauthor
where titles.title_id = titleauthor.title_id
   AND authors.au_id = titleauthor.au_id
   AND pub_id is NOT NULL
order by pub_id, type
COMPUTE avg(ytd_sales) BY pub_id, type
COMPUTE avg(ytd_sales) BY pub_id


GO


CREATE PROCEDURE reptq3 @lolimit money, @hilimit money,
@type char(12)
AS
select pub_id, type, title_id, price
from titles
where price >@lolimit AND price <@hilimit
  AND type = @type OR type LIKE '%cook%'
order by pub_id, type
COMPUTE count(title_id) BY pub_id, type


GO


CREATE TRIGGER employee_insupd
ON employee
FOR insert, UPDATE
AS
--Get the range of level for this job type from the jobs table.
```

```
declare @min_lvl tinyint,
    @max_lvl tinyint,
    @emp_lvl tinyint,
    @job_id smallint
select @min_lvl = min_lvl,
    @max_lvl = max_lvl,
    @emp_lvl = i.job_lvl,
    @job_id = i.job_id
from employee e, jobs j, inserted i
where e.emp_id = i.emp_id AND i.job_id = j.job_id
IF (@job_id = 1) and (@emp_lvl <> 10)
begin
    raiserror ('Job id 1 expects the default level of 10.',16,1)
    ROLLBACK TRANSACTION
end
ELSE
IF NOT (@emp_lvl BETWEEN @min_lvl AND @max_lvl)
begin
    raiserror ('The level for job_id:%d should be between
        %d and %d.', 16, 1, @job_id, @min_lvl, @max_lvl)
    ROLLBACK TRANSACTION
end

GO
```

Glossary

ad hoc connector name—The **OpenRowset** function in the **FROM** clause of a query, which is used to make a one-time connection to an external data source.

aggregate functions—Functions that produce summary values. The aggregate functions are: AVG, COUNT, COUNT(*), MAX, MIN, STDEV, STDEVP, SUM, VAR, and VARP.

aggregate query—Any query using an aggregate function.

alert—A system-administrator-defined response to a SQL Server event.

alias—An alternative name for a table or column in expressions.

American National Standards Institute (ANSI)—The organization of American industry and business groups that develops trade and communication standards for the United States.

anonymous subscription—A pull subscription that enables a server that is known to the Publisher to receive a subscription to a publication, but only for the duration of the connection.

API server cursor—A server cursor built indirectly by calling an application programming interface (API), such as ODBC, OLE DB, ADO, and DB-Library.

application log—A Windows NT file that records events. SQL Server can be configured to use the Windows NT application log.

application programming interface (API)—A set of routines that an application can call.

application role—A SQL Server database role in which the application takes control of security. This role is activated by a password.

article—The basic unit of replication. An article can be a table or a stored procedure.

authentication—The process of identifying users and verifying permissions while connecting to SQL Server.

authorization—The process of verifying permissions and access rights for a user after connecting to SQL Server.

automatic recovery—The automatic process of either rolling transactions forward or rolling transactions back when SQL Server is restarted. Automatic recovery is used to guarantee the consistency of databases.

automatic synchronization—An automatic replication process that synchronizes a Subscriber to a Publisher when a subscription is created.

back end—The processing performed by the database server.

backup—The process of making a copy of a database, transaction log, file, or filegroup to a tape, named pipe, or hard disk.

backup device—A tape, disk file, or named pipe that is used to either back up a database or restore a database.

backup file—A file that contains a backup.

backup media—Types of backup storage devices. You can use a file, tape, or named pipe to store a backup set.

backup set—The backup media that is used for a single backup operation.

base table—An underlying table that makes up a view.

batch—One or more SQL statements that are executed by SQL Server.

bcp utility—A DOS-prompt utility that copies data between a SQL server table and an operating system file in a format that the user specifies.

binary datatype—A SQL Server datatype used to store hexadecimal numbers. The binary datatype can store from 0 through 8,000 bytes.

binary large object (BLOB)—A SQL Server data type for binary data, such as graphics, sound, or compiled code. This data type can contain up to 2GB of data.

bit data type—A SQL Server data type that stores either 1 or 0.

blocks—One or more SQL statements between a **BEGIN** statement and an **END** statement.

Boolean expression—Any expression that returns a true, false, or null value.

candidate key—Any unique identifier for a row of data. A candidate key is also called a *surrogate key*.

Cartesian product—The result when two tables are joined together with no join arguments. A Cartesian product returns all the possible combinations of rows from the tables involved in a join operation.

cascading delete—A process that deletes all the related rows (or columns) in dependent tables.

cascading update—A process that updates all the related dependent rows (or columns).

character set—The set of characters that SQL Server stores in **char, varchar,** and **text** data types. Every character set contains 256 letters, digits, and symbols specific to a country or language. The first 128 characters are the same for all character sets.

char(n) data type—A SQL Server data type that holds from 0 through 8,000 characters.

CHECK constraint—A constraint that verifies the values being stored in a column match the domain.

checkpoint—A SQL Server system event that causes all changed data pages to be written to disk.

client—A process (a program or a task) that requests a service from a server application. Also, on a local area network, a computer that accesses shared network resources provided by a server.

client cursor—A cursor that is implemented on a client by an API.

client/server computing—A branch of computing in which processing is distributed between *clients* (programs typically optimized for user interaction) and *servers* (programs that provide centralized data management and network administration and security) on a local area network. Client/server architecture offers increased processing power and more efficient use of processing power than older architectures offer.

clustered index—An index in which the data is sorted in the order of the index values.

code page—See *character set*.

column—An individual piece of data in a row.

column-level constraint—A constraint that enforces column integrity.

commit—The act of saving changes to a database.

composite index—An index that consists of more than one column.

composite key—A key that consists of more than one column.

concatenation—The process of joining two or more character strings, expressions, or binary strings into one.

concurrency—Multiple users accessing SQL Server at the same time.

connection—Any successful login to SQL Server.

connectivity—The capability of multiple processes to intercommunicate.

constant—Any static value that can be used in a query not including functions, columns, or database objects.

constraint—A property of one or more columns in a table, limiting the values that can be stored in the column(s).

control-of-flow language—T-SQL statements that control execution flow of SQL statements.

correlated subquery—A subquery that uses values from the outer query to determine what rows are returned by the subquery.

cross join—A join that produces a Cartesian product as its result.

cursor—The processing of a result set one row at a time. Cursors can be either client—the tables or database structure.

data dictionary—The system tables that describe the database objects.

data file—A file that contains the data that makes up a database, as opposed to the files used to store the transaction log.

data integrity—The process of ensuring that data is accurate and reliable.

Data Manipulation Language (DML)—The SQL statements that insert, update, delete, or select data.

data migration—The movement of data from one data source to another. Also called *data transfer*.

data source—Any data that can be accessed through SQL Server.

data transformation—The process that changes the data's structure or values when migrating data.

Data Transformation Services (DTS)—A SQL Server component that can import, export, and transform data.

data type—An attribute of a column describing what sort of information can be stored in the column. Also referred to as datatype.

database catalog—The system tables that contain the information describing the objects in the database.

Database Consistency Checker (DBCC)—A SQL Server statement used to check the logical and physical consistency of a database and to perform other system functions.

database diagram—A graphical representation of either the complete database schema or any part of a database schema.

database file—Either a data file or a transaction log file.

database management system (DBMS)—A program that controls access to data.

database name—A name that uniquely identifies a database on a SQL Server.

database object—Any one of the following database elements: table, index, trigger, view, key, constraint, default, rule, user-defined data type, or stored procedure.

database object owner—The database user that created a database object.

database owner (dbo)—The user that owns a database; he or she does not have to own the objects in the database.

datetime data type—A SQL Server data type that stores date and time information. A **datetime** data type consists of two 4-byte integers.

DB-Library—A series of high-level language application programming interfaces (APIs) for the client in a client/server system.

deadlock—A situation in which two or more users have a resource locked and are waiting for the other users to release their locks.

decision support system—A database used to analyze data.

default database—The database that a login switches to when connecting to SQL Server.

default language—The language that a login will use to communicate with SQL Server.

denormalize—The process of adding redundant data into a database. This process will change the normal form of a table.

deny—A response that specifically states that a user or role does not have permissions to access an object or perform a task.

differential database backup—A database backup that dumps only the rows that have changed since the last full database backup.

dirty read—A read that retrieves data that has been changed, but not committed to the database.

distributed database—A database that is physically implemented on multiple database servers.

Distributor—In the Publish and Subscribe model of replication, the server that holds the distribution database.

domain—The set of valid values for an attribute.

domain integrity—The processes of ensuring that all attributes must be a valid member of their domain.

dump—A backup.

dynamic cursor—A cursor in which the result set is not static. That is, as you scroll through the result set, any data modifications made to the underlying data will show up in the result set.

dynamic locking—The SQL Server process that evaluates the most effective locking schema to use with every query.

entity integrity—A process that ensures that a table has a unique primary key.

equality join—A join based on a comparison of scalar values (=, >, >=, <, <=, < >, !<, and !>).

error log—An operating-system ASCII file in which SQL Server records messages.

event log—An NT system file that contains messages from any process that is on the computer.

exclusive lock—A lock that prevents any other process from obtaining a lock on rows of data currently being locked.

explicit transaction—A situation in which an application requests that a transaction does not start until the application commits or rolls back the transaction.

expression—Any column, function, variable, subquery, or any combination of column names, constants, and functions connected by an operator that evaluates to a single value and is used in place of a column in a SQL statement.

extended stored procedure—A function in an external DLL that is executed as if it is a SQL Server stored procedure.

extent—The unit that SQL Server uses to allocate space to a table or index. An extent is eight contiguous pages from one file, for a total of 64K of storage.

fetch—A process that retrieves a row or a set of rows during cursor processing.

field—A column in a database table.

file—An operating-system storage unit. A SQL Server database consists of two or more operating-system files.

filegroup—One or more data files in a database that are named to ease administration.

fill factor—An attribute used to reserve free space in an index when the index is created. Fill factors reduce page splitting when a table grows.

fixed database role—A predefined role that controls access in a database.

fixed server role—A predefined role that controls access at the server level.

float data type—A data type used to hold floating-point numbers.

foreign key (FK)—One or more columns in a table that match the primary key of another table. In SQL Server, a foreign key can match any unique constraint of the other table.

forward-only cursor—A cursor in which rows can be read only in sequence from the first row to the last row.

front end—Any program that is used to access a database.

full outer join—An outer join that returns all the rows in both tables, even if the join conditions do not produce a matching row.

full-text catalog—The mechanism that stores a database's full-text index. A full-text catalog is stored external to SQL Server in an operating-system file.

full-text index—A special index on a table that, when enabled, allows a full-text search to be performed against the table. Unlike regular indexes, a full-text index does not automatically keep track of changes to the data.

full-text query—A SELECT statement that uses fuzzy logic and imprecise matches.

full-text service—The SQL Server component that is used in full-text queries.

grant—A setting that allows a user or role to access a database object or perform an activity.

guest—A special SQL Server user account that allows any SQL Server login access to a database.

heterogeneous data—Data that comes from two or more data sources that originate from different providers.

homogeneous data—Data that comes from one data source that is from one data provider.

horizontal partitioning—A physical design process that splits one table into multiple tables based on selected rows.

identifier—The name of a database object. An identifier must be unique within its scope.

identity column—A system-generated column that has the identity property. There can be only one identity column per table.

identity property—An attribute that identifies which column will be an identity column and specifies that its values will be generated by SQL Server.

image data type—A SQL Server data type used to hold binary data. An image data type can hold up to 2GB of data.

implicit transaction—SQL Server's normal transaction processing, in which a SQL statement outside of a transaction is implicitly in a transaction by itself.

implied permission—The standard permissions that apply to a server-wide role and to a standard database role. The implied permissions can't be changed.

index—A database object that allows SQL Server to access data faster than scanning every row of data in a table for the results.

index page—A database page containing the data that makes up an index.

inner join—A join that combines two tables using join fields to determine the results.

insensitive cursor—A cursor with a result set that does not change as the underlying data changes.

int (integer) data type—A SQL Server data type that can be any integer from 2,147,483,647 through –2,147,483,648. Storage size is 4 bytes.

integrated security—Another name for Windows NT Authentication Mode.

intent lock—A lock that SQL Server places on data in an object to indicate that it wants to acquire a shared or exclusive lock.

isolation level—An attribute used to control the locking behavior of SQL Server.

join—The act of combining data from two or more tables, views, or procedures.

join condition—Any clause that is used to control how tables are joined together.

kernel—The core SQL Server processing.

key—One or more columns that either uniquely identify a table or identify the relationships between two tables.

keyset-driven cursor—A cursor that doesn't show the effects of inserts and deletes to the underlying data. However, a keyset-driven cursor does show all data modifications to the underlying data.

left outer join—An outer join in which all the rows for the first table are returned, even if there are not any related rows in the second table.

linked server—A remote OLE DB data source that has been identified to the local SQL Server.

local server—The SQL Server to which the user is currently connected.

local variable—A user-defined variable.

locale—Information that describes the language and country that a login will use when connecting to SQL Server.

lock—A restriction that affects another connection's capability to access resources.

lock escalation—The process in which multiple locks generated by a SQL statement can escalate to a higher locking level.

log file—A file or set of files that contains a record of the transactions that were run in a database.

Log Reader Agent—A process that replicates information from a database's transaction log to another database.

logical name—The internal name that SQL Server uses to identify a file.

logical operators—The **AND, OR,** and **NOT** operators.

login—Any operating-system user that can connect to SQL Server, or, if using SQL Server standard security, a login is an account that can connect to SQL Server. Login is also the processes of connecting to SQL Server.

login identification—The account name that must be passed to SQL Server when standard SQL Server security is used.

login security mode—The type of security allowed when connecting to SQL Server. You can either use Windows NT Authentication Mode or Mixed Mode.

many-to-many relationship—A relationship in which each row in the first entity has many related rows in the second entity, and each row in the second entity has many related rows in the first entity.

MAPI—An email application programming interface (API).

master database—The SQL Server system database that keeps track of server-wide resources.

Merge Replication—A replication type that allows data to be changed on multiple databases and merged back into a central database.

metadata—The data that describes the other database objects. *See* system catalog.

Mixed Mode—A security mode that allows users to connect using both Windows NT Authentication and SQL Server standard security.

model database—A system database that is used as a template for every new user-defined database.

money data type—A SQL Server data type used to store money values with an accuracy of four decimal places. A **money** data type can store values from 922,337,203,685,477.5807 through –922,337,203,685,477.5808.

named pipe—An interprocess communication (IPC) mechanism that permits access to shared network resources.

nchar data type—A SQL Server data type used to store up to 4,000 Unicode characters.

nested query—A query that contains one or more subqueries.

Net-Library—A library that controls the communication with SQL Server for a specific network protocol.

noise words—Words that do not take part in a full-text query.

nonclustered index—An index in which the physical order of the data isn't the same as the order of the index.

nonrepeatable read—A transaction isolation level in which a transaction can read the same table twice and get different results.

normalization rules—The rules that describe how to remove redundant data from an entity.

ntext data type—A SQL Server data type used to store Unicode data containing up to 1,073,741,823 characters.

NULL—An unknown value or a column in which there is no value.

nullability—An attribute that determines if a column must have a value or if it can allow nulls.

nvarchar data type—A SQL Server data type that can store up to 4,000 Unicode characters.

Object Linking and Embedding (OLE)—An application programming interface (API) for sharing objects among applications.

object owner—The user account that created an object.

object permissions—The permissions that have been granted or denied on a table or view.

ODBC driver—A DLL that allows an application to connect to an ODBC (Open Database Connectivity) data source.

OLE DB—A COM-based application programming interface (API) for accessing data. OLE DB can access data in any data-storage format—databases, spreadsheets, text files, and so on—for which an OLE DB provider is available.

OLE DB provider—The software that accesses the data source using the OLE DB API.

one-to-many relationship—A relationship in which every row in the first table can have many rows in the second table, but every row in the second table can have only one row in the first table.

one-to-one relationship—A relationship in which every row in the first table can have only one row in the second table, and every row in the second table can have only one row in the first table.

online analytical processing (OLAP)—An application and database designed to analyze data. An OLAP system normally has a few users performing reporting queries.

online transaction processing (OLTP)—An application and database designed to perform a specific business function. An OLTP system will normally perform multiple well-defined queries.

Open Database Connectivity (ODBC)—An application programming interface for database material, which is aligned with the ANSI and the International Organization for Standardization (ISO) standards for a database Call Level Interface.

outer join—A join that returns rows even when the join conditions do not find a matching row in the other table.

package—A Data Transformation Services (DTS) object that defines the steps to perform while importing and exporting data.

page—SQL Server's internal storage mechanism. A SQL Server page is 8K.

page split—A situation in which inserting or updating data causes the rows on a page to grow to a size larger than a page. When a page split occurs, half of the rows will move to a new page.

parameter—In a stored procedure, a placeholder for a value that is going to be filled in when the procedure is executed. A parameter can be set to a constant or a variable.

Performance Monitor—A Windows NT application that provides status information about system performance and can be used to monitor SQL Server.

permissions—The authorizations that have been granted or denied on an object or statement.

permissions validation—The process that SQL Server uses to check whether a user has permissions to perform the SQL statement he or she is trying to execute.

positioned update—An update, insert, or delete that is performed on a row at the present cursor position using server cursors.

primary key (PK)—The candidate key that was chosen to be the main identifier of a row of data in a table.

projection—The relational algebra function that allows you to retrieve a subset of the columns in a table.

proximity search—A full-text query that looks for words that are near each other in a column.

publication—One or more articles that are replicated as a unit.

Publication Access List—The logins that have access to a publication.

publication database—A database containing data that is being or can be replicated to other databases.

publish—The act of marking a set of data as being available for another database to subscribe to during the replication processes.

Publisher—In the Publish and Subscribe model of replication, the server that contains one or more publication databases.

pubs database—One of SQL Server's sample databases.

pull subscription—A type of replication in which the Subscriber requests the data changes from the Publisher.

push subscription—A type of replication in which the Publisher controls when the data changes are sent to a Subscriber.

range query—A query that looks for data rows in which a column is in a range of values.

ranking—In a full-text query, a value indicating the degree of matching of each word that is determined to match in a full-text query. 0 represents a low degree of matching; 1,000 represents the highest degree of matching.

RDBMS—See *relational database management system*.

read-only replication—When the replicated data is not allowed to be updated or changed by the Subscriber. This is also called a *read-only snapshot*.

real data type—A SQL Server data type used to store numbers with seven-digit precision.

record—Another name for a row.

recovery interval—The estimated time for a database to come back online when SQL Server is restarted after the system has abnormally shut down.

recursive relationship—A relationship in which a table is related to itself. This is also called a reflective relationship.

referential integrity (RI)—The rules that ensure that foreign keys have related primary keys.

relational data model—A data model based on set theory, relational algebra, and relational calculus.

relational database—A database based on the relational data model.

relational database management system (RDBMS)—A program that supports a relational database.

relationship—A situation in which one entity refers to the primary key of another entity.

remote data—Any data that is stored outside the SQL Server you are currently connected to.

remote procedure call (RPC)—An execution of a stored procedure that isn't on the local server.

remote server—A SQL Server on the network that can be accessed through a user's local server.

remote stored procedure—A stored procedure on a remote SQL Server that can be executed through the local SQL Server.

remote table—A table that is external to the local SQL Server.

replication—The process of keeping data on one SQL Server in sync with the data on another SQL Server (through duplication).

result set—The rows returned from a **SELECT** statement.

return parameters—Parameters in a SQL Server that can return data to the caller.

revoke—The act of cancelling a granted or denied permission.

right outer join—An outer join that returns all the rows in the second table, even when the join conditions do not find a matching row in the first table.

role—A SQL Server security unit that can be applied to users or logins to link together similar users.

roll back—The act of cancelling a transaction and returning the data modified in the transaction to its original state.

roll forward—A database recovery feature that causes committed transactions to be applied to the data and uncommitted transactions to be rolled back when a SQL Server starts up.

row—A set of one or more columns. A row is equivalent to a record.

row aggregate—The results of a row aggregate function.

row aggregate function—An aggregate function that generates summary data in separate rows of a result set. A row aggregate function is used in a **COMPUTE** or **COMPUTE BY** clause.

row lock—The result when SQL Server locks one row in a table for a query.

rule—A database object used to specify the data that can be in a column.

savepoint—A user-defined marker that allows a transaction to be partially rolled back.

scalar aggregate—A function applied to all the rows in a table, generating an aggregate value as one of the columns returned.

scheduled backup—A backup that SQL Server Agent accomplishes automatically when the backup is defined and scheduled as a job.

schema—A description of a database using DDL.

scroll—A cursor that can move only forward.

search condition—A part of a **WHERE** or **HAVING** clause that limits the rows being returned.

security identifier (SID)—A unique value that identifies a user who is logged on to the SQL Server.

SELECT—A SQL statement that returns data from a SQL Server database.

select list—The elements that are returned in a **SELECT** statement.

select query—A query that uses the **SELECT** statement.

self-join—A table that is joined to itself.

sensitive cursor—Another name for a dynamic cursor.

server cursor—Any cursor that is performed using the SQL cursor statements.

server name—The name by which a SQL Server knows itself or other data sources. It can also be the name a client uses to identify a SQL Server.

shared lock—A lock that allows other users to read the data that is being locked.

smalldatetime data type—A SQL Server data type used to store date and time information to the minute.

smallint data type—An integer data type used to store whole numbers from 32,767 through –32,768.

smallmoney data type—A SQL Server data type that stores monetary values. These values range from 214,748.3647 through –214,748.3648, to four decimal places.

Snapshot Replication—A type of replication that takes periodic snapshots of the published data and applies them to the Subscriber database.

sort order—The order in which SQL Server evaluates character strings.

SQL—See *Structured Query Language.*

SQL-3—The latest version of the SQL standard; currently, it has not been approved.

SQL-92—The latest approved version of the standard for SQL, published in 1992; also referred to as SQL-2. It is sometimes referred to as ANSI SQL in the United States.

SQL Mail—SQL Servers interface to MAPI mail systems. It allows SQL Server to send and receive mail.

SQL Server Agent—A component of SQL Server that creates and manages local or multiserver jobs, alerts, and operators.

SQL Server Authentication—The process of verifying connections to SQL Server.

SQL Server login—See *login.*

SQL Server user—A database security account that allows SQL Server logins to use a database.

standard security—See *SQL Server Authentication.*

statement permission—The permission to execute T-SQL statements.

static cursor—A cursor that shows the data as it looked when the cursor was opened.

stored procedure—A collection of one or more T-SQL statements that are stored on SQL Server.

Structured Query Language (SQL)—A database query and programming language.

subquery—Any **SELECT** statement that is used to make up another query.

subscribe—The act of agreeing to receive a publication as part of replication.

Subscriber—In the Publish and Subscribe model of replication, the server that holds copies of published information.

surrogate key—In Microsoft terminology, a candidate key. In everyone else's terminology, an artificially generated key.

system administrator—Any user with the sysadmin role.

system catalog—The system tables in the master database that contain information about SQL Server. They do not contain information about tables in a database.

system databases—Four databases that are provided on a fresh SQL Server installation: master, tempdb, model, and msdb.

system stored procedures—A set of stored procedures provided by SQL Server that are used to access the system tables.

system tables—The tables that make up the system catalog and the database catalog.

table—A database object that stores data in a tabular (that is, in a collection of rows and columns) form.

table lock—A lock that locks the complete table.

tabular data stream (TDS)—SQL Server's internal data-transfer protocol.

tempdb database—A system database used to store working objects.

temporary stored procedure—A stored procedure created in tempdb by prefixing the procedure's name with a number sign (#).

temporary table procedure—A table procedure created in tempdb by prefixing the procedure's name with a number sign (#).

text data type—A data type used to hold character data up to 2GB in size.

timestamp data type—A datatype that generates a unique value for a database. Every new value generated will be one larger that the last value generated.

tinyint data type—An integer data type used to store whole numbers from 0 through 255.

Transact-SQL (T-SQL)—SQL Server's implementation of the ANSI SQL-2 standard and SQL Server's extensions to the standard.

Transact-SQL cursor—A server cursor that uses the T-SQL extensions to the **DECLARE CURSOR** statement.

transaction—A logical unit of work.

transaction log—A specialized database file in which all changes to the database are recorded before the data changes are written.

trigger—A component similar to a stored procedure, except that a trigger is automatically executed when data is modified.

tuple—The proper name for a row of data.

Unicode—A set of characters that are stored in the **nchar, nvarchar**, and **ntext** data types.

Unicode collation—The sort order for Unicode data.

union query—A query that merges results from two or more queries into one result set.

UNIQUE constraint—A constraint that enforces the fact that the constrained column(s) are unique in a table.

unique index—An index that uniquely identifies a row in a table.

uniqueidentifier data type—A SQL Server data type containing a globally unique identifier (GUID) number, stored as a 16-byte binary string.

update—The act of modifying data by adding new data, removing existing data, or changing existing data.

user databases—Any SQL Server database other than the four system databases.

user-defined data type—A data type that was created by a user. This data type must be based on one of the SQL Server standard data types.

username—The name that a login uses when the computer is using a database.

varbinary data type—A data type used to store binary data up to 8,000 bytes in size.

varchar data type—A data type used to store character data up to 8,000 bytes in size.

variable—An object used to temporarily store values. A variable name starts with an at symbol (@).

vertical partitioning—A physical design practice that splits a table into multiple tables for different sets of columns. Every row in the original table has a row in each of the new partitioned tables.

view—A logical table made from a **SELECT** statement that retrieves data from one or more tables.

wildcard characters—The characters used in pattern matching with the **LIKE** keyword in the **WHERE** clause.

Windows NT Authentication—A process that enables a user with an NT user account to connect to SQL Server.

Windows NT Event Viewer—A Windows NT application that views events.

Windows NT Performance Monitor—A Windows NT utility that can help system administrators monitor the activity of Windows NT and processes, including SQL Servers that run on NT.

write-ahead log—The transaction logging method used by most RDBMs. In this method, the data changes are written to the log before the changes are made to the data.

Index

Bold page numbers indicate sample exam questions.

A

Ad hoc distributed queries, 251–252
Adaptive exams, 7, 280, 283–285
Administration. *See* Automated administration.
Alert Properties dialog box, 189–190
Alerts, 185, 188–189
Aliases, 60
ALTER DATABASE command, 85–87, **92**
Ambiguity on exams, 281–282
ANSI SQL, 17
AppleTalk ADSP, 28
Application architectures, 14–18
Application roles, 66, **72**
Architectures
    applications, 14–18
    client/server, 14–15, **19, 20**
    SQL Server, 15–18, 21
Authentication, 54–59
Automated administration, **195–197**
    about, 184, 186
    alerts, 185, 188–189
    Database Maintenance Plan Wizard, 187
    jobs, 184–185, 186–187, 192
    logging, 194
    master servers, 185
    multiserver administration, 185
    notifications, 187–188, 189, 192
    operators, 185, 187–188, 189, 192
    SQL Enterprise Manager, 188–194
    target servers, defined, 185

B

Backing up data, **138–140**, **287, 289, 297, 302**
    See also Restoring data.
    backup, defined, 126
    BACKUP command, 130–137, 265–267, **275, 287, 297**
    BACKUP DATABASE command, 128–129
    BACKUP LOG command, 129–130
    devices, adding, 126–128
    differential database backup, 132, 137
    dump, defined, 126, **138**
    strategy, choosing, 137, **138**

    transaction log backup, 126, **138**
    troubleshooting, 265–267, **275, 287, 297**
    types of backups, 126
Backup, defined, 126
BACKUP command, 130–137, 265–267, **275, 287, 297**
BACKUP DATABASE command, 128–129
Backup devices, adding, 126–128
BACKUP LOG command, 129–130
Backup set verification, 153–154
Banyan VINES, 28
bcp, 107–112, **121, 122, 303**
bcp optimizer hint, 111
BEGIN DISTRIBUTED TRANSACTION statement, 255–256
Budgeting your time on exams, 6
Bulk Copy Program, 107–112, **121, 122**
BULK INSERT statement, 104–107, **119**

C

-c startup parameter, 42
Careful reading of exams, 7–8
Certification exams
    adaptive exams, 7, 280, 283–285
    ambiguity, 281–282
    budgeting your time, 6
    careful reading, 7–8
    checkboxes, 4
    exam-readiness, 2
    exhibits, 5
    fixed-length exams, 5–6, 280, 284
    guessing, 6, 7
    marking questions for later, 5, 282
    memorizing, 283–284
    multiple choice format, 3–5, 280
    online resources, 9–12
    partial credit, 5
    practicing, 9, **279–303**
    preparing, 2, 9–12, 284
    process of elimination, 8, 280–281
    question format, 4–5, 280
    radio buttons, 4
    strategies, 5–6, 7, 8
    taking notes, 283
    testing center environment, 3, 282–283
    time allowed, 3, 280